Réjane Dreifuss, Simon Hagemann, Izabella Pluta (eds.)
Live Performance and Video Games

Theatre Studies | Volume 165

Réjane Dreifuss has worked as a dramaturge and project manager for the theatre company sonimage. Together with the author and director Igor Bauersima, she has written and directed theatre plays under the pseudonym Réjane Desvignes, in which digital technologies play a crucial role in the creation of narratives. Since 2016, she has been researching the influence of digitalization on theatre, with a particular focus on the generation of new narrative forms. She is a lecturer and researcher in the Department Performing Arts and Film at the Zürcher Hochschule der Künste.

Simon Hagemann is a lecturer in communication at the IUT of Saint-Dié-des-Vosges (University of Lorraine) and an associate researcher at Crem (Centre de recherche sur les médiations). He also holds a doctorate in theatre studies (Université Sorbonne Nouvelle-Paris 3). His work focuses on video games, theatre, history and media innovations.

Izabella Pluta is a researcher in the performing arts (PhD in theatre and cinema), theatre critic and translator as well as associated researcher at the Center of Theatre Studies (University of Lausanne). She has been granted advanced research fellowship Fernand Braudel IFER/Marie Curie at Université Lyon 2 and ENSATT (2013-2014) and Directeur d'études associé (DEA) at several laboratory's spaces in France such as Atelier Art/Science or Studio Fresnoy.

Réjane Dreifuss, Simon Hagemann, Izabella Pluta (eds.)

Live Performance and Video Games

Inspirations, Appropriations and Mutual Transfers

[transcript]

This Open Access edition was published with the support of the Zurich University of the Arts (ZHdK).
This volume is published as volume 31 of the subTexte series.

Bibliographic information published by the Deutsche Nationalbibliothek

This work is licensed under the Creative Commons Attribution-NonCommercial-NoDerivatives 4.0 (BY-NC-ND) which means that the text may be used for non-commercial purposes, provided credit is given to the author.

To create an adaptation, translation, or derivative of the original work and for commercial use, further permission is required and can be obtained by contacting rights@transcript-publishing.com
Creative Commons license terms for re-use do not apply to any content (such as graphs, figures, photos, excerpts, etc.) not original to the Open Access publication and further permission may be required from the rights holder. The obligation to research and clear permission lies solely with the party re-using the material.

First published in 2024 by transcript Verlag, Bielefeld
© Réjane Dreifuss, Simon Hagemann, Izabella Pluta (eds.)

Cover layout: Kordula Röckenhaus, Bielefeld
Cover illustration: "Can You See Me Now?" (2001) by Blast Theory
Printed by: Majuskel Medienproduktion GmbH, Wetzlar
https://doi.org/10.14361/9783839471739
Print-ISBN: 978-3-8376-7173-5
PDF-ISBN: 978-3-8394-7173-9
ISSN of series: 2700-3922
eISSN of series: 2747-3198

Contents

subTexte 9

Acknowledgements 11

Introduction

Live Performance and Video Games: Introduction
to an Interdisciplinary Field of Research
Réjane Dreifuss, Simon Hagemann and Izabella Pluta 15

Potential and Critique of a Gamified Theatre

'It's (Not) Only a Game'... some Game-Changing Potentials of Game-Based Theatre
Josephine Machon with Munotida Chinyanga and Persis-Jadé Maravala 39

Video Games, Flow, and Immersive Theatre:
Participatory Arts in the Ultraliberal Era
Olivia Levet 61

Ludic Neuro-Performances: An Approach Towards Playful Experiments
Margarete Jahrmann 73

New (Game) Technologies for the Theatre

Directing Avatars in Live Performances –
An Autonomy Simulacrum of Virtual Actors
Georges Gagneré 87

Unreal Engine in the Theater: New Challenges for the Lighting Designer
Victor Inisan 105

Combining Layers of Reality. Video Game Elements in Live Performance
Christophe Burgess 117

Working at the Interface of Games and Performance

Gaming in Performance. Between Research and Artistry
Matt Adams, Blast Theory, interviewed by Helen W. Kennedy 131

Machina eX: Working Collectively at the Interface
of Theatre and Video Games. In Conversation
with Clara Ehrenwerth and Anton Krause
Réjane Dreifuss and Simon Hagemann 147

What Even Is Video Game Performance?
A conversation between Marleena Huuhka and Harold Hejazi 159

(Digital) Play as Performance

Play, Performance, Agency: Prompt Injections and Playful Misuses of AI
Miguel Angel Sicart 171

Operations & Encounters: Playing Out Performativity
Mary Flanagan 183

From Home to Stage: How Speedrunners Negotiate
Performance, Relation to the Audience, and Spectacle
in Live-Streaming Speedrun Marathons
Sacha Bernard and Fanny Barnabé 195

Understanding Video Games through a Performative Gaze

The Dramaturgy of Videogames: A Dialogue
Mike Sell and Michael M. Chemers 219

On Time Compression and *Déjà vu*: Remastering, Remaking, Modding, and Performing *Final Fantasy*
Darshana Jayemanne and Cameron Kunzelman 237

Video Games as Material Performances
Michael Nitsche 255

subTexte

The *subTexte* series of the IPF-Institute for the Performing Arts and Film, is dedicated to presenting original research within two fields of inquiry: Performative Practice and Film. The series offers a platform for the publication of texts, images, or digital media emerging from research on, for, or through the performative arts or film. The series contributes to promoting practice-based art research beyond the ephemeral event and the isolated monograph, to reporting intermediate research findings, and to opening up comparative perspectives. From conference proceedings to collections of materials, *subTexte* gathers a diverse and manifold reflections on, and approaches to, the performative arts and film.

Published so far:

subTexte 01 Attention Artaud. Zürich 2008.

subTexte 02 Wirklich? – Strategien der Authentizität im aktuellen Dokumentarfilm. Zürich 2009.

subTexte 03 Künstlerische Forschung. Positionen und Perspektiven. Zürich 2009.

subTexte 04 research@film. Forschung zwischen Kunst und Wissenschaft. Zürich 2010.

subTexte 05 Theater Vermittlung Schule. Ein Dialog. Zürich 2011.

subTexte 06 Wirkungsmaschine Schauspieler. Vom Menschendarsteller zum multifunktionalen Spielemacher. Zürich-Berlin 2011.

subTexte 07 Ästhetische Kommunikation im Kindertheater. Zürich 2012.

subTexte 08 Akustik des Vokals – Präliminarien. Zürich 2012.

subTexte 09 Michael Tschechow. Lektionen für den professionellen Schauspieler. Berlin 2013.

subTexte 10 Disembodied Voice. *Alexander Verlag*. Berlin 2015.

subTexte 11 Freilichttheater. Eine Tradition auf neuen Wegen. *hier + jetzt*. Zürich-Baden 2015.

subTexte 12 Acoustics of the Vowel. Preliminaries (Dieter Maurer). *Peter Lang*. Bern 2016.

subTexte 13 Wiederholung und Ekstase (Milo Rau, Rolf Bossart). *Diaphanes*. Zürich-Berlin 2017.

10 Live Performance and Video Games

subTexte 14 Impro Talks. https://www.zhdk.ch/publikationsreihe-subtexte. open access. Zürich 2017.

subTexte 15 ausgewandert – eingetanzt (Fumi Matsuda). *Zytglogge.* Basel 2018.

subTexte 16 IPF – Die erste Dekade. 10 Years of Artistic Research. *Theater der Zeit.* Berlin 2018.

subTexte 17 Ausweitung der Spielzone (Yvonne Schmidt). *Chronos.* Zürich 2020

subTexte 18 Minor Cinema: Experimental Film in Switzerland. *JRP Edition/Ringier.* Zürich 2020.

subTexte 19 DisAbility on Stage //disabilityonstage.zhdk.ch. *Hybrid Media Publication.* Zürich 2020.

subTexte 20 Sinn und Sinne im Tanz. Perspektiven aus Kunst und Wissenschaft (Margrit Bischof/Friederike Lampert). *transcript.* Bielefeld 2020.

subTexte 21 Performative Sammlungen (Stefanie Lorey). *transcript.* Bielefeld 2020.

subTexte 22 Trotz allem. Gardi Hutter. Biografie (Denise Schmid). *hier + jetzt.* Baden 2021.

subTexte 23 Filmen, Forschen, Annotieren. Handbuch Research Video (Gunter Lösel, Martin Zimper). *Birkhäuser.* Basel 2021.

subTexte 24 Dance and Costumes. A History of Dressing Movement (Elna Matamoros). *Alexander.* Berlin 2021.

subTexte 25 Fertig gibt's nicht. Bühnenbild. Prozesse (Michael Simon). *Theater der Zeit.* Berlin 2022.

subTexte 26 Michael Tschechow. Der Schauspieler ist das Theater (Anton Rey et al.). *Alexander.* Berlin 2022.

subTexte 27 Actor & Avatar. A Scientific & Artistic Catalog (Dieter Mersch et al.). *transcript.* Bielefeld 2023.

subTexte 28 Unsichtbares und Ungesagtes (Bernadette Kolonko). *Schüren.* Marburg 2023.

subTexte 29 Die dunkle Seite des Spiels (Gunter Lösel). *transcript.* Bielefeld 2023.

subTexte 30 Acoustics of the Vowel (Dieter Maurer). *Peter Lang.* Bern 2024.

subTexte 31 Live Performance & Video Games (Réjane Dreifuss et al.). *transcript.* Bielefeld 2024.

In Preparation:

subTexte 32 Michael Chekhov (ed. Hugo Moss). The Paris Manuscript. *Bloomsbury London* 2025.

subTexte 33 gezeichnet (Manuel Fabritz). *edition Stefan Witschi.* Zürich 2024.

s.: www.subtexte.ch

Acknowledgements

We would like to thank everyone who has helped make this publication possible. Above all we are grateful to all the researchers and artists who have generously contributed chapters, enriching this book with their contrasting approaches. Thank you to Anton Rey, Head of the *Institute for the Performing Arts and Film* and to Esther Zaugg and the team of the *Medien- und Informationszentrum*, both at the Zurich University of the Arts, for their precious advice and their financial support. Thank you to the publishing house *transcript Verlag* and especially to Luisa Bott. Thank you to Rebecca Eacho and Graeme Currie, who helped with the editing of the English-language contributions. Thank you to Blast Theory for the cover picture and to the photographers who permitted us to publish their pictures. Finally, a big thanks to Dieter Mersch, who opened the door to researching the influence of digital culture on theatre at the Zurich University of the Arts.

Réjane Dreifuss, Simon Hagemann, Izabella Pluta

Introduction

Live Performance and Video Games: Introduction to an Interdisciplinary Field of Research

Réjane Dreifuss, Simon Hagemann and Izabella Pluta

Introduction - Context, intentions, and origins of this volume

Narrative strategies, immersion, interaction, identification, multimodality, characters, the relationship between the physical and virtual worlds: The fields of investigation into the complex relationship between live performance and video games are many and varied. Since the early 2000s, video games have become the economically dominant medium of our world, and their cultural importance has only kept rising since then. It is, therefore, easy to understand why an increasing number of creators of live performances are interested in video games: be it to expand the possibilities of the theatre, or to tune in to the media reality of a theatre audience that is ever more immersed in ludic culture. On the one hand, references to video games can arise on very different conceptual, thematic, and technological levels. On the other hand, video games also draw on aesthetic features of older media. Though references to cinema probably dominate, there are also repeated allusions to theatre and other forms of live performance. Furthermore, especially with the success of e-sports and live streaming of gameplay, questions about the staging of gaming itself have increasingly taken centre stage.

In the research literature, a few pioneering works on the connections between play and performance (Richard Schechner) or on computer software and theatre (Brenda Laurel) can be found, but it was only with the rise in social significance of video games in the 2000s and the emergence of immersive theatre that references to video games began to be found in theatre studies. In the young discipline of game studies, which is considered to have begun in the early 2000s, little attention was paid to the aspect of performance until the end of the first decade, as the discipline initially focused more on narrativity and media specificity. Since then, a few articles have appeared on the complex relationship between video games and live performance in the two research disciplines.

The primary function of this book is to gather together the scattered approaches to this topic in one place. To the best of our knowledge, it is the first academic edited volume on this subject. It follows a consistently interdisciplinary approach, bringing together experts from theatre and performance studies with specialists from game studies, researchers, and art-creating researchers with researching artists. The book evokes several hybrid formats such as game theatre, game performance, the use of avatars and VR/AR technologies on stage, e-sport, speed running, and reflects on notions such as play, games, performativity, theatricality, dramaturgy, immersion, participation, and interaction, which are discussed in terms of theatre and in video games.

This volume is based on the online symposium *Live Performance and Video Games*, which was held from 5–7 October 2022 by the Institute for the Performing Arts and Film, Zurich University of the Arts (ZHdK, Switzerland) in cooperation with the Digital Images and Virtual Reality Laboratory (INREV), Université Paris 8 (France); the Research Centre on Mediation, Communication – Language – Art – Culture (CREM), Université de Lorraine (France); GameLab UNIL-EPFL, Université de Lausanne; Ecole polytechnique fédérale de Lausanne (Switzerland); and the Association Theatre in Progress (Switzerland). The volume has also been enriched by several other important contributions. It should be noted that the ZHdK already has a certain tradition of reflecting on the relationship between live performance and video games, as two international symposia on this topic have already taken place here, in 2016, *Gamification: Digitale Ausrahmung des Theaters* and in 2018 *Ludification in Theater. Neue Utopien des Theatralen*, both organised by Dieter Mersch and Réjane Dreifuss.[1]

While the various articles included in this book deal with a variety of – sometimes very specific – aspects of the relationship between video games and live performance, the introduction aims to provide a brief overview of the general relationship between these two arts and/or media.[2] First, we will discuss the growth of gamification in live performance in recent years and the underlying causes of this development, as well as the specific format of game theatre. This is undertaken with reference to performances in an artistic context, mostly theatre performances (Schechner 2002, 31). Second, the application of a performative perspective to the playing of video games will be discussed. Video games are games that are played on a video screen, and we are of course talking about digital games in this case. Here the concept of performance is interpreted broadly, in the sense of Richard Schechner, who differentiated between eight different kinds of performance, of which play is one

---

1   The two symposia were part of the research project *Ludification in Theater: zur digitalen Ausrahmung des Theaters*, 2016–2020, conceived at the Institut für Theorie, Zurich University of the Arts, under the direction of Prof. Dieter Mersch.

2   There is a whole series of academic articles on both the artistic character of video games and the medial character of theatre or performance, but these cannot be discussed further here for reasons of space.

(Schechner 2002, 31). Due to mediatisation, liveness must also be understood more generally and not in the sense of a strict physical co-presence of actors and performers as in the traditional concept of performance in theatre studies.[3] Finally, we briefly present the structure of the book and introduce the individual contributions.

Gamification of live performance

Crucial turning points in contemporary live performance

When looking at changes in live performance in the western world in recent decades, a few general trends can be observed.

First of all, the 'hybridization of the arts' has, for the most part, vindicated the idea that the arts have a tendency to 'fray' (Adorno 1970). This tendency towards the 'ongoing dissolution of the arts' (Wellershoff 1989),[4] the 'de-framing of the arts' (Klotz 1999, Belting 2002) and the notion that the arts are, finally, 'dissolving their limits' (Fischer-Lichte, Hasselmann, Rautzenberg 2010) has been observed for well over 60 years. The concept of the dissolution of the arts touches on multiple aspects of artistic experience. Theorists have spoken of 'intertextuality' (Plett 1991) which has been extended to a broader concept of 'intermediality' (Rajewsky 2002, Bay-Cheng 2010). Theatre, no less than the other arts, is also influenced by the phenomenon of 'hybridisation'. This involves the aesthetic crossover of live performance with other forms from different artistic fields, such as plastic arts, film, installation, and digital art. The theatrical elements and the new components are placed in a contemporary configuration, in a single art form, which may be characterised by a fusion of these elements and components or by their tension (Manovich 2001, Pluta 2010).

Second, the 'performative turn' in theatre has led to a shift from representation based essentially on the text towards a theatrical 'event', which focuses on corporality, co-presence, staging, and performance as well as tendencies towards 'postdramatic' theatre (Auslander 1997, Lehmann 1999, Fischer-Lichte 2004). The deconstructionist praxis deployed here has transformed the theatre itself into an object of reflection, questioning the division of space, text, roles, characters, presence, etc. Those reflections have led to the rethinking of the traditional setting of stage and audience as well as the relationship between authorship, production, scene, and drama – through collective productions, 'de-dramatised' and 'de-symbolised' plots (Balme

---

3   A concept that has also been repeatedly challenged by various artists through experiments with multimedia theatre.

4   Unless otherwise indicated, this and all other quotations from texts that are cited in bibliographies in languages other than English are translations by the authors.

2003, Sermon 2012). The book *Performative Stories* by Nina Tecklenburg shows in detail how new narrative practices have emerged since the beginning of the 21st century, including 'collective games, theatre installations, extensive autobiographical performances, immersive role-playing and audio-video walks' (Tecklenburg 2022).

Third, the 'digital turn', with increasing use of digital technologies in the theatre in recent decades, has also contributed to expanding the possibilities of theatre, both aesthetically and in terms of content (Blake 2014, Wiens 2014, Masura 2020). This digital transformation is a multi-faceted phenomenon. The range of technical devices is particularly complex today. The following devices can be mentioned: screens (panoramic, multi-screen, concave, convex); VR headsets (such as Oculus Rift); cameras (small digital cameras, 16mm cameras, surveillance cameras, surround-view and 360° cameras, Kinect); sound devices (headphones, sensors); mobile media (mobile phones, tablets); robotic objects (arms, exoskeletons); robots (androids, robotic puppets, domestic robots) (Mersch et al. 2023, Pluta 2022). Software and interfaces, meanwhile, are particularly abundant these days: The most widely used software includes Max/MSP (real-time), Isadora (programming software, can work with video and interactive media), Sunlight (DMX interface and software environment), Hephaestos (multiple audio interfaces, multi-track, can generate spatialization, automation, lighting and electronics linked to Arduino boards), Videostage (video broadcasting software) and many others (Dixon 2007, Salter 2010).

Fourth, with the development of digital technology, two important concepts that invoke the idea of audience participation are placed at the centre of artistic interest: interactivity and immersion (Couchot 1998). Theatres have been experimenting with the idea of audience participation since at least the 1920s. The overcoming of the 'fourth wall' has been discussed since the early avant-garde, and, in the course of the politicisation of theatre formats in the 1960s and 70s, interactive and participatory formats with the direct involvement of the audience were also tried out (action theatre, street theatre) with audiences being invited to participate, provoked, and used as the object of observation or questioning. Similarly, the renewed radicalisation of participatory models in the context of the performative turn and postdramatic theatre of the 1990s explicitly thematised the passive role of the audience. On the one hand, various attempts were made to dissolve the separation of the stage and audience while, on the other, the creation of entire environments or theatrical spaces as artificial environments using new media was proposed.

Digital technology transforms ideas of interaction and participation from early forms of the dissolution of boundaries in theatre. Interactivity, we should note, is a characteristic of computerised media that can be summed up as the creation of a 'more or less advanced dialogue with the user' (Poissant 1997). Interactivity can have different levels of interaction, varying from a closed model to an increasingly complex format. Here it is the viewer that interacts with the system of the work of art and enables it to come to fruition. In theatre, contemporary forms of interactivity and immersion have become highly popular. In his article 'Contour du Théâtre Immersif' (1990–2010), the stage-designer Marcel Freydefont defines immersive theatre as follows: 'Immersive theatre [...] is a spatial, three-dimensional stage that aims to break away once again from the two-dimensional stage, the tableau stage (*la scène-tableau*), by following the dynamics of all this research but also by taking other paths' (Freydefont 2011, 2).[5]

Immersive theatre,[6] a format that unites actors and spectators in the same space, has become a significant subcategory of theatre since the 2000s, especially in the UK, where many theatre companies have pursued it, including pioneers *Punchdrunk*. Immersive theatre can be considered a further development of participatory theatre, amalgamating participation with immersion (Bieger 2007). The amalgamation works because participation creates the emotional 'involvement' that appears to be decisive for immersive experiences, while immersion and involvement promote genuine participation. The concepts of 'participation' and 'immersion' bring together different aesthetics or 'strands of discourse' (Ryan 2001, Bouko 2016), which appear relevant to investigating the gamification of theatre.

Gamification of society and performance

The term that remains at the heart of the debate on the intersection of live performance and video games is gamification. According to Gabe Zichermann and Joselin Linder, gamification '[...] uses concepts from games, loyalty programmes and behavioural economics to stimulate user engagement' (Zichermann, Linder, 2013, 123). The term was introduced by computer programmer Nick Pelling in 2002 and was preceded by a more general discussion of games and the gamification phenomenon following a presentation by Jesse Schell at the annual Design, Innovate, Communication, Entertainment conference in 2000. In this presentation Schell set out his hypothesis about the future of society, in which everyday actions would be subject to a system of points and rewards. From this conference onwards, gaming and ludic activity have been associated with areas of social life that incorporate ludic mechanisms into domains usually considered as 'non-play' (Schell, 2000).

Gamification, i.e. the transfer of elements of a game structure into non-game environments, mainly draws on two different streams of research: firstly, game the-

---

5   'Le théâtre immersif [...] constitue une scène spatiale et tridimensionnelle qui entend rompre à nouveau avec la scène bidimensionnelle, la scène-tableau, en se situant dans la dynamique de toutes ces recherches tout en empruntant d'autres voies.'

6   Catherine Bouko (2016) proposes a definition of immersive theatre with respect to the 'spectator' in 3 steps: 1. Physical integration in space, 2. sensorial and dramaturgic immersion and 3. Confusion between the real and the fictional world.

ories originating from the humanities and social sciences, and secondly, applied research in the field of design, using computer games as an example. This game structure is based on engagement, individual and/or collective progress, and creativity. Outside of the arts, applications of gamification in society are on the rise in many fields: Health, education, work, media, culture, emotional relationships, and other areas have all been affected by gamified practices. In order to analyse the trend of 'gamification in theatre', it is important to highlight the ongoing gamification of society as a whole (Cotta 1980, Vinck 2016, Stalder 2016, Le Lay 2021, Salter 2022).

The rapid growth of social media platforms where the line between art-consumer and art-creator is blurred reflects the increasing importance of gamification for modern audiences. The practices of personal representation, self-staging, playing with different identities, on blogs, YouTube, Twitter, or Facebook in ways that often resemble theatrical 'events' seem to have influenced contemporary theatre. The same applies to TV reality shows, which can also be seen as a form of 'theatricalisation' of everyday life. Perhaps even more if one thinks of online platforms such as Second Life, in which the user assumes a different identity in the game and experiences an adventure as 'someone else' in a digital parallel universe. As Ulf Otto has also shown in his book *Internetauftritte. Eine Theatergeschichte der neuen Medien* (2013), such network-based games exert an influence on theatre, because they have contributed to establishing participatory practices both inside and outside the theatre.

The gamification trend is also noticeable in the theatre. It is integrated in different ways and on various levels. Theatre can be inspired by new formats. Constanza Blanco notes that the theatre has taken up elements from live action role playing games, theme parks, and escape rooms (Blanco 2021). It can use technologies from the gaming world such as the Unreal Engine or Unity game engines or VR or AR technology, for example. Elements from digital games are also used in world-building, in reflecting on how the audience is perceived, in creating dramaturgies using game rules, and plays with 'quests' and 'levels'. This can be considered a 'theatricalisation' of the logic of digital game formats. The use of digital game technologies and game rules systems here can be seen as part of the digitalisation of theatre, even where the process is entirely analogue (Machon 2013, Kolesch, Schütz, Nikoleit 2021).

Different theatre companies apply the concept of gamification in various ways. This type of performance has many facets: It transposes the aesthetics of video games to the stage (Susanne Kennedy & Markus Selg, Nationaltheater Reinickendorf); it immerses the spectator in a fictional yet material world (Punchdrunk, SIGNA, Yan Duyvendak, Björn Bicker, Madame Lupin); it includes the use of game controllers or video game images (Rimini Protokoll, Extraleben); it explores interactivity between actors and avatars (Georges Gagneré); or it invites the audience on a life-size collective experience involving the interactive unfolding of a story (Blast Theory, Alan Borek, machina eX).

Towards a game theatre

The relationship between live performance and video games is still rarely studied, and relatively few research articles have been devoted to these issues (Homan 2014, Annis 2019, Männel 2018, Büscher 2018, Pluta 2022). A few dissertations and doctoral theses have been completed in relation to this theme, such as Michael St. Clair's dissertation, *Acts of Play: Games as Experiential Performance* (2013) or Greg Foster's PhD thesis, *Towards a Theatre for Gamers: A new paradigm of practice in contemporary live performance as a response to games and interactivity in digital media and performance culture* (2017).

The German theatre critic Christian Rakow has investigated theatrical performances in Germany that adopt interactive game mechanics for their own stage fictions. He coined the term '*Game Theater*' in the online theatre journal nachtkritik.de, adding it to the website's glossary (2012). In his article 'Playing Democracy', he describes several works involving audience participation developed by theatre collectives such as machina eX and SIGNA and argues that those live performances draw inspiration directly from video games (Rakow 2013, see also 2015).

The defining feature of game theatre is that it substitutes 'dramatic structures' with 'program design'. The latter generally comprises an initial situation and an open set of rules that serve as springboards for the development of play situations and scenes that integrate entire environments (off-spaces, industrial wastelands, neighbourhoods, basements, etc.). In designing/creating collective worlds (*Weltentwerfen*) (Borries 2016), game theatre formats require that all participants are equally actors, players, and co-creators, who are involved, engaged, and ethically concerned about the Other. By this means, game theatre produces narratives that can be concretely experienced by participating individuals. Thus, game theatre discards a series of distinctions that have structured the theatre over the centuries in various ways (including the binaries: inside/outside, actor/audience, role/action, drama/text). The distance established by the stage/audience binary gives way to direct action, involvement, and experience, because everyone present takes part in the action and has the capacity to influence the course of the game with their decisions. Participants get caught up in the events, have to take positions in group situations, can try to solve problems in different ways, and can engage in parallel activities, all the while having to take responsibility for the effects their actions have on other 'players'. In game theatre, these participants are charged with collectively solving a task and 'co-creatively' 'coming up with' a story that cannot be separated from their own personal 'experience' of the process (Drewes 2010, Birch 2012, Biggin 2017, Frieze 2017).

The German artist collective machina eX 'integrates modern technologies with elements of classical illusion theatre to create playable theatre pieces that are simultaneously accessible as computer games' (see website machina eX[7]). The collective builds its game theatres by working with a system based on precise game rules which define how the theatre space and the audience are treated, as is the case in a point-and-click videogame. In *Toxik* (2015), ten audience members had 90 Minutes to find out who murdered a policewoman. In *Patrol* (2019), they become employees of a fictitious company where they are supposed to work. In these games, the group experience becomes social and political as the group is constantly challenged to make decisions that are discussed collectively.

If machina eX builds its games in the tradition of point-and-click video games, there are theatre companies which draw inspiration from other types of games, such as Open World Games, embracing the idea of letting the spectator move freely in an artificial world with a wide range of choices over factors such as how and when to achieve their objectives. SIGNA, an Austrian-Danish collective, develops non-stop performance-installations which are built to be self-contained worlds, like miniaturised model-societies, in which the participants/visitors can enter, experiment, and explore. These performative installations are inhabited by actors with whom the visitors can engage. While the visitor must respect certain rules, evolve within a certain framework, within that they can then do 'whatever they want': move from one space to another, stay or move on, enter into contact with other people (actors and other visitors), and, by means of the choices they make, take a position and influence the course of the show. Depending on the concept, the length of time the audience spends in a performance can range from two and a half hours to several days (see website SIGNA[8]). *Das Halbe Leid* (Half the Suffering) (2017) took place in the halls of a disused machine factory in the Hamburg suburbs, which was converted into a fictitious emergency shelter where 50 spectators, i.e. visitors, were invited to share life with the shelter's inhabitants (played by the actors) all night long. In *Das 13. Jahr* (The 13th year) (2023) SIGNA built a village 'surrounded by dense fog' in which the visitors are transported back to their 13th year of life and assigned to one of the village's families.

The effects of the coming together of live performance and video games include increased interdisciplinary co-operation between different professional groups and the development of new technical and artistic skills. In some forms of game theatre we can observe the collaboration of professions from traditional theatre and professions new to theatre such as computer scientists and game designers. Many of these collaborations enable new ways of both thinking about theatre and of making video games, which can find inspiration in live performance.

---

7 See https://machinaex.org/en/

8 See https://signa.dk.

Gaming as performance

The integration of performance and video games: A question of perspective

Shifting perspective to look at the relationship between live performance and video games from the gaming side, we can observe many instances of inspiration, appropriation, and transfer.

Here the concept of 'liveness' is significant. In performance studies, a liveness debate was largely initiated by Peggy Phelan (1993) and Philip Auslander. In his book *Liveness: Performance in a Mediatised Culture* (1999), Auslander demonstrates the historicity of the concept, arguing that it is not an ontological condition, but has emerged since the development of recording technologies, as a historical condition of certain representations. As Auslander points out, following the establishment of the dichotomy between 'live' and 'recorded', our understanding has continued to change with the emergence of new formats such as live broadcasts or even live recordings.[9] In a later essay, Auslander (2012) develops these ideas further. For digital technologies, which could easily include games, Auslander argues that liveness is an interaction produced through our engagement with the object and our willingness to accept its claim (2012, 9). Following this logic, when we play games, we expect real-time interactions with a machine that we can perceive as live. The concept of liveness must therefore be understood as something more comprehensive in the context of video games. Nevertheless, there are several different ways to mix live performance and video games.

Mixed art forms such as mixed-media performances or alternate reality games can be considered either from the point of view of live performance or from that of games, since both elements are included though, depending on the project, one or the other may predominate. The *framing medium* (Müller 2000), through which everything is ultimately perceived, is sometimes quite difficult to define. Alternate reality games often link the virtual and the physical worlds using GPS tracking. Mixed-media performances (Giannachi 2004) can exploit new potentials created by the use of augmented reality (AR) and virtual reality (VR) technology. Escape room games are a related category. They may contain performative elements and many draw inspiration from video games. However, escape room games are primarily perceived as sui generis and thus represent a framing medium in their own right.

---

9   While the co-presence of actors and spectators was often assumed to be constitutive of theatre performances, live performances today have to be defined more broadly. In various theatre performances, the shared co-presence has also been called into question by the fact that the audience and performers were in different places and communication was only possible via media technology, usually video.

While references to game culture, the use of video game technology and game design elements may seem optional in some live performances, other live events are inconceivable without elements drawn from video games, such as concert performances of game music. This is even clearer when gaming is the central element of a live event, as in e-sports or speedrun events. Even if the framing medium is live performance, gaming is the central element here.[10] The same applies to gaming performances on Twitch, even if these are mediatised and feature both greater interaction via chat and a slightly different role for the performers, who also take on the role of commentators. So even though gaming is the central element here, another major focus is on entertainment and performance as it is at some e-sport events.

Another hybrid situation is *virtual theatre* (Giannachi 2004, Dixon 2007). This form, which gained popularity in the 1990s and attempts to transport a theatrical experience into the virtual world, allows the 'spectators' to meet the actors in the form of avatars on a virtual stage. In this format, audience interaction means that each performance is different, and the levels of playfulness and performativity within those interactions may vary widely.

Marlena Huuhka (2020) provides one of the most complete overviews of the various possible combinations of video games and performance. She distinguishes five approaches to interweaving video games and performance. The first considers video games as an aesthetic resource in performances. Equally, performances can be used as an aesthetic resource within games, such as the theatre you can visit in *Red Dead Redemption 2* (Rockstar Games, 2018). The second approach examines video games as a structural category in performances and in various forms of immersive theatre, an approach already discussed above. Conversely, video games can be structured around essentially performative elements as in the *Just Dance* game series (Ubisoft, 2009–) where players are required to perform dance moves. The third approach focuses on performances staged within video games, such as the 2019 Marshmello concert attended by ten million spectators in *Fortnite* (Epic Games, 2017). The fourth category, 'performances made with video games' encompasses mixed-media performances and alternate reality games by artists such as Blast Theory. Huuhka analyses the concept of 'gameplay as performance' in the fifth category. For gameplay to be considered as performance, the player needs to abandon the ordinary goals and plot elements of the game and play it with a different purpose. However, considering only such 'counterplay' as performative may be a little bit too restrictive.

---

10   The question of the domination of one medium over another or even the incorporation of the latter in the former has been widely debated in studies of intermediality and performance (Chapple, Kattenbelt 2006/ Bay-Cheng et al. 2010).

The performative view of games and gaming

Besides counterplay, various other forms of play in video games can also be considered as performative. Since Brenda Laurel's *Computers as Theatre* (1991), attempts have been made to apply methods from theatre and performance studies to gain new insights about computer software. In a pioneering text in game studies, Espen Aarseth (Aarseth 1997, 21) identifies a 'performative aspect' in what he calls 'ergodic literature', which challenges the reader to interact. Another pioneer, researcher and game designer Gonzalo Frasca, has been trying to develop video games inspired by Augusto Boal's theatre work and to reflect on them rigorously since his Master's thesis (2001). Various researchers have since tried to fine-tune these approaches to gain a better understanding of various aspects of computer games.

Many researchers refer to the classical literature of performance studies: John L. Austin's speech act theory and the reality-generating qualities of language, John R. Searle's focus on intentionality, Jacques Derrida's counter-position and focus on the historical linguistic context, Erving Goffman's performance of social identities and Judith Butler's gender performance, Richard Schechner's performing as 'showing doing' and his concept of 'restored behaviour', and Erika Fischer-Lichte's concept of the transformative potential of performance. According to Erika Fischer-Lichte, the lowest common denominator of all performativity theories is that performative processes are always self-referential and reality-constituting (Fischer-Lichte 2021, 157).

Clara Fernández-Vara (2009) was one of the first to propose a more systematic framework for analysing computer games with the help of insights from performance theory and theatre studies. In her approach, the players take on the roles of both performer – via their interaction with the game – and the spectator, who makes sense of the videoludic sign system (Fernández-Vara 2009, 6). This idea was further developed by Britta Neitzel, who described the avatar controlled by the players as a 'point of action', which is always accompanied by a 'point of view' from which the data body can be observed by the players (Neitzel 2018, 184). In his dissertation, *Acts of play: Games as experiential performance* (2013), Michael St. Clair develops, without referring to Fernández-Vara, but in a similar direction, a performance studies approach to games which 'should focus on games principally as things people do, and only secondarily as media objects or technological artifacts' (St. Clair 2013, 4). He places particular emphasis on analysing physical aspects of the players' practice. As research focuses more on the players, gaming is increasingly being considered as an embodied performative practice. Darshana Jayemanne's concept of 'performative multiplicities' (2017) is one of the most recent comprehensive attempts to apply a performative approach to video games. Due to the large number of possible performances in games, this approach is deliberately comparative and not typological (Jayemanne 2017, 2). One feature of this approach is the distinction between diachrony and synchrony, in which narration can be described as a synchronising element that brings together different performances (Jayemanne 2017, 26).

Performance theory is often applied to the study of video game characters. Some researchers have discussed the relationship between players and character avatars in terms of performance. The parallels between controlling avatars and manipulating puppets have been identified at least since Emma Westecott's paper 'The Player Character as Performing Object' (2009). Performance studies theory is also often applied to role-playing games. Pen and paper RPGs have been identified as performative at least since Daniel Mackay (2001). As Hoover, Simkins, Deterding et al. point out 'though modern role-playing games (RPGs) sprouted more from military wargames than from theatre, from the beginning, RPGs were seen as an interesting way of telling stories, playing characters, exploring themes and recasting performance rituals in a new and personal light' (Hoover, Simkins, Deterding et al. 2018, 213). RPG participants are considered to be simultaneously actors and spectators (Hoover, Simkins, Deterding et al. 2018, 217), especially in massively multiplayer online role-playing games, in which roles are performed in front of a large number of other players.

While a performative view of games often centres on questions of (role-)play, embodiment, and incorporation (Calleja 2011), other aspects like acting, dramaturgy, temporality and spatiality are also addressed. For example, to get a better understanding of video game space, Andre Westerside and Jussi Holopainen propose using site-specific performance theory (2019). Michael Nitsche looks at actions of the video game players in reference to improvisational theatre (Nitsche 2014, 390), while Magdalena Leichter, in her case study of *Tacoma* (Fullbright 2017), searches for performative elements in some games on the intradiegetic level, which she recognises above all in the development of a self-referential reality and requests to the players to co-create and complete the game world (2019).

As the numerous interactions between game studies and performance studies show, an exchange can be extremely fruitful and lead to new approaches and insights. While intermediality has been an important field of research in theatre studies, more publications address explicitly the topic of intermediality in game studies (Neitzel 2015, Fuchs, Thoss 2019). The performative view on games and gaming can help us to better understand video games, their elements, and their effects, but also the practice of playing and the various possibilities for staging gaming. As Michael Nitsche points out 'any introduction of an established discipline into the field of game studies not only opens up new opportunities but can also lead to misconceptions and mismatches in terminology and methodology' (Nitsche 2010, 11). It is not always possible to simply adopt approaches from the other discipline, as the specific characteristics of each medium must always be considered. As the terms gamification and, above all, performance or performativity have been interpreted very comprehensively and historically in many different ways, it is always important to describe which aspects are being referred to precisely in each case. However, as many video games and live performances are themselves becoming increasingly hybrid, interdisciplinary approaches are becoming more and more necessary.

The sections and articles of this volume

In the fifteen different contributions included in this book, a number of international authors attempt to shed further light on various aspects of the complex relationship between video games and performance. Some contributions were written alone, others are polyphonic, some are formulated as essays, others in the form of a dialogue or interview. Some concentrate more on the gamification of live performance, others focus more on performativity in games and still others more on the interfaces that arise from the interplay of the two forms. As almost all contributions address a variety of topics, categorising them into different areas was anything but easy. The division into different sections should therefore not be understood as restrictive, but rather as the creation of resonance spaces in which the individual articles illuminate common points from different directions.

Entitled *Potential and Critique of a gamified Theatre*, section one brings together diverse approaches to a theatre enriched with game elements. First, the conversation entitled 'It's (Not) Only a Game'... some (game-changing) potentials of game-based theatre' between Josephine Machon and the practitioners Munotida Chinyanga and Persis-Jadé Maravala shows how playing or gaming can go beyond a simple game-based theatre and become dramaturgical methods for establishing 'communities' within live performance. The performance events created by those two artists seek to rebuild physical connection across neighbourhoods and set up ways for creative and critical transformation in the society. Second, in 'Video Games, Flow and Immersive Theatre: Participatory Arts in the Ultraliberal Era' Olivia Levet, by contrast, shows a darker side of gamified theatre, arguing that the concept of the 'flow state', as used in video games and extended to immersive theatre, leads to an ideological shift in participatory processes. Taking up Adam Alston's thesis (2013), she considers that while they could originally lead to emancipation, participatory processes are now mainly being diverted in favour of individual sensational experiences, which seem to adopt the values of ultraliberal ideology. Third, applying her idea of a 'ludic neuro-method', the artist and researcher Margarete Jahrmann presents in 'Ludic neuro-performances: An approach towards playful experiments', a concept of artistic research that understands play as a process of questioning research methods, experimental rules, or technologies. Against this background, she discusses two of her own performances that test new forms of play using technologies such as neural interfaces or AI.

The second section, entitled *New (game) technologies for the theatre*, focuses on the theatrical use of technologies that play a major role in the gaming sector. It addresses the new possibilities, but also the challenges that these technologies bring with them, as well as artists' desire to respond to the audience's world outside the theatre. Georges Gagneré, in 'Directing Avatars in Live Performances – an Autonomy Simulacrum of Virtual Actors', reviews the history of virtual actors before going on to discuss theatre work with avatars, above all reflecting his own artistic praxis. The question of the autonomy of virtual actors emerges as a central aspect, alongside the new possibilities that arise for theatre makers in terms of presence and human-computer interaction. In 'Unreal Engine in the theatre: New challenges for the lighting designer', Victor Inisan deals with the very specific question of the potentials and challenges of using the game engine Unreal Engine for theatre lighting. The use of Unreal Engine 5 is compared to other visualisation software, and discussed in terms of how it can change the work of the lighting designer and influence theatre aesthetics. 'Combining layers of reality. Live performance and video game elements in performance' by theatre director Christophe Burgess addresses the use of VR technology in theatre, taking his own immersive performance *Brainwaves* (2021) as an example. He explains the various technical and artistic motivations and challenges involved in the work with VR, motion capture, and avatars as well as collaboration with artists from different disciplines.

Section three, entitled *Working at the interface of games and performance*, brings together a variety of interviews and conversations with artists influenced by theatre and video games who design artworks mixing the two media/artforms. In 'Gaming in performance. Between research and artistic approach', Helen W. Kennedy interviews Matt Adams, who explores some of the key influences and trajectories underpinning the work of Blast Theory, an internationally renowned artists' group at the forefront of innovative interactive storytelling. The interview shows how the artistic practices of Blast Theory make use of and advance the possibilities of play, games, and live performance. In 'Machina eX: Working collectively at the interface of theatre and video games' researchers Réjane Dreifuss and Simon Hagemann talk to Clara Ehrenwerth and Anton Krause, two current members of machina eX, pioneers of game theatre in Germany. They look back at some of their shows over the last thirteen years and address various questions about the interplay between video games and theatre: the role of the audience, the artistic input of games, different venues, the role of technology, and the political dimension of games. Finally, 'What even is video game performance?' is a conversation between performance scholar Marleena Huuhka and live artist Harold Hejazi about video games as a medium of performance. Through examples from their own practice, they discuss contemporary video game performances as well as gameplay as performance and the possible futures of these intermedial artistic forms.

Play is a key term in both theatre and (video) games. Section four, entitled *(Digital) play as performance*, focuses on the performative dimension of, mainly digital, play in various configurations. In 'Play, Performance, Agency: Prompt Injections and Playful Misuses of AI' Miguel Sicart deals with the contemporary practice of prompt injections in generative AIs. It is Sicart's stated intention to change our perspective on generative AIs by no longer seeing them as independent, function-driven systems, but as agents we must enter into a relationship with, appropriating these new technologies in ways that are creative and playful, but also ethically conscious. This also suggests that a playful approach does not have to be limited to the magic circle of a game but can also have an effect beyond it. 'Operations & Encounters: Playing Out Performativity' by Mary Flanagan discusses performativity in digital and non-digital play through the lens of media archaeology and spans the arc of various media art projects, especially her own pioneering artistic works, from virtual theatres of the 1990s to more recent interactive activist artworks. She shows that already early net artworks can be regarded as highly performative. Flanagan notes that her own work has increasingly moved offline because, as she explains, our everyday experiences are so dominated by a technology that has yet to adequately address its own biases and shortcomings (from commercialism to addiction to data collection). Finally, Fanny Barnabé and Sacha Bernard in 'From Home to Stage: How Speedrunners Negotiate Performance, Relation to the Audience, and Spectacle in Live-Streaming Speedrun Marathons' explore a staged form of play using the example of charity speedrun marathons. The article, methodologically based on an analysis of a series of interviews with various actors, including speedrunners, commentators, entertainers, and reviewers, shows how this specific performance of gaming is perceived and how this perception is determined by a variety of factors or frames of reference.

The fifth section, *Understanding video games through a performative gaze*, proposes a new understanding of video games by looking at their performative qualities, in terms of dramaturgy, temporality, and materiality. In 'The Dramaturgy of video games: A Dialogue' Mike Sell and Michael M. Chemers attempt to extend their conception of theatre dramaturgy to video games. An essential feature of their discussion is that the video gamer should be understood as operating a dramaturgy, like an actor, director, or dramaturg. Computer games thus become an *improvisational dramaturgy*, in which the various systems of the game are used in an experimental way to create meaningful experiences. The second article in this section, 'On Time Compression and Déjà vu: Remastering, Remaking, Modding and Performing Final Fantasy' by Darshana Jayemanne and Cameron Kunzelman, is based on the concept of performative multiplicity initially developed by Jayemanne in *Performativity in Art, Literature and Videogames* (2017) but is extended here with a special focus on temporal dynamics and taking into account new phenomena such as the *platformification* of cultural production. The performative perspective can help us to better understand the different temporal dynamics in such diverse forms as remakes, demakes, remasterings, and mods in reference to the *Final Fantasy* game series. Finally, in 'Video Games as Material Performances', Michael Nitsche argues for the perspective of object theatre to be brought to bear on video games. Drawing on aspects of puppetry, Human Computer Interaction (HCI), and New Materialism, Nitsche argues game objects should be viewed as performing pieces with their own agency. Finishing with a case study of *Tetris* (Pajitnov, 1985–) he argues that players can be considered as a species of puppeteers, also showing how gameplay can also be understood as a co-emergent performance between human action and the actions of the game objects.

References

Aarseth, Espen J. 1997. *Cybertext. Perspectives on Ergodic Literature*. Baltimore and London: Johns Hopkins University Press.

Adorno, Theodore W. 1970. *Ästhetische Theorie*. Frankfurt am Main: Suhrkamp.

Alston, Adam. 2013. *Beyond Immersive Theatre: Aesthetics, politics and productive participation*. Basingstoke: Palgrave Macmillan.

Annis, Heather Marie, Amy Lee, and Byron Laviolette. 2019. 'The Scripting of Unscripted: The Game of Making Theatre and the Theatre of Making a Game.' *Canadian Theatre Review* 178 (Spring): 14–19. https://doi.org/10.3138/ctr.178.003.

Auslander, Philip. 1997. *From Acting to Performance: Essays in Modernism and Postmodernism*. London, New York: Routledge.

———. 2008. *Liveness: Performance in a Mediatized Culture*, Second Edition. New York: Routledge.

———. 2012. 'Digital liveness: A historico-philosophical perspective.' *PAJ: A Journal of Performance Art* 34, No. 3 (Fall): 3–11. https://doi.org/10.1162/PAJJ_a_00106.

Balme, Christopher, Erika Fischer-Lichte, and Stephan Grätzel, eds. 2003. *Theater als Paradigma der Moderne? Positionen zwischen historischer Avantgarde und Medienzeitalter*. Tübingen and Basel: A. Francke Verlag.

Bay-Cheng, Sarah, Chiel Kattenbelt, Andy Lavender, and Robin Nelson, eds. 2010. *Mapping Intermediality in Performance*. Amsterdam: Amsterdam University Press.

Belting, Hans. 2002. *Das Ende der Kunstgeschichte. Eine Revision nach zehn Jahren*. München: C. H. Beck.

Bieger, Laura. 2007. *Ästhetik der Immersion. Raum-Erleben zwischen Welt und Bild*. Bielefeld: transcript.

Biggin, Rose. 2017. *Immersive Theatre and Audience Experience. Space, Game and Story in the Work of Punchdrunk*. London: Palgrave Macmillan.

Birch, Anna, and Joanne Tompkins, eds. 2012. *Performing Site-Specific Theatre: Politics, Place, Practice*. Basingstoke: Palgrave Macmillan.

Bishop, Claire. 2012. *Artificial Hells. Participatory Art and the Politics of Spectatorship*. New York: Verso.

Blake, Bill. 2014. *Theater and the Digital*. Basingstoke: Palgrave Macmillan.

Blanco Jessen, Constanza. 2021. 'Performative game or theatre gamification? What a gameformance is and why interactive theatre should be interested in it.' *Estudis Escénics* 46 (Fall):1–13.

Bouko, Catherine. 2016. 'Le théâtre immersif : une définition en trois paliers.' *Société* 134, no. 4: 55–65. https://doi.org/10.3917/soc.134.0055.

Borries, Friedrich. 2016. *Weltentwerfen. Eine politische Designtheorie*. Berlin: Suhrkamp.

Büscher, Barbara. 2018. 'Gaming-Strategien im Theater: Spiel-Situationen, dokumentiert und notiert. Methodische Überlegungen zur (Aufführungs-)Analyse.' In *Digitale Spiele. Interdisziplinäre Perspektiven zu Diskursfeldern, Inszenierung und Musik*, edited by Christof Hust, 193–204. Bielefeld: transcript.

Calleja, Gordon. 2011. *In-Game: From Immersion to Incorporation*, Cambridge, Mass. London: MIT Press.

Chapple, Freda, and Chiel Kattenbelt, eds. 2006. *Intermediality in Theatre and Performance*. Amsterdam, New York: Rodopi.

Cotta, Alain. 1980. *La société ludique: la vie envahie par le jeu*. Paris: Grasset.

Couchot, Edmond. 1998. *La technologie dans l'art: de la photographie à la réalité virtuelle*. Nîmes: Jacqueline Chambon.

Dixon, Steve, with contributions by Barry Smith. 2007. *Digital Performance. A History of New Media in Theater, Dance, Performative Art, and Installation*. Cambridge, Massachusetts: The MIT Press.

Drewes, Miriam. 2010. *Theater als Ort der Utopie. Zur Ästhetik von Ereignis und Präsenz*. Bielefeld: transcript.

Fernández-Vara, Clara. 2009. 'Play's the Thing: A Framework to Study Videogames as Performance', Proceedings of DiGRA.

Fischer-Lichte, Erika. 2004. *Ästhetik des Performativen*. Frankfurt am Main: Suhrkamp.

———. 2021. *Performativität. Eine kulturwissenschaftliche Einführung*, Fourth edition. Bielefeld: transcript.

Fischer-Lichte, Erika, Kristiane Hasselmann, and Markus Rautzenberg, eds. 2010. *Ausweitung der Kunstzone. Interart Studies –Neue Perspektiven der Kunstwissenschaften*. Bielefeld: transcript.

Foster, Greg, 2017. *Towards a Theatre for Gamers : a new paradigm of practice in contemporary live performance as a response to games and interactivity in digital media and performance culture*. (Thesis). University of Salford.

Frasca, Gonzalo. 2001. 'Videogames of the oppressed. Videogames as a means for critical thinking and debate.' MA Thesis, Atlanta Georgia Institute of Technology.

Freydefont, Marcel. 2010. 'Les contours d'un théâtre immersif (1990–2010).' *Agôn* (en ligne) 3: *Utopies de la scène, scènes de l'utopie*. https://doi.org/ 10.4000/agon.1559.

Frieze, James. 2017. *Reframing Immersive Theatre: The Politics and Pragmatics of Participatory Performance*. Basingstoke: Palgrave Macmillan.

Fuchs, Michael, and Jeff Thoss, eds. 2019. *Intermedia Games—Games Inter Media: Video Games and Intermediality*. New York: Bloomsbury.

Giannachi, Gabriella. 2004. *Virtual theatres. An Introduction*. London and New York: Routledge.

Homan, Daniel, and Sidney Homan. 2014. 'The Interactive Theater of Video Games: The Gamer as Playwright, Director and Actor.' *Comparative Drama* 48, no.1/2 (Spring & Summer): 169–186. https://doi.org/10.1353/cdr.2014.0000.

Hoover, Sarah, David Simkins, Sebastian Deterding, David Meldman, and Amanda Brown. 2018. 'Performance Studies and Role-Playing Games.' In *Role-Playing Game Studies: A transmedia approach*, edited by José P. Zagal and Sebastian Deterding, 213–226. New York: Routledge.

Huuhka, Marleena. 2020. 'Playing is Performing: Video Games as Performance', In *Einspielungen. Neue Perspektiven der Medienästhetik*, edited by Markus Spöhrer, and Harald Waldrich. Wiesbaden: Springer VS. https://doi.org/10.1007/978-3-658-3 0721-9_3.

Jayemanne, Darshana. 2017. *Performativity in Art, Literature and Videogames*. Cham: Palgrave Macmillan.

Klotz, Heinrich. 1999. *Kunst im 20.Jahrhundert: Moderne, Postmoderne, Zweite Moderne*. München: C.H. Beck.

Kolesch, Doris, Teresa Stütz, and Sophie Nikoleit, eds. 2021. *Staging Spectators in Immersive Performances. Commit yourself!* London: Routledge.

Laurel, Brenda. 1991. *Computers as theater*. Reading: Addison-Wesley.

Lehmann, Hans-Thies. 1999. *Postdramatisches Theater*. Frankfurt am Main: Verlag der Autoren.

Le Lay, Stéphane, Emmanuelle Savignac, Jean Frances, and Pierre Lénel, eds. 2021. *Gamification of Society*, Volume 2. London: Wiley.

Leichter, Magdalena. 2019. 'Zwischen Passivität und Involvierung: Elemente der Performance im Computerspiel am Beispiel von "Tacoma".' *Paidia: Computer Game Research Journal* (Summer). https://paidia.de/zwischen-passivitaet-und-i nvolvierung-elemente-der-performance-im-computerspiel-am-beispiel-von-t acoma/.

Machon, Josephine. 2013. *Immersive Theaters: Intimacy and Immediacy in Contemporary Performance*. Basingstoke: Palgrave Macmillan.

Mackay, Daniel. 2001. *The Fantasy Role-Playing Game: A New Performing Art*. Jefferson: McFarland & Company.

Männel, Juliane. 2018. '"Put theater at play": Spielanordnungen im Theater Aktuelle Tendenzen und methodische Fragen an Aufführungen als Spiel-Situationen.' In

Digitale Spiele. Interdisziplinäre Perspektiven zu Diskursfeldern, Inszenierung und Musik, edited by Christof Hust, 205–218: Bielefeld: transcript.

Manovich, Lev. 2001. *The Language of New Media*. Cambridge, Massachusetts and London: MIT Press.

Masura, Nadja. 2020. *Digital Theater. The Making and the Meaning of Life Mediated Performance, UK & US 1990–2020*. New York: Springer International Publishing.

Mersch, Dieter, Anton Rey, Thomas Grunwald, Jörg Sternagel, Lorena Kegel, and Miriam Laura Loertscher, eds. 2023. *Actor & Avatar. A Scientific and Artistic Catalog*. Bielefeld: transcript.

Müller, Jürgen E. 2000. 'L'intermédialité, une nouvelle approche interdisciplinaire: perspectives théoriques et pratiques à l'exemple de la vision de la télévision.' *CiNéMAS* 10, no.2–3 (Winter): 105–134. https://doi.org/10.7202/024818ar.

Neitzel, Britta. 2015. 'Performing Games: Intermediality and Video Games.' In *Handbook of Intermediality. Literature – Image – Sound – Music*, edited by Gabriele Rippl, 584–604. Berlin/Boston: de Gruyter.

———. 2018. 'Videospiele(n) als Aufführung(en) und Aufführungen in Videospielen.' In *Digitale Spiele. Interdisziplinäre Perspektiven zu Diskursfeldern, Inszenierung und Musik*, edited by Christof Hust: 179–192. Bielefeld: transcript.

Nitsche, Michael. 2010. 'Games as Structures for mediated Performances.' In *Logic and Structure of the Computer Game*, edited by Stephan Günzel, Michael Liebe, and Dieter Mersch: 110–129. Potsdam: Potsdam University Press.

———. 2014. 'Performance.' In *The Routledge Companion of Video Game Studies*, edited by Mark P. Wolf, and Bernard Perron: 388–396. New York: Routledge.

Otto, Ulf. 2013. *Internetauftritte. Eine Theatergeschichte der neuen Medien*. Bielefeld: transcript.

Phelan, Peggy. 1993. *Unmarked: The Politics of Performance*. London and New York: Routledge.

Plett, Heinrich F., ed. 1991. *Intertextuality*. Berlin: De Gruyter.

Poissant, Louise. 1997. *Dictionnaire des arts médiatiques*. Sainte-Foy: Presse de l'Université du Québec.

Pluta, Izabella. 2010. 'Hybridity.' In *Mapping Intermediality in Performance*, edited by Bay-Cheng S., Chiel Kattenbelt, Andy Lavender, Robin Nelson: 186–187. Amsterdam: Amsterdam University Press.

———. 2022. 'L'enjeu épistémologique du dispositif technologique sur la scène contemporaine. Exemple de *Game-Theatre*.' In *Observer le théâtre, pour une nouvelle épistémologie des spectacles*, edited by Sandrine Dubouilh and Pierre Katuszewski: 71–83. Bordeaux: Presses universitaires de Bordeaux.

———. 2022. 'Introduction. Artistes de la scène à l'épreuve des dispositifs technologiques. Topographie de la pratique scénique et de la pensée théorique.' In *Scènes numériques. Anthologie critique. Digital Stages. Critical Anthology*, edited by Izabella

Pluta, in collaboration with Margot Dacheux, Simon Hagemann, Hervé Guay, and Eugénie Pastor : 19–42. Rennes: Presses universitaires de Rennes.

Prinz, Mathias. 2022. 'Au croisement du théâtre et des jeux vidéo: vers un spectateur-joueur. Entretien réalisé par Réjane Dreifuss.' In *Scènes numériques. Anthologie critique. Digital Stages. Critical anthology*, edited by Izabella Pluta, in collaboration with Margot Dacheux, Hervé Guay, Simon Hagemann, and Eugénie Pastor: 409–414. Rennes: Presses universitaires de Rennes.

Rajewsky, Irina. 2002. *Intermedialität*. Tübingen: Francke.

Rakow, Christian. 2012. 'Die Ritter der Interaktivität. Computerspiele und Theater – Wie die neue Medienkunst die Bühnenwirklichkeit verändert,' *Nacht Kritik*, November 15, 2012. https://nachtkritik.de/index.php?option=com_content&view=article&id=7452:computerspiele-und-theater-wie-die-neue-medienkunst-die-buehnenwirklichkeit-veraendert&catid=101:debatte&Itemid=84.

———. 2013. 'Playing Democracy', *Nacht Kritik*, 9 November 2013. https://nachtkritik.de/portraet-reportage/a-presentation-about-the-new-game-theatre-and-its-political-relevance-at-the-conference-replayce-thecity-in-zuerich.

———. 2015. 'Game Theater', *POP. Kultur und Kritik*, Heft 6, Frühling: 88–93. https://doi.org/10.25969/mediarep/821.

Ryan, Marie-Laure. 2001. *Narrative as virtual reality: immersion and interactivity in literature and electronic media*. Baltimore: The Johns Hopkins University.

Schechner, Richard. 2002. *Performance Studies. An introduction*, second edition. New York: Routledge.

Sermon, Julie and Jean-Pierre Ryngaert,. 2012. *Théâtres du XXIe siècle: commencements*. Paris: Armand Colin.

Salter, Chris. 2010. *Entangled. Technology and the Transformation of Performance*. Cambridge, Massachusetts, London: The MIT Press.

———. 2022. *Sensing Machines: How Sensors Shape our Everyday Life*. Massachusetts: MIT Press.

St. Clair, Michael Aaron. 2013. 'Acts of play: games as experiential performance,' PhD diss., Stanford University.

Stalder, Felix. 2016. *Kultur der Digitalität*. Berlin: Suhrkamp.

Tecklenburg, Nina. 2022. *Performing Stories. Narrative as Performance*. Kolkata: Seagull Books.

Vinck, Dominique. 2016. *Humanités numériques: la culture face aux nouvelles technologies*. Paris: Le Cavalier bleu.

Wellershoff, Dieter. 1989. *Die Auflösung des Kunstbegriffs*. Frankfurt am Main: Suhrkamp.

Westecott, Emma. 2009. 'The Player Character as Performing Object.' Proceedings of DiGRA.

Westerside, Andrew, and Jussi Holopainen. 2019. 'Sites of Play: Locating Gameplay in Red Dead Redemption 2.' Proceedings of DiGRA.

Wiens, Birgit. 2014. *Intermediale Szenographie. Raum-Ästhetiken des Theaters am Beginn des 21. Jahrhunderts*. Paderborn: Wilhelm Fink Verlag.

Zichermann, Gabe, and Joselin Linder. 2013. *The Gamification Revolution: How Leaders Leverage Game Mechanics to Crush the Competition*. New York: McGraw-Hill.

Biographies

Réjane Dreifuss has worked as a dramaturge and project manager for the theatre company SONIMAGE. Together with the author and director Igor Bauersima, she has written and directed theatre plays under the pseudonym Réjane Desvignes, in which digital technologies played a crucial role in the creation of narratives. Since 2016, she has been researching the influence of digitalization on theatre, with a particular focus on the generation of new narrative forms. She is lecturer and researcher in the Department Performing Arts and Film at the Zurich University of Arts.

Simon Hagemann is a lecturer in communication at the IUT of Saint-Dié-des-Vosges (University of Lorraine) and an associate researcher at CREM (Centre de recherche sur les médiations). He also holds a doctorate in theatre studies (Université Sorbonne Nouvelle-Paris 3). His work focuses on video games, theatre, and media innovations, and he is currently working on the representation of history in video games. He is the author of *Penser les médias au théâtre, des avant-gardes historiques au théâtre contemporain* (L'Harmattan, 2013) and co-author of *Quels rôles pour le spectateur à l'ère numérique?* (Epistémé, 2024).

Izabella Pluta is a researcher in performing arts (PhD holder in theatre and cinema), a theatrical critic and translator, and an independent researcher associated with the Centre of Theatre Studies (University of Lausanne). She is the recipient of a Fernand Braudel/Marie Curie Cofound fellowship and has undertaken research at Université Lyon 2 and Ecole Nationale Supérieure des Arts et des Techniques du Théâtre (2013–2014). In 2020, she has been Associate Director of Studies (DEA) founded by Fondation Maison des Sciences de l'Homme and visited several laboratories and research institutions in France, including Atelier Art/Science in Grenoble and Studio Fresnoy in Tourcoing (Lille). She is the author of *L'Acteur et l'intermédialité* (L'Age d'homme 2011), coedited a special issue of the journal *Ligeia* entitled 'Théâtres Laboratoires' with Mireille Losco-Lena (January 2015). Her other publications include *Metteur en scène aujourd'hui – identité artistique en question?* (a collaboration with Gabrielle Girot, PUR 2017), '*Salle d'attente' de Krystian Lupa* (Antipodes, 2019) and a collective book of artistic manifestos *Scènes numériques. Digital Stages* (PUR 2022). In

2024, she co-edited *Quels rôles pour le spectateur à l'ère numérique* with Simon Hagemann (Epistémé 2024). (www.izabellapluta.com)

Potential and Critique of a Gamified Theatre

'It's (Not) Only a Game'...
some Game-Changing Potentials
of Game-Based Theatre

Josephine Machon with Munotida Chinyanga and Persis-Jadé Maravala

> Play is as essential as food, air, sleep,
> whatever else we have to do to stay alive
> *(Cas Holman: Design for Play)*

Abstract *This conversation between Josephine Machon, Munotida Chinyanga and Persis-Jadé Maravala surveys some potentials of game-based theatre. We consider how play, gaming and gameshow, as aesthetic methods for establishing 'communities' within live performance, resonate with Joan Littlewood's 'Fun Palace' ideals, as illustrated by State of the [Art]'s How To Build [The City] (2021/2022) and ZU-UK's Pick Me Up (& Hold Me Tight) (2020), Project Perfect Stranger/PlagueRound (2021) and Radio Ghost (2021-).*

Introduction

This chapter began as a 'keynote-conversation', with contexts, themes, and provocations framed by Josephine Machon, to which Munotida Chinyanga (Co-founder, Co-artistic Director of State of the [Art]) and Persis-Jadé Maravala (Co-founder, Artistic Director of ZU-UK), responded through reflection on their practice.[1] State of the [Art] and ZU-UK, in comparable and contrasting ways, construct performance 'playgrounds' and offer models for the potentials of game-based theatre in reimagining social relationships; an ethos that was necessarily exercised and re-examined during the crisis of Covid-19. The conversation offers reflections on the appropriations, inspirations, and mutual transfers of play, game, and gaming *in*

---

1   For information on State of the [Art] see, https://chinyangam.wixsite.com/stateoftheart/ho me, and for ZU-UK and all works referenced see, https://zu-uk.com/.

and *as* theatre. We consider how play, gaming, and gameshow, become dramaturgical methods for establishing 'community' within live performance, as illustrated by State of the [Art]'s *How To Build [The City]* (H2BTC, 2021/2022) and ZU-UK's *Pick Me Up (& Hold Me Tight)* (2020), *Project Perfect Stranger/PlagueRound* (2021) and *Radio Ghost* (2021–).

Framed and edited by Machon in the spirit and style of its original form, names have been abbreviated to Jo, Munotida, and Persis-Jadé and a conversational style and layout maintained. Any text that appears in quotation marks without academic citation belongs to the named practitioner, indicated within the sentence. Other sources are referenced accordingly.

Play as ethos, discipline, training

State of the [Art] is an international collective, co-founded and co-artistically directed by Munotida, based in London, and Simone Giustinelli in Rome, with a multicultural ensemble of Associate Artists. It was set up as an artist development programme in 2018, evolving out of the MA Theatre Arts at Middlesex University to give underrepresented emerging artists based in the UK the opportunity to train and develop work around Europe. It quickly found its 'antidisciplinary' approach, combining intercultural, multilingual, physical storytelling and gamified narratives within diverse relational aesthetics. Its focus is twofold; facilitating interactive experiences for audiences that do not identify as 'citizens of the arts'; and, for the collective, continuing to 'redefine the relationships and rules of practice'.

Anglo-Brazilian ZU-UK, founded by Persis-Jadé and Jorge Lopes Ramos as Zecora Ura Theatre Network in 2005 and known as ZU-UK since 2012, works at the intersection of performance, games, and technology. Persis-Jadé designs experiences that are playable, interactive, and always driven by the political. Situating art in places that 'non-arty people go', the company plays inventively with readily available *and* cutting-edge tech. Played out across public spaces, ZU-UK's work mediates the space between strangers; scaling intimacy by forging playful, sometimes deeply meaningful, connections.

Persis-Jadé: I make player-centred experiences, creating dialogic spaces for players. We use the term 'hacking the familiar' because we're looking at how people 'play games' already in day-to-day social situations in all kinds of ways; hacking, as in, accessing and emphasising everyday behaviours and attitudes. We adjust and repurpose the existing tacit rules we live by to create new perspectives. For this reason, we tend to put our work in clubs, car parks, bingo halls, malls, or public transport, unpicking and replaying the games that are already at work in those spaces. We also work in the digital space, with ubiquitous technology. I've used communication technology and text-messaging to matchmake people in paired performance experiences, generating playful and intimate connections between strangers, for about 15 years; making instruction-based games on Conductor since 2015 and WhatsApp since 2018. When the pandemic happened, that brought games and intimacy into a different, more immediate frame, which fed into the game app we created called *Radio Ghost* (2021–), a three-player game for shopping malls.

I come from a tradition of games as used in interactive theatre and applied drama. When I started out with my own company, ParaActive, I often ended up bartering my skills for rehearsal space, offering after-school workshops for children in return for use of the school hall or community centre. Retrospectively, I realise I was laying the ground for my mid-career work around games and participation. I would have to devise new games every week for them to level up and remain interested. It taught me so much about games and how they're transformative experiences. From there it was the methods and games of Brazilian practitioner Augusto Boal that influenced me.[2] He devised a specific way of politicising people through games, which stayed with me forever. I was inspired by Joan Littlewood's Theatre Workshop and her approach to ensemble-making, forging temporary communities in a short space of time. Clive Barker's theatre games and Keith Johnstone's improvisation games and methods were also influential. I'd later go back to Johnstone's techniques and re-evaluate them through the one-on-one work that I developed, in terms of the discipline and the listening it takes to play more open-ended games with people.[3]

Jo: Munotida, since starting out in 2018, State of the [Art] has spent five years actively investigating games and gameplay as a means of establishing a performance collective and, in turn, a means of that collective establishing a performance vocabulary to interpret an epic text. At the heart of this runs your own fascination with wrestling as a performance convention mixing wrestling terms, techniques, and mythologies with parallel aesthetics and archetypes found in K-Pop.[4]

---

2   For the background and practice of Augusto Boal (1931–2009) and the way play lies at the heart of his 'Theatre of the Oppressed', see *Games for Actors and Non-Actors* (2002), as used by Maravala.

3   We go on to discuss the mission and practice of Joan Littlewood (1914–2002) further below, and recommend her autobiography, *Joan's Book* (1995) for context. Keith Johnstone (1933–2023) was a renowned improviser and pedagogue, whose writings and workshops on improvisation as a performer-training *and* performance-making process continue to influence writers, performers, and educators, especially in Britain and North America. Johnstone's *Impro* (2018) is referenced here by Maravala. For more on the radical working-class advocacy and playful theatre practice of UK performer, actor training coach, and academic, Clive Barker (1931–2005), refer to his *Theatre Games* (2010).

4   K-pop, short for 'Korean Popular Music' is a form of popular music originating in South Korea, made widespread since the late 1990s by social media platforms. For a straightforward explanation of K-pop see Erklärt Tapakapa's video (2016), available at: https://www.youtu

Munotida: I'm a director and sound designer, with a technical mindset for how you can heighten moments using sound, set, space, dimension, and using bodies in that space. I spent much of my childhood watching wrestling. In retrospect, I realise I was engaging with spectacle that was all play. This was my first experience of 'theatre'. There's a lot of talk about wrestling being 'fake', but by examining wrestling as a discipline I saw how it created worlds, performance playgrounds, that are scripted and choreographed. I use wrestling terminology alongside K-pop references and translate that into the space of theatre to interpret epic texts, such as *Gilgamesh*.[5] K-pop terms such as, 'Visual', 'My/Ultimate Bias', 'Stan', 'Fancam', 'Fan Chants', serve as a shorthand among the ensemble.[6] They became references and tools for developing characters, games, or structuring scenes and audience interaction during rehearsals. For instance, each member of a K-pop band has specific roles, including the role of 'Visual', assigned to those who best fit a strict Korean beauty standard. In *H2BTC21*, we had performers on stage and artists engaging with the public outside. The performers on stage were the 'Visuals' because they had the most contact time with the audience, carried them through the show. They had a responsibility to be watched and become the 'popular kids', characters the audience wanted to befriend, to facilitate that relationship. Another example is 'Bias', which defines a K-pop fan's favourite band member. 'Ultimate Bias' is the absolute favourite across all the bands. 'Stan' refers to an extreme K-pop fan and is used as a verb and a noun, 'I stan…', or 'I'm a K-pop stan'. 'Fancam' is unofficial footage taken by these fans. During rehearsals we like to incorporate the 'choose-your-character/player' concept found in video games. This allows performers to develop unique characters, which encourages audiences to develop attachments throughout the show. It's like wrestling, where fans have favourite wrestlers with their own set of rules for engagement, gestures, taunts, catchphrases, including 'Fan Chants'. This elevates each character and encourages audiences to support them physically, vocally. We challenge the audience to engage beyond clapping and traditional theatre behaviour, in ways that are closer to sports events or concerts. We also encourage the audience to take videos during the show; through that video content, we see who they 'stan'. Performers play to the cameras, resulting in 'fancam' edits that we use.

I also paint the picture of what I'm envisaging through wrestling terminology as shorthand for archetypes or archetypical routines; terms and techniques I've ab-

---

be.com/watch?v=_S7XXvQNong. For K-pop archetypes and aesthetics, see Taylor Glasby's overview (2018).

5   *Gilgamesh*, told in the ancient Akkadian language, is the collected tales of the eponymous Mesopotamian hero's odyssey in pursuit of eternal life. See Stephen Mitchell's translation (2005) or Surayo Field Fiorio's and Amir Houshang Moein's animated adaptation (2021).

6   Jason Pham's overview provides a summary and explanation of K-pop terms cited here by Chinyanga (see Pham 2020).

sorbed by watching documentaries, reading books, obsessing about the practice. We use wrestling terms to explain intention and motivation as much as to establish games, movement, postures; Hot Tag, Heel, Main Event, Gimmick, Put Over, or Taunt.[7] If there's a villain, we'll use the term 'Heel' as the ensemble knows the history of 'Heel', which unlocks so many different sequences of actions, intentions, and motivations that then build character or a scene. Because we make work in short and intense timescales, the terminology in performance and those references within design help us to establish performance moments quickly, unlock ways to create the show and communicate meaning.

We also investigate 'play' within the rehearsal room and on stage. In the early days there were times where we'd been working seriously on the text and we'd spontaneously have to break, play a game, have a singalong. Those were the moments where we saw and felt the company's identity. We wanted to translate that within our interpretation of *Gilgamesh*, taking it from the epic to the contemporary, interpreting its seriousness by applying authentic play; examining what it means to play within the shows, keeping it fresh. When it comes to playing as an ensemble, playing *seriously*, there must be an understanding of the science of play. We spend a lot of time reading about gameplay to gamify all aspects of our practice. Everything becomes a game during the process, even when we're sitting for lunch and eating, there's continuous talk of how we can gamify those situations, riffing on ideas in books we've shared that look at ways in which you can turn moments, situations, the rules of games, into experiences. For instance, we transposed management theory to theatre following a shared reading of *Gamestorming* (Grey, Macanufo, Brown 2010).[8] By applying the games to building a collective, a democratic ensemble, we shifted the strategies and gameplay away from any capitalist ideals in the book to uncover the fun of emergent play, where the play alone is the focus and outcome. By identifying the fundamentals and interrelations of any game, we could then explore and expand those ideas to interpret a story with an audience, through competitiveness as much as playfulness in shared dramaturgical composition. Working with and against each other in small groups the ensemble interprets sections of *Gilgamesh* as a game that's entertaining to watch. It helps us to make sense of the themes, to challenge the narrative and in turn that translates into key scenes to present to an audience.

---

7   For the wrestling drills and terminology referenced by Chinyanga here, see Bill Welker's handbook (2013). For historical and critical contexts of wrestling as a performance practice see Sharon Mazer's ethnographical study (2020) or Chow et al. (2016). Wikipedia provides a useful overview for 'Heel', which expands on Chinyanga's subsequent example: see https://en.wikipedia.org/wiki/Heel_(professional_wrestling).

8   *Gamestorming* is a practical handbook, authored by Dave Gray, Sunni Brown and James Macunfo, outlining games for use in the workplace designed to encourage better communication and idea-generation among teams. There is also a website to accompany the book: https://gamestorming.com/ (accessed 21 March 2024)

Similarly, Edward de Bono's *Six Thinking Hats* (2016) enables us to investigate an idea, see if a concept works by using different ways of thinking within the room.[9] Those references in our process, applied in a gamified way, help us understand the limitations and all possible outcomes of whichever scenes we're trying to create. It's a continuous process; those theories inform the creation of new games, becoming a game cycle that evolves, keeps us authentic, and allows us to tell stories without acting (see figure 1).

Figure 1: Gilgamesh *games in H2BTC (2022). Photo: State of the [Art].*

---

9   De Bono's 'Six Hats'® is a creative problem-solving technique based on the human brain's different modes of thinking. In teams, individuals or groups are assigned figurative coloured 'hats' to 'wear': The white hat is facts and data driven; the black hat is caution-led, identifying risks and negatives; yellow hats consider benefits and potential uses of any suggestions; green is creativity, emphasising existing possibilities and alternative ways for developing the ideas generated; red uses feelings, intuition, gut instincts in response, while blue is process-driven, focused on planning and action, summarising findings and identifying next steps. Time limits for each hat enable individuals or groups to 'try on' other hats, which encourages everyone involved to consider the idea from different perspectives.

Gameplay mechanics in the work of ZU-UK and State of the [Art]

Jo: You both inventively deploy gameplay mechanics and tech in performance contexts, to establish performance composition, as well as inviting impromptu or improvised audience engagement in the work.

Persis-Jadé: The important thing about game mechanics in performance is that they should be aligned to the narrative or the theme; the story that's being told. I don't mean a full-on fiction necessarily, but the scenario and trajectory you want participants to experience, goals you want them to engage with. If we're telling the story through game mechanics, the hard work of it is where you try to bring those two things together into a seamless whole. That can happen in quite simple ways. A project that's been running since January 2020, *Pick Me Up (& Hold Me Tight)* rings all the pay phones in the UK at the same time. The tech is set up to call at the annual national peak of suicides, the 1st of January of each year at 11am. There are around 19,000 still working. It takes an enormous amount of tech for the simple mechanic of a phone being triggered to ring, which becomes an invitation for any passer-by to become a player by picking up. When you pick up the phone there's an audio track that you respond to by pressing buttons on the dial pad. We carefully thought through the significance of that central play mechanic. The interactive framework is built around one simple concept that is itself an act of listening, which is what the piece is about; creating better listening and addressing loneliness by asking people to think, just for fifteen minutes, about what it really means to listen to others. That's what I mean when I say the mechanics need to align with the intentions; the actions and the framework can't just be incidental, just for the sake of doing something game-y. It's a strong example of where the mechanic *is* the message. Picking up the phone, pressing the buttons, *is* a commitment to listening, *is* the theme conveyed and behaviour we're promoting. It's all baked in together.

Radio Ghost (2021–), a game for three people to play in shopping malls, explores how we might find a way out of consumer trauma; questions how, in the West, we square our existence, knowing it costs the global majority (see figure 2). Climate research proves it would be dangerous simply to stop consuming, but what we need to do is slow down. With the game, I was committed to building it around the mechanic of physically slowing down, as a literal and metaphorical act of resistance. I was married to that idea and insisted on that trajectory. The game begins by asking players to walk fast, gradually requires them to slow their pace, and ends with the challenge of totally stopping still for 60 seconds in the middle of a mall. The aim is an embodied realisation of slow down, stop, think, and connect to the question, 'What is it that we agree to when we buy something?' The mechanic was working in close relationship to the concept. The tech facilitates integration of meaning and mechanics. We use an accelerometer and a pedometer in a way that is ever-so-gently gamified, engaging people in this gradual slowing down of their walking pace until they finally come to a stop. Using apps and technology in meaningful but invisible ways, in this instance to physically, literally, make the player slow down and think about their actions.[10]

Figure 2: Imagine & Play. *An audience-player in ZU-UK's Radio Ghost 2021. Photo: ZU-UK*

---

10   An in-depth conversation with Maravala and Ramos, discussing the game mechanics and experience of *Radio Ghost* is available on *Voices of VR* (Bye, 2022).

Jo: Munotida, you incorporated cross-platform composition in *How To Build the [City]*, 2021 (*H2BTC21*). Questioning how we might 'build the city back better', you focused this locally, in collaboration with Battersea's Omnibus Theatre, rebuilding social relationships through solution-led play, kicking off by using a 'Hackathon' (Tauberer 2017). Originating in the tech industry, where teams compete in intensive timeframes to create software solutions, you redeployed Hackathon as a dramaturgical device; a means of critiquing *and* constructing performance.

Munotida: We had two central concepts at the start of *H2BTC21*. The first explored how to involve the audience within the rehearsal room while developing the show. We were interested in how we could involve the audience in the creative process rather than at its culmination; how we could make every rehearsal a performance. Opening up our rehearsal space related to questions we had about reopening theatres coming out of lockdown in London. We were keen to play with the positive significance of online interactive experiences and social media broadcasting during the pandemic, where anyone could be invited into everybody's home via live stream. We were also inspired by the *Pokémon GO* craze where people were using GPS and smart technologies in the outside world. Instead of being trapped in your room, we wanted to use tech to connect and interact with nature, with social spaces, with architecture. These were ambitious concepts and questions for us; how to create a show that is full of interactive games for an audience, that culminates in a one-off performance for ticketed audience members, which itself connects these ticketed audience members and performers to unsuspecting members of the public outside. We answered that by using phone messaging, livestreaming, GPS as tools for live interaction between audiences and members of the ensemble inside the studio with those based outside.

Our R&D involved researching how tech start-ups and global tech companies, such as Facebook and Amazon, dealt with problem-solving. This led to a Hackathon as a way for our collective, at that time spread across the UK, Barcelona, Portugal, Italy, to come together via any means. We put a call out for creatives, such as my niece Gabrielle who's a coder, friends who were doctors, poets working across written and visual composition, then split the rehearsal activity into three interdisciplinary groups. Each group was given tasks to create a game that had a different foundation, location, and tools. One group was tasked with being outside and in motion, using GPS and any means of overground transport, including walking. The next group had to imagine a space that connects people, reimagining a sense of home through sport. The third group had to create a game in a cafe that used the rules of any board game as its base. The combinations were randomised to create a challenge and to see what unexpected result we would get. Each group would go away for two hours, create a game, then come back but instead of sticking with the games they'd made, we would then switch people within the groups, establishing

Potential and Critique of a Gamified Theatre

new groups that would then scaffold up those original formats, which could include dismantling ideas. It resulted in about seven groups across a day, with the continual mixing and switching, bringing new eyes to the game. At the end of the day, we came together to play the final outcomes. The Hackathon found creative solutions to how we could reinterpret *Gilgamesh* through scenes that were simultaneously games to be played on both the inside and outside of the performance space (see figure 4). For example, a game of cat-and-mouse with performer-players inside the performance space collaborating with a ticketed audience member and using GPS and messaging to direct another performer, located nearby outside, to locate and 'catch' a performer who was on the other side of London. To ensure progress in bringing that performer in, we would continually re-sculpt the context and narrative around Gilgamesh's odyssey and eventual return for the group giving instructions from the inside.

Jo: The whole process was multilayered gameplay; gamifying the rehearsal room *and* the live performance event while simultaneously connecting the company to members of the community as an audience; connecting those members of community to other community members on the outside; connecting the community once again with its outdoor spaces.

Munotida: Gabrielle, observing us, came up with a solution for how to package all this, to document the experience, collecting all the responses and games, all the opinions and results the hackathon had produced. She coded this into a website live on stage during the final show that would then be gifted to the ticketed audience members and to the people passing by outside who had contributed to the creation of this game. It became a live ephemera for the experience, this moment we created together. It was a reference to how social media was vital in linking us, exhibiting our daily connections, and holding memories. Gabrielle's live coding became coding in-and-as performance; a live digital process that both opened up and fleetingly archived this complicated concept.

Playing the Game(show): Aesthetics, mechanics, care, and caretaking

Whether implicit or explicit, rules were fundamental to the live 'on-boarding' for performer-players and audience-players for State of the [Art] and ZU-UK's projects during the global lockdowns of 2020 and 2021. These rules enabled an understanding of and respect for consent, with a continual renegotiation of permission as play progressed. Tacit or explicit 'contracts for participation' constituted acts of caretaking and were vital in securing the constructs and governing principles of the world of each performance; facilitating *willingness* to participate as much as estab-

Josephine Machon with Munotida Chinyanga and Persis-Jadé Maravala: 'It's (Not) Only a Game' 49

lishing structures by which audience and artist safety was supported (Machon 2013, 99–100).

ZU-UK's *PlagueRound* (2020–) and State of the [Art]'s *How to Build the [City]* (2022) both used the formulae of gameshows as a scaffolding for play, shaping the experience as entertainment while gently nudging audience-players to rethink their participation in the social contract through this play. As a format it allowed State of the [Art] and ZU-UK to move from the 'silly' (a term used by both Munotida and Persis-Jadé to describe the form) to the 'serious':

Figure 3: PlagueRound *(2020) Photo: ZU-UK*

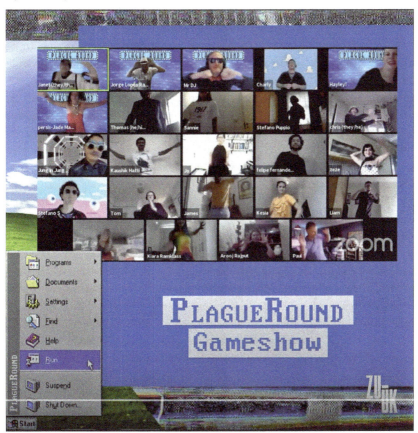

Persis-Jadé: I think that 'silly' isn't the opposite of 'serious'. The key thing about using silly as a methodology is that silliness doesn't have to deny the gravity of the situation, and at that time we were in a grave situation. 'Silly' aesthetics can be used to get

50 Potential and Critique of a Gamified Theatre

to a place of norm-shedding, of doing things in unusual and unexpected ways, that will often open our eyes to a new way of seeing the world and ourselves. *PlagueRound* was a gameshow experience on Zoom (see figure3), with *Project Perfect Stranger* being a separate experience that fed into it by connecting pairs of anonymous strangers via WhatsApp through a series of playful tasks and questions. We were encouraging people to 'norm-shed' by inviting them to break their 'norms'; instead of eating at the table, eat underneath it, sleep in unusual places in the house. Being housebound, it seemed like an important moment to be interrogating what house and home mean to us, how they mean radically different things depending on who you are, and where you are. We were provoking people, through silliness, to rethink the rules and behaviours that go with those spaces. It was also about identity and relationship to local spaces. We had participants wearing other people's clothes or wearing their clothes inside out, or going for a walk blindfolded. There's a lot published on how humour and playfulness can function as ways of reframing a situation and can act as mechanisms to create psychological distance from negative events. Cultivating a sense of the absurd became crucial for us in terms of dealing with that moment, coming in and out of lockdown into a lot of social fear. It was helping weather all that uncertainty. Later versions of *PlagueRound* took the question of how and when our society might get to a place that is 'post-normal' (Sardar 2010). We lost our normalities but were also acknowledging that what had been 'normal' was seriously messed up: What new ways of doing things are we going to take with us and how can we turn uncertainty into an asset?

There's something about 'silly' that's also providing a resistance to the forces of capitalism, isn't there? The screeching at you that if you don't have goals, you're a morally bankrupt person and you're only worth what you produce. Being silly and gameplaying offers something 'contra' to that mode of capitalism. People find it hard to switch into playfulness from that stressful, goal-focused state. When you're playful, when you're being silly, it's not the same as being stupid. You need a lot of skills to be properly silly. You need to be observant, you need to be a little bit innovative, you need to be quick, able to see things from a different perspective, you need to be a risk-taker, really responsive, able to read the room. Those skills that you have when you allow yourself to be playful function well as an approach to solving problems or managing relationships, teaching, presenting information, even conflict resolution. I was hoping with that project that we could find a new language to express our appreciation of the silly. I wanted it to be something that could look a little bit like freedom, even if it was illusory.

Jo: Munotida, with *H2BTC* at Rich Mix, in London (2022), the rules of play were visibly and verbally introduced in a quiz-style set-up as the performance, a reinvention of *Gilgamesh*, progressed. The performer-players knew these rules in advance, including being able to ask you directly for advice and to renegotiate how the rules work. You were physically present running the technical design, (projections, live feed, music, and sound), as well as opening the show with a rap to set the scene, giving verbal instructions from behind the desk. In this way, the audience become immediately familiar with how 'the play' was being constructed, in both senses of the word. The audience quickly learned we had to take turns in volunteering to play each game, plot each scene, to get to the end of the show. The informality of the space allowed audience-players to come and go to the bar as they chose, like a pub-quiz, to shout and participate from their seats as much as on stage.

Munotida: The way we build the show is different to a traditional set-up where departments take responsibility for different areas; directors, performers, designers, audience, all do 'their thing'. We build a show only at the point that we get into the venue, which could be the night before. We have blueprints, the foundations that are seen and investigated together by the full collective; everyone has a stake in what we're building and so everyone has an understanding and awareness of how dangerous it could be if rules aren't followed. We discuss every possible outcome within this multiverse so that we can play safely but also know that there are required points of uncertainty that allow us to play with the unknowns, to take risks in a safe environment. For example, several performers were unable to come for rehearsals. Given we'd only a day to get a show on, we used the need for improvisation in the live event as an opportunity to teach those performers the rules of the game *as it played*. The game itself in turn builds the scene, tells the narrative and so interprets pivotal moments in *Gilgamesh* as it unfolds. We shared the rules of each game live with the audience as the performance was being constructed. Additionally, the enforced limitation of performers not being able to make rehearsals became a safeguarding rule; using their vulnerability, the very real sense of 'I don't know what's happening' as an authentic and supportive moment to guide, to teach the rules and outcomes of the scene. The one rule that is always known in advance is that performers can bend these rules where needed, in response to the audience, because of the informal style. It keeps an energy in the playing of each moment; ensemble members, as much as the audience, are learning the rules of each game. That language and that way of interacting creates a shared space with negotiated boundaries that allows for a freedom *to play with and within* the uncertain, to protect each other and the audience.

Figure 4: Gaming Gilgamesh *in H2BTC (2022). Photo: State of the [Art]*

Persis-Jadé: The emotional safety of our participants is a priority for me, but I don't really talk about 'safeguarding', because, as you say, Jo, of the job done by clear but playful contracting. I try to establish, through a series of explicit and implicit opt-ins and a human presence on the part of the artwork (whether that's via a physically present performer or a digitally accessible facilitator), responsibility from the artist and from participants. At some point there's always a tacit acknowledgement that we're all adults, that we'll all behave with care and consideration, that we've all agreed to participate in something that's bringing people, usually strangers in the case of my work, up against each other in very intimate and unusual encounters and that that entails a degree of emotional risk. What's important to me about this process of contracting is that it's never separate from the artwork itself; it's part and parcel. It's not an add-on, an extra form where you tick a few boxes, or some kind of waiver. It comes into the language of how the performance-worlds are conveyed.

Instructional work in public space builds respect for those others in that space who aren't part of the event, within the nature and language of the instructions. In *Radio Ghost*, for example, I understand there's a wider public in the mall that has no idea that people around them are playing a game; like 'non-player characters' (NPCs). I create imperatives in the audio instructions to observe those 'NPCs' with compassion, as fellow human beings; to observe details that show their humanity, that endear, noticing details in which we might find our shared woundedness.

Project Perfect Stranger, which pairs strangers via a series of WhatsApp instructions, hinges entirely on language, as the piece itself just consists of texts. The text instructions and framing are premised on a shared understanding of decency and ethics. But that's always also risky, partly because interpretations always vary. I think the biggest danger is when things aren't clear. We try to make the language simple and straightforward. Importantly, there's always a figure present who acts like a guide. In *Project Perfect Stranger*, facilitated entirely via WhatsApp, it's important that we have a human facilitator as the guide, sending out the instructional messages and responding in real time to people's queries and concerns, offering adaptations to tasks, within reason, if people report difficulties with them. Along those lines, it's important to all our work in digital space that we keep the humans behind the tech tangible, accessible. It means that, though people have signed up to a contract of what's involved and what's expected of them, there's always room, within the bounds of the artwork, for responsiveness and a degree of opt-out. I do want to avoid the potentially patronising excess of 'safeguarding' in arts and theatre, when the situation is already a very clear opt-in. I want to respect people's decisions as adults and agents to have taken on the challenge of the experiences we're inviting them to.

Playing together, 'in-it-togetherness': Temporary community and *communitas*

Playing together was a crucial device in creating temporary communities through *Project Perfect Stranger/PlagueRound* and *H2BTC21*. These temporary communities were examples of *communitas* in practice. *Communitas*, a Latin term, defines both *the spirit of* community, involving a feeling of intense solidarity and togetherness, and/or a community in which there is solidarity and equality amongst members. Victor Turner, cultural anthropologist and theorist of serious play in ritualised interactions, asserted theatre is ripe for 'Spontaneous Communitas', when there is 'a direct, immediate and total confrontation of human identities', and a 'liberation of human capacities of cognition, affect, volition, creativity' (Turner 1982, 44).

Communitas can be seen in the visionary principles of Littlewood's 'Fun Palaces'. Speculatively designed in 1961 in collaboration with architect Cedric Price, Fun Palaces were conceived as inclusive cultural spaces (Littlewood 1995, 701–754; Bonet Miro 2018 and Matthews 2016). According to architectural scholar Stanley Matthews, Price's blueprint for Littlewood's concept resonates with game design, inspired by the then 'emerging sciences of cybernetics, information technology, and game theory' alongside theatre (Matthews 2006, 39). Integrating concepts of 'technological interchangeability with social participation and improvisation':

> The three-dimensional structure of the Fun Palace was the operative space-time matrix of a virtual architecture. The variable 'program' and form of the Fun Palace were not conventional architecture but much closer to what we understand today as the computer program: an array of algorithmic functions and logical gateways that control temporal events and processes in a virtual device (Matthews 2006, 39).

Unlike conventional theatres, where, as Littlewood put it, audiences 'escape up their own assholes in the dark', Fun Palaces were to be 'where the British worker' would take back agency and creativity, realise 'self-expression' via this 'university of the streets [...] playground for adults' (in Matthews 2016) . Beyond a reimagining of what a cultural venue should and could be, this was a socialist shift in thinking around those audiences that the spaces would be for. These would be arts institutions open to all but targeted at those to whom cultural experience had been denied for perceived reasons of entitlement and education as much as related to economic exclusion. Here all were invited to be citizens of that experience, to *become* that cultural experience. Where Fun Palaces in concept 'represented an unprecedented architectural synthesis of technology, cybernetics, and game theory, these were the means but never the objective', instead, they enabled 'the convergence of site and human event' (Matthews 2006, 47). Littlewood imagined a practice where divisions between place, space, art, education, and leisure were blurred within an interdisciplinary, intermedial playground; one that celebrated 'high' and 'low' art forms (Littlewood 1995, 628).[11]

Jo: Littlewood's ideals for fusing communal recreation, egalitarian artistic experiences, and silly-serious collaborative play clearly exist in each of your practices and were proactively implemented during the Covid lockdowns. Munotida, your projects offered you new ways of thinking about playgrounds and theme parks as places of fun and discovery and drew you to positive social relationships that could be encouraged when transiting public spaces, to the potentials of transitory space.

Munotida: During the pandemic I was influenced by the YouTube channels, Beta Squad and Jubilee, who play 'guess the odd one out' styled games.[12] The concept brings random people together to play in a studio setting, encouraging them to connect in a way that serves as a commentary on society, on identity politics, on

---

11 Though Littlewood and Price's designs were never physically realised, those original blueprints are available via: https://funpalaces.co.uk/about-fun-palaces. Rather than a building, Littlewood's legacy and its contemporary reinvention continues through 'Makers' of Fun Palaces, their annual activity sited in existing community buildings.

12 See Beta Squad: https://www.youtube.com/@BetaSquad and Jubilee: https://www.youtube.com/@jubilee.

social perception and expectation. They also took the games into the real world, surprising passengers with quiz shows in packed buses or lifts, with an unknowing and sometimes unwilling audience. I found it interesting how this activated these transit spaces and moments of waiting and what that encouraged between people.

I watched a wrestling documentary about how Seth Rollins, in response to a career-threatening injury, redesigned, reclaimed and rebuilt himself in order to play at his best (Rollins 2016). I took those principles and translated it into what we were doing with *H2BTC21* to question how we might redesign, rebuild, and reclaim our relationships and our community spaces post-pandemic. Significantly, we were asking how State of the [Art] might rebuild our connections with a wider community of artists. It became important to me and Simone to examine and activate the spaces in which we work; attending to the ways we interact not just as artists but as humans sharing space and place. We've continued with those principles, to expand our 'playground' and to imagine what that might still become. We're constantly wanting to connect with people, to create spontaneous communities and interactions. An aim is to highlight that there's positivity to interaction through technology.

Jo: Jadé, you believe games transform people, that transformations in play correspond to transformations in 'reality'.

Persis-Jadé: I've seen games that change what people know and how people think about things. People can transform in incredible ways through games, but, importantly, what I've learned is that people only change when they *feel* things. They don't change because you tell them to, they don't change because they ought to, they change because they *feel* something, they've been affected. It must connect on an emotional level. For me, that relates to the spaces where these things happen. A big part of that is how people come across your work; does it just circulate around the same middle class, white circles of exclusivity, or can it happen in places where ordinary people will be able to access that work? We use rituals, playful actions, to invite people into an experience, and these rituals and invitations are always familiar; they wouldn't alienate people. Knowing that a ringing phone is an invitation to pick it up is an understood action, albeit in this instance ritualised, for people to latch onto. Similarly, most people understand how to enter a shopping mall and the activities you might expect to do there.

Whether or not the work genuinely transforms people often depends on who's being reached. Arts aficionados who've already been to several ground-breaking interactive digital experiences that year and are already 'woke' are unlikely to change their shopping habits because of *Radio Ghost*. Which isn't to say you can't transform those people but to stress that it's important to acknowledge *who* is making the work and who they're making the work for. My position is important as well when we're talking about the kinds of play and the kinds of invitations I'm offering as transformational. I'm trying to create a practice and a culture that refutes the normal hierarchies of patriarchy, of capitalism, and of white supremacy. It's important that you're taking care of where your art happens and with whom you're playtesting. Munotida mentioned something about making work *with* people. Similarly, I'm concerned that when we playtest, we recognise the image we have of who the 'Everyman' is. When we first started making work, I was imagining someone as this neutral recipient of it, but who is that someone? Usually, in our heads it's a white, middle-class, male player yet that isn't the 'Everyman', that's a minority. Re-framing *how* we make work is the most important part of what it means to be 'transforming' people.

Conclusion: Game-changing play – Translations, transitions, transformations

State of the [Art] and ZU-UK both interweave the tools and mechanisms of digital-gaming with long-established play protocols of board games, choose-your-own-adventure literature, team and performance sports, playground recreation, along with the spectacle and fun of gameshows. This mash-up, played out across the on-line realm, public spaces and in the communal areas of cultural venues, foregrounds team-participation within stage interaction as a *show* of in-it-togetherness. Not 'only a game' but instead an inter/anti-disciplinary fusion of theatre, team-building exercise, and social event; a practice of *communitas*.

State of the Art and ZU-UK's work is gamified theatre that deploys everyday tech imaginatively, to make meaningful connections rather than to accentuate alienation. It illustrates how game in/as performance only has the potential to be game-changing if all players understand and feel invited into – give consent to and have respect for – the 'rules of play' to enable *the play of possibility*. The performance events discussed sought to rebuild physical connection across cities, establishing both silly and serious routes for creative and critical transformation. Participation in the game of each project supported individual risk-taking as much as individual fun, yet always in association with others sharing the physical or virtual play. In so doing, as models of gameplay *in and as* performance practice, these projects emphasise and celebrate the ways in which individual input and outcome directly feed into collective responsibility and reward.

References

Barker, Clive. 2010. *Theatre Games: A New Approach to Drama Training*. London: Bloomsbury.

Boal, Augusto. 2002. *Games for Actors and Non-Actors*. London: Routledge

Bonet Miro, Ana. 2018. 'From filmed pleasure to Fun Palace'. arq: Architectural Research Quarterly, 22, no. 3 (September): 215–224. https://doi.org/10.1017/S1359135518000519

Bye, Kent. 2022. 'Site-Specific Immersive Audio Piece "Radio Ghost" Changed the Way I See Malls', Voices of VR (Podcast and Transcript). #1085, May 16. Available at: https://voicesofvr.com/1085-site-specific-immersive-audio-piece-radio-ghost-changed-the-way-i-see-malls/

Chow, Broderick, Laine, Eero and Warden, Claire (Eds). 2016. *Performance and Professional Wrestling*. London: Routledge.

De Bono, Edward. 2016. *Six Thinking Hats*. London: Penguin Life.

Field Fiorio, Soraya and Houshang Moein, Amir, 2021. *The epic of Gilgamesh, the king who tried to conquer death*. Educator, Soraya Field Fiorio. Director and Animator, Amir Houshang Moein. Ted-Ed Animations, Ted-Ed Channel, YouTube, 1 June: Available at: https://www.youtube.com/watch?v=BV9t3Cp18Rc

Glasby, Taylor, 2018. 'The A-Z of K-pop'. The Guardian, June 5. Available at: https://www.theguardian.com/music/2018/jun/05/the-a-z-of-k-pop-know-your-sasaengs-from-your-monster-rookies

Grey, Dave, Brown, Sunni, Macanufo, James. 2010. *Gamestorming: A Playbook for Innovators, Rulebreakers, and Changemakers*. California: O'Reilly.

Holman, Cas. 2019. 'Cas Holman: Design For Play', Abstract: The Art of Design. Series 2: Episode 4. Netflix. 25 Sep: https://www.netflix.com/watch/0?origId=802370

Johnstone, Keith. 2018. *Impro: Improvisation and the Theatre*. London: Bloomsbury.

Littlewood, Joan. 1995. *Joan's Book – Joan Littlewood's Peculiar History As She Tells It*. London: Minverva.

Machon, Josephine. 2013. *Immersive Theatres – Intimacy and Immediacy in Contemporary Performance*. London: Palgrave.

Mathews, Stanley. 2006. 'The Fun Palace as Virtual Architecture: Cedric Price and the Practices of Indeterminacy.' Journal of Architectural Education (1984–), 59, no. 3 (February): 39–48. https://doi.org/10.1111/j.1531-314X.2006.00032.x.

———. 2016. 'The Fun Palace at Fifty.' Art in America. 1 (October): The Fun Palace at Fifty

Mazer, Sharon. 2020. *Professional Wrestling: Sport and Spectacle*. Jackson: Uni. Mississippi Press.

Mitchell, Stephen. 2005. *Gilgamesh*. London: Profile Books.

Pham, Jason. 2020. '25 K-Pop Fandom Words Every K-Pop Stan Should Know', Stylecaster. https://stylecaster.com/feature/k-pop-fandom-words-1153522/

Ramos, Jorge Lopes, Dunne-Howri, Joseph, Maravala, Persis-Jadé & Simon, Bart. 2020. 'The Post-immersive Manifesto'. International Journal of Performance Arts And Digital Media.16, No.2 (July): 196–212. https://www.tandfonline.com/doi/full/10.1080/14794713.2020.1766282

Rollins, Seth. 2016. 'Redesign. Rebuild. Reclaim' WWE Network, 30 May: https://watch.wwe.com/episode/Seth-Rollins-1764

Sardar, Ziauddin, 2010. 'Welcome to postnormal times', Futures 42, 5. (June): 435–444. https://doi.org/10.1016/j.futures.2009.11.028

Tauberer, Joshua, 2017. 'How to run a successful Hackathon': https://hackathon.guide

Tapakapa, 2016. 'K-pop Explained': https://www.youtube.com/watch?v=_S7XXvQNong

Turner, Victor. 1982. *From Ritual to Theatre – The Human Seriousness of Play*. New York: Performing Arts Journal Publications.

Welker, Bill (Ed.). 2013. *The Wrestling Drill Book*. USA: Human Kinetics.

Biographies

Josephine Machon is a writer, researcher and educator specialising in immersive practice and is one of the first appointed Research Residents at Guildhall School of Music & Drama, London. She is the author of *The Punchdrunk Encyclopaedia* (2019), *Immersive Theatres: Intimacy and Immediacy in Contemporary Performance* (2013), *(Syn)aesthetics: Redefining Visceral Performance* (2009, 2011) and has published widely on experiential and interactive performance. She is Joint Editor of the Palgrave Macmillan Series, Palgrave Studies in Performance and Technology, and on the Editorial Boards for the *International Journal of Performance Arts & Digital Media* (IJPADM) and *Body, Space & Technology* (BST).

Munotida Chinyanga is an 'antidisciplinary' practitioner creating work through multimedia direction, sound design, and international collaborations. She is Co-Founder and Co-Artistic Director, with Simone Guistinelli, of the international arts collective, State of the [Art]. She has worked with leading companies and directors including Katie Mitchell and Headlong at Barbican, with Kwame-Kwei Armah at The Young Vic, and The Gate Theatre, Pleasance Theatre and Oxford Northwall.

Persis-Jadé Maravala is co-founder and Artistic Director of ZU-UK, creating work that sits at the intersection of games, performance, and technology. She has won awards and nominations in the fields of interactive theatre, hybrid art, and innovation. Her most acclaimed project, *Hotel Medea* (2006–12), is considered a pioneering moment in immersive theatre and became the standout hit of the 2011 Edinburgh Fringe. She is the director and writer of all ZU-UK productions including *Goodnight Sleep Tight*, *Binaural Dinner Date*, *Pick Me Up (& Hold Me Tight)*, *Project Perfect Stranger/ PlagueRound*, and *Radio Ghost*.

Video Games, Flow, and Immersive Theatre: Participatory Arts in the Ultraliberal Era

Olivia Levet

Abstract *The 'flow state', in video games, designates an optimal, immersive, and pleasant experience, based on stimulating challenges (Chen 2006). Extended to immersive theatre, it highlights, in line with Adam Alston's analysis (2013, 2016), the ideological shift of participatory processes. While they could originally lead to emancipation, distancing, and liberation, they are now mainly diverted in favour of exciting, sensational, and gamified experiences, which seems to convey values in line with the ultraliberal ideology.*

Introduction

Technological innovations change our relations to the world and to society; virtual reality, augmented reality, robotics, artificial intelligence, cryptocurrency, and the metaverse are currently shaping our daily lives and outlining a future characterised by velocity, performance, flexibility, and fluidity. Industrially produced video games mirror these values: Designers aim to create worlds that are more and more fluid, open, immersive, and exciting. Flow, a concept theorised by Mihaly Csíkszentmihályi in the field of positive psychology and then applied to video game design by Jenova Chen in 2006, fulfils this ambition. It is widely used in the video game industry as a recipe to optimally engage players and avoid boredom or frustration in a gaming experience. However, the 'flow state' can also be used to analyse contemporary 'immersive theatre', specifically plays of the kind that companies such as Punchdrunk (2000) produce, which attempt to create interactive, playful, and stimulating settings. This approach is in line with that of Josephine Machon, who refers to game studies to understand the 'total immersion' specific to immersive theatre (Machon 2013, 59–63).

Contemporary immersive theatre can be considered to focus on creating an '*expérience à vivre* [experience to be lived]' (Freydefont 2010) which viscerally involves the participants. Audience participation is not approached here from an emancipatory, distancing, and critical perspective, as it could be in the participative and political theatre of the 1960s and 70s. Rather, immersive theatre values challenge, excitement, stimulation, or entertainment, in other words, a 'flow state'. The use of flow to engage and immerse the audience in a playful drama is not a coincidence. The ideological values behind this concept are today aligned with the domination of ultraliberal ideology, which consciously or unconsciously irrigates a set of artistic and cultural productions. In this paper, ultraliberal ideology is considered the culmination of the mutations of the 'new economy', driven by Silicon Valley and the technological innovations of the 1960s, as criticized by Fred Turner (2006). This economic, philosophical, and political ideology, in the tradition of theorists such as Milton Friedman, shows an ideological shift from valuing participation, independence, freedom, and autonomy as emancipatory values to stressing the skills required of employees in a flexible and deregulated labour market.

1. The flow state: Toward an optimal, total, and visceral experience

The multiplication of theatrical works that claim to be – or are designated as – 'immersive' reflects the contemporary quest for exciting, disorienting, and sensorial experiences. From *Stranger Things: The Experience*[1] to The Banksy Museum,[2] via Onyo's *bulles de déconnexion* [disconnection bubbles],[3] immersion is now a valuable commodity, whether in theatre, entertainment, museography, tourism, cinema, or even at work. If the boundaries of immersive theatre are difficult to define precisely (Freydefont 2010, Machon 2013), Punchdrunk can be considered as a key example. The group's aesthetic is playful, drawing on and revitalising the techniques of first-person adventure video games. Punchdrunk's plays place the audience at the heart of the action, immersing them viscerally in the scenography. While spectators wear masks, maintaining an invisible fourth wall (Pearce 2021) between actors and audience, they can freely wander among the actors, in a physical scenography that

---

1   *Stranger Things: The Experience* is an immersive and interactive experience based on the Netflix series *Stranger Things*. It is available in several major cities: Toronto, London, New York, Paris. https://strangerthings-experience.com/paris/

2   The Banksy Museum in Paris is hosting the permanent exhibition "The World of Banksy" dedicated to the work of the street artist. The scenography is designed to immerse the spectators in an urban atmosphere, recreating the different cities and periods through which the artist passed. https://museebanksy.fr/

3   Onyo is a company that offers individuals and professionals immersive and sound experiences available in several forms: online ('*Je suis DRH, et j'offre une pause aux salariés de mon entreprise*' [I am a HRD, and I offer a break to the employees of my company]), or in the form of installations intended to take place in shopping malls, train stations, trade fairs, but also in companies, within workshops ('*Je suis en charge du séminaire sur la transformation de mon entreprise.*' [I am in charge of the seminar on the transformation of my company.]) https://www.wedogood.co/onyo/

spreads over several rooms. The narration is arborescent and environmental (Jenkins 2004). The audience members can access the story in a fragmented way by walking through the different rooms, exploring the set, deciding to follow one actor or another. Felix Barrett, the artistic director of the company, claims to be inspired by video games, comparing Punchdrunk's play *The Drowned Man* to the gaming experience of *Skyrim*. In an article in *The Guardian*, the journalist and writer Thomas McMullan, who has also written for theatre companies, says:

> There are two ways of watching *The Drowned Man*. Either you can follow one character and treat it as a completely linear show, or you can follow your instincts, treat it as free-form exploration and let the beats of architectural detail lead you. [...] It's similar to how in *Skyrim* you can follow a character and go on a mission, or you can explore the landscape, find moments of other stories and achieve a sense of an over-arching environment (Mcmullan 2014).

This level design[4] approach allows artists to combine the spectators' free exploration with a coherent and meaningful narration. Steve Gaynor, the co-founder of the Fullbright video game studio, which developed the adventure game *Gone Home* (2013), goes so far as to qualify Punchdrunk's scenography as level design: 'I mean, this entire experience is level design. Lighting directs you to stuff that's important, there are main thoroughfares, etc. This is a video game level, period.' (Jakob-Hoff 2014, Biggin 2017, 173).

Flow, in its original definition, identifies a set of conditions that help an individual to devote themselves fully and without disturbance to a task. The task must have clear goals, be adjusted to the skills of the person performing the task, and provide immediate feedback. When all these conditions are fulfilled and the person is focused on the activity, the flow state occurs and everyday life frustrations disappear; self-consciousness; and the perception of time, place, and everything outside the activity fade away. This state provides a feeling of control, and, moreover, a deep sense of pleasure, accomplishment, and plenitude (Csíkszentmihályi 2004, 79–80). In level design, the flow state is the moment when the player is completely absorbed by the game. This absorption is due to a perfect balance between the challenges encountered and the skills deployed. The game should not be too complex or too easy. If it is too complex, players may experience anxiety and frustration; but if it is too easy, they may become bored and lose interest. As a result, games are designed so that their difficulties and challenges evolve in line with the progression curve of the player.

---

4   In video games, level design refers to the conception of levels, the building of stages and spaces traversed by players.

The flow's ability to initiate a pleasant and comfortable state in which the perception of time and place is disrupted, and which provides a sense of control and agentivity seems to fit well with the ideals of immersive theatre. It could offer a way to put the audience at the heart of the work, inviting them to act and be hyperfocused on the fiction being played around them. In this form of theatre, the immersants' (Machon 2013) mental and emotional engagement seems to be enhanced when their actions or movements lead to an immediate and satisfying result, and when they are fully involved in the storytelling. Immersive theatre offers the participants an active place in the aesthetic experience. The purpose is to achieve the dream of a fluid, cathartic, and enjoyable interactive narrative, in line with the pioneering publication *Computers as Theatre* (Laurel 1991) on the relation between human-machine interaction and theatre: a narrative that adapts dynamically and coherently to the player's actions, providing a feeling of control and freedom, similar to flow. Furthermore, the live dimension of immersive theatre allows actors to improvise and react to the audience's actions to guarantee fictional coherence, in contrast to computer-based non-player characters. This aspect matches perfectly with the aspiration of some designers and players for ever freer and more open worlds, and, above all, enjoyable and exciting ones. In these virtual worlds, the notions of time, daily worries, and frustrations that would break the game's fantasy disappear. Beyond the specific mental and cognitive engagement of a flow experience, immersive theatre also brings a visceral experience of 'physical *praesence*, the participant's physical body responding within an imaginative, sensual environment' (Machon 2013, 61). This physical dimension creates a direct and organic relationship between the audience and the events surrounding them and amplifies their emotional and sensory engagement in the fiction.

Rose Biggin, in *Immersive Theatre and Audience Experience: Space, Game and Story in the Work of Punchdrunk*, highlights the multiplicity of engagement and immersion modalities of this type of theatre. Beyond immersion based on the flow state, which leads to the idea of 'experience as "skill"' (Biggin 2017, 29), immersive theatre achieves an 'overwhelming, visceral sensation of sublime experience' through an encompassing and multisensory scenography (Biggin 2017, 32). Yet the pursuit of a flow state seems to create some contradictions in immersive theatre:

The idea that there is no 'wrong way' to experience a production becomes problematic if there is also an implicit need to work towards experiencing aesthetic 'flow' by being able to match a challenge or work towards a clearly defined goal. An immersive production's (unspoken or implied) rules might become hypervisible for audience members who sense these rules need to be discovered and followed to have the better experience [...] What these rules are taken to be in turn suggests what is being *valued* in a piece of immersive theatre (Biggin 2017, 29–30).

Behind the desire to offer total freedom and free exploration to the audience, the search for a flow state and a dynamic system leads the designers to set up challenges and rewards, or at least to establish a set of rules to be followed. Following these rules facilitates engagement with the fiction and provides access to narrative rewards and a full experience. As an implicit contract established between the work and the audience, these rules contribute directly to the aesthetic, artistic and cultural meaning of the work, just as procedural rhetoric helps to express values, ideas, and messages in video games (Bogost 2007). Like the narrative, the scenography, or the performance of the actors, they convey a certain point of view towards society. In the context of an ultraliberal society, where the notions of participation, reward, risk-taking, or initiative are largely valued, this observation leads us to question the ideological impact of these processes.

2. Injunction to happiness and participation in the ultraliberal era

Several authors have criticised the prescriptive aspect of flow, particularly in its reappropriation by Jenova Chen (Serdane 2014). The concept turns the pursuit of an optimal, balanced, and fun experience into an injunction and seems to eclipse any other form of engagement. Through the flow, experience must provide immediate pleasure in the completion of a task or an action. It condemns any exit from the game, any 'reflexive hindsight in the course of action' (Caïra 2018)[5], promoting an individual experience 'that largely overlooks the collective' (Caïra 2018)[6]. This observation matches Adam Alston's research on immersive theatre: He analyses 'how immersive theatre shares particular values with neoliberalism, such as entrepreneurialism, as well as the valorisation of risk, agency and responsibility' (Alston 2013). He identifies the main concern of the immersive theatre as the pursuit of hedonism, with no other end in itself: Participation provides a sensational, exciting, and enjoyable experience, rather than perspective-taking, collective debate, or critical thinking. This analysis reflects the autotelic nature of the flow state, in which commitment comes from immediate feedback. When performing a task in a flow state, a feeling of pleasure and control occurs in the simple act of being engaged in the activity. This search for happiness as the only goal is a feature of the positive psychology and ideology of personal development that prevails today, especially in managerial methods. The emergence of new professions such as happiness managers or *funsultants*, whose role is to keep employees happy at work, is a symptom of this phenomenon, which eludes any political criticism of a managerial organisation. It fits the contemporary happiness injunction, where responsibility

---

5   '*recul réflexif en cours d'action*', translated by the author of this article.
6   '*qui fait largement l'impasse sur le collectif*', translated by the author of this article.

for achieving happiness lies solely with the individual, not on a collective and political dimension: 'the experience is all about you, the participant' (Alston 2013). This criticism goes hand in hand with Olivier Caïra's critique of flow: The experience focuses only on the players' 'G-spot' (Caïra 2018).

In this context, Alston defines the audience participation in immersive theatre as an 'entrepreneurial participation', 'a kind of participation based on self-made opportunity' (Alston 2013). As Rose Biggin has also pointed out, Punchdrunk's theatre does not offer the audience free roaming within the fiction; it establishes a set of implicit rules, which, if understood and followed, influence the aesthetic experience. Participation here is not free, like an aimless walk through the scenography, but necessary at all costs. Adam Alston uses the example of the *one-on-ones* to support his point: these are specific scenes in Punchdrunk's theatre, where a spectator can share a special moment with an actor. It gives this person the feeling for a few minutes that the whole production is about them. These moments sound like rewards for the most curious spectators: Showing initiative and holding the attention of the actors are highly valued actions. They are part of a logic that is specific to the concept of flow as seen through the prism of level design, and, more broadly, to the gamification mechanisms that are today colonising all of our activities and all of society (Siegel 2015). Some audience members, as soon as they enter the play, work towards the goal of having a one-on-one. They go so far as to consult online guides – analogous to video game guides – that describe the best way to experience the work and access all of its secrets. The ideal spectator of immersive theatre becomes 'the entrepreneur: the self-starter, the independent, autonomous, motivated subject who is capable, self-reliant and conscientious' (Alston 2016, 130). As the entrepreneur fantasised by neoliberalism, he takes risks, overcomes challenges and obstacles, and, in a meritocratic way, reaches happiness and its objectives thanks to his motivation and efforts.

Immersive theatre, according to Alston's analysis, fits perfectly into the zeitgeist that also irrigates the video game industry: the production of large-scale experiences, ever more realistic, immersive, and free, turning players into heroes of sensational adventures. In an economic, political, and social era in which new technologies are reshaping consumer habits, the spectator – or gamer – is akin to the 'neoliberal consumer' (Alston 2016, 16) in what B. Joseph Pine II and James H. Gilmore call the 'experience economy' (Pine II and Gilmore 1999). Pursuing a marketing strategy structured on the customer experience, productions make the audience's reception, their absorption in the fiction, and the pursuit of a flow state the work's main objective. This demonstrates the need to hold the audience's attention in an economy ruled by zapping, over-solicitation, and consumerism. Alston's conclusion is based on the observation 'that a pleasurable or challenging experience is not just a fortunate by-product of the theatre event, but is, in many respects, immersive theatre's raison d'être' (Alston 2013) but also focuses on Punchdrunk's various partnerships with Belgian beer manufacturer Stella Artois, in which the advertising relies entirely on the theatre company's aesthetic processes.

A core feature of the experience economy is the 'activation' of consumers as producing consumers, either in terms of an affective engagement with a product or a brand that serves as a source of profit, or in terms of consumer participation in the production of a product (Alston 2016, 146).

All of these experiences tend to empty the participatory processes of the theatrical avant-gardes of their critical, subversive, and emancipatory potential in order to make them the tools of a dominant order. They seem 'entirely oppositional to the aware, distanced, critical and decisive mindset behind the engagement of, for example, a Theatre of the Oppressed spect-actor' (Biggin 2017, 25–26), in which audience activation is designed for political and revolutionary ends.[7] However, this observation is not limited to certain contemporary works of immersive theatre: Augusto Boal's *Theatre of the Oppressed*, used by Biggin as an example of emancipatory participation, seems to have difficulties nowadays resisting this ideological shift and maintaining its role as a countervailing power. In *Forum Theatre*, one of the *Theatre of the Oppressed* methods, the audience goes from spectator to spect-actor, freeing itself and assuming agency. The aim is not to favour a cathartic and sensational immersive aesthetic, but rather a critical distance inherited from Brecht. The stage becomes a space for political and critical experimentation. Although this theatre was originally intended to convey a radical political message, its various techniques are now widely misused, and show the domination of ultraliberal ideology.

While Adam Alston discusses the affinity between immersive theatre and the 'experience economy', revealing the ideological values behind these productions, Julian Boal, Augusto Boal's son, and a Forum Theatre theorist and practitioner, criticises the affiliations between Forum Theatre and human resources departments. Forum Theatre is nowadays mainly used as a management and team building strategy, to foster team cohesion and employee performance – far from Augusto Boal's revolutionary ambitions.

[...] what seems much more disturbing for us to investigate is why so many games, exercises, and forms of TO have been so easily recruited by countless human resources services worldwide. Such research would undoubtedly reveal

---

7   The *Theatre of the Oppressed* is a set of theatrical methods theorised and practiced by Augusto Boal in the 1960s and 70s in Brazil, in the political context of the 1964 *coup d'état*. At its origin, the practice of the *Theatre of the Oppressed* was an aspect of Boal's militant and political activity: It was developed as a political tool with a strong social dimension. Its ambition is to embody a 'weapon of liberation' and revolution. This liberation begins for Boal with a radical critique of the passive position of the Aristotelian theatre audience.

68 Potential and Critique of a Gamified Theatre

unwanted affinities between this method of critical theatre and the present state of our subjugation (Boal 2019, 609–10).

He emphasises that, beyond a conscious depoliticization of some theatrical processes, such as the use of Forum Theatre for managerial purposes, it is the relationship between the processes and the context in which they take place that must be questioned. If these processes could be a tool for social emancipation in the original political and historical context, they no longer have the same ideological meaning in times of ultraliberalism, where autonomy, action, freedom, and participation are valued by the dominant ideology.

These observations illustrate the systematic use of flow to design immersive fiction. The immersant becomes the hero of fluid, exciting, and stimulating worlds. This echoes the *uberisation* of society, which promotes deregulation, self-employment, flexibility, and individual action. The revolutionary hero promoted by Forum Theatre as the immersive theatre audience acts, takes initiative, and faces up to obstacles. This figure fits perfectly, without criticism, with the 'micro-entrepreneur imperative' (Boal 2019, 610), of the individual who must show autonomy and self-control in a flexible labour market.

It then becomes a matter of paying close attention, as artist and designer, to the political impact of the processes used in a work. As Olivier Neveux says, the shift of this political dimension in the contemporary theatre must be understood 'in light of a specific – determined – intelligence of the present' (Neveux 2019, 17).[8]

Conclusion

Despite all this, some designers do conceive of video games in artistic, critical, and political terms and approach participation in a different way. In contrast to audience participation through immersion, the flow state, and an 'entrepreneurial participation', they allow us to reconnect with the emancipatory dimension of interactive systems.

For example, the *Artgame* movement, which considers video games in their counter-cultural, experimental, and expressive dimensions (Siegel 2015),[9] calls for the restoration of the political potential of interactivity and participatory processes,

---

8   The original quotation in French: 'à la lumière d'une intelligence spécifique – déterminée – du présent', translated by the author of this article.

9   The artgame movement emerged in the 2000s at the intersection of digital art and independent video game culture, and in opposition to the industrial mainstream. It aims to establish games as expressive art media, able to convey a critical point of view with artistic and counter-cultural dimensions (Siegel, 2015).

away from their hegemonic – and meaningless – use. Artgames approach player engagement not in terms of a fluid, immersive experience, but rather as a matter of social and political commitment. This enables the creation of slow, confusing, or uncomfortable experiences that seek the distancing effect that the flow state seems to deny.

In a similar vein, several theatre companies are questioning the political and ideological meaning of playful and immersive systems in the 21st century. The GK Collective, a 'theatrical research group' founded in 2009 by Gabriella Cserháti, uses these processes from a critical and emancipatory perspective. It aims to renew political theatre in the light of the challenges facing technological society:

> Theatre shouldn't be a museum. Everything must be flexible. [...] The new illusion machine, that of the new digital reality (with its tendency to disperse attention and generalized entertainment) calls for its own theatre. Internet and the virtual are expanding immersion into everyday life. What is the role of theatre in the digital immersion era? What function can theatre still have? (Cserháti 2017a, 10).[10]

Although the collective uses immersive methods to produce fully immersive pieces, it claims to be far removed from the 'Anglo-Saxon traditions' of immersive theatre, exemplified in particular by the Punchdrunk company. The central issue is not immersion in sensational sets and environments, but rather reconnection with a human dimension; a sensitive and intimate relation to reality. The GK Collective's approach stands in the tradition of Augusto Boal's Theatre of the Oppressed: It reconfigures the theatrical methods of immersion for political or even revolutionary purposes. The 'THéâTRe CaCHé', a method created by Gabriella Cserháti in 2009, is very much like Augusto Boal's 'invisible theatre' (Boal 1996). It aims to 'give a new legitimacy to theatre, in a society overloaded with generators of illusions (the virtual, the internet, interactivity, and 3D)' by taking place directly in public space (Cserháti 2017b, 1).[11]

Like immersive theatre, it blurs the boundary between fiction and reality. But the ambition is not, as in a flow experience, to make people forget their self-con-

---

10   The original quotation in French: 'Le théâtre ne doit pas être un musée. Tout doit y être mobile. [...] La nouvelle machine à illusion, celle de la nouvelle réalité numérique, (avec sa part de dispersion de l'attention, et de divertissement généralisé) réclame son théâtre. Internet, le virtuel répand l'immersion au quotidien. Quel est le théâtre, là, au moment de l'immersion numérique ? Quelle fonction peut encore avoir le théâtre ?', translated by the author of the article.

11   The original quotation in French: 'donner une nouvelle légitimité au théâtre dans une société surchargée de générateurs d'illusions (le virtuel, internet, l'interactivité et la 3D)', translated by the author of the article.

sciousness and perception of time and place, but rather to assert and revitalize their relationship to it – and to social reality – through play. This drives us to question the game in its capacity to simulate new horizons and take a critical look at our daily lives and society.

References

Alston, Adam. 2013. 'Audience Participation and Neoliberal Value: Risk, agency and responsibility in immersive theatre.' *Performance Research* 18, no. 2 (April): 128–38. https://doi.org/10.1080/13528165.2013.807177

———. 2016. *Beyond Immersive Theatre: Aesthetics, Politics and Productive Participation*. London: Palgrave Macmillan.

Biggin, Rose. 2017. *Immersive Theatre and Audience Experience: Space, Game and Story in the Work of Punchdrunk*. Cham: Palgrave Macmillan.

Boal, Augusto. 1996. *Théâtre de l'opprimé*. Translated by Dominique Lémann. Paris: La Découverte/Poche.

Boal, Julian. 2019. 'Theatre of the Oppressed in neoliberal times: from Che Guevara to the Uber driver.' In *The Routledge Companion to the Theatre of the Oppressed*, edited by Kelly Howe, Julian Boal and José Soeiro, 598–628. London: Routledge.

Bogost, Ian, 2007. *Persuasive Games: The Expressive Power of Videogames*. Cambridge: The MIT Press.

Caïra, Olivier. 2018. 'Les dimensions multiples de l'engagement ludique.' *Sciences du jeu* 10, no. 10 (October): 1–13. https://doi.org/10.4000/sdj.1149

Chen, Jenova. 2006. 'Flow in Games.' MFA thesis, University of Southern California.

Couchot, Edmond, and Norbert Hilaire. 2003. *L'Art numérique*. Paris: Flammarion.

Cserháti, Gabriella. 2017a. 'Manifeste en infrason, pour un théâtre du 21ème siècle.' GK Collective manifesto (December): 1–15. http://gkcollective.org/wp-content/uploads/2020/10/Manifeste-Infrason-24_12_17-mep.pdf

———. 2017b. 'THéâTRe CaCHé. Règles et illustrations' GK Collective (July): 1–3.

Csíkszentmihályi, Mihaly. 2004. *Vivre, La psychologie du bonheur*. Translated by Léandre Bouffard. Paris: Robert Laffont.

Freydefont, Marcel. 2010. 'Les contours d'un théâtre immersif.' *Agon* 3. no. 3 (January): 1–51. https://doi.org/10.4000/agon.1559

Jakob-Hoff, Tristan. 2014. 'At the Gates of Temple Studios: Where gaming and theatre collide.' *Eurogamer*, 2 May 2014. https://www.eurogamer.net/how-punchdrunk-created-a-virtual-world-in-the-heart-of-central-london

Jenkins, Henry. 2004. 'Game Design as Narrative Architecture.' In *First Person, New Media as Story, Performance and Game*, edited by Noah Wardrip-Fruin and Pat Harrigan, 118–30. Cambridge: The MIT Press.

Laurel, Brenda. 1991. *Computers as Theatre*. Reading, MA: Addison-Wesley.

Levet, Olivia. 2021. 'Théâtre immersif et jeu vidéo : Éléments d'analyse sociocritique du processus de création participative', *Appareil* 23, no. 23 (March), 1–16. https://doi.org/10.4000/appareil.3991

Machon, Josephine. 2013. *Immersive Theatres: Intimacy and Immediacy in Contemporary Performance*. Basingstoke: Palgrave Macmillan.

Mcmullan, Thomas. 2014. 'The immersed audience: how theatre is taking its cue from video games.' *The Guardian*, 20 May 2014. https://www.theguardian.com/technology/2014/may/20/how-theatre-is-taking-its-cue-from-video-games

Neveux, Olivier. 2019. *Contre le théâtre politique*. Paris: La Fabrique.

Pearce, Celia. 2021. 'Introduction: Building a plane in mid-air.' *Well Played. A Journal on Video Games, Values, and Meaning* 10, no. 2 (July): 1–11. https://doi.org/10.1184/R1/14919645.v5

Pine II, B. Joseph, and Gilmore, James H. 1999. *The Experience Economy: Work is Theater & Every Business a Stage*. Boston: Harvard Business School Press.

Serdane, Thierry. 2014. 'Le jeu vidéo, un art mécanique ? Se réapproprier la contre-culture.' PhD diss., Université Paul-Valéry Montpellier.

Siegel, Claire. 2015. 'L'Artgame, un jeu utopique à l'ère de la gamification ?' PhD diss., Université Paul-Valéry Montpellier.

Turner, Fred. 2006. *From Counterculture to Cyberculture, Stewart Brand, the Whole Earth Network, and the Rise of Digital Utopianism*. London: University of Chicago Press.

Biography

Olivia Levet holds a PhD in Plastic Arts and Video Games from Paul-Valéry University in Montpellier, where she also is a lecturer. Moreover, she is a game designer; her PhD research led to the creation of *Brèche*, an *artgame* that hybridizes video games and theater in an attempt to reinvest the utopian and emancipatory processes of the Augusto Boal's *Theatre of the Oppressed* in a critical, experimental, and political way. Her work focuses on the mutual influences of video games and theater, immersive experiences, and the ideological shift of participatory processes in the ultraliberal era.

Ludic Neuro-Performances: An Approach Towards Playful Experiments

Margarete Jahrmann

The Ludic as a method for game-based design sheds light on the human condition. It allows dynamic change, free play with art, science, and game rules. A new conceptual ludic art explores rules of play, systems of investigation and knowledge acquisition through an open-ended game mechanic in the design process. The fundamentals of perception, experience and cognition are considered (Jahrmann, 2021).

Abstract *Building on the ludic method as an approach to artistic research, the concept of ludic neuro-performance is explained via the description of two performative plays developed as part of the artistic research project Neuromatic Game Art: Critical Play with Neurointerfaces (2020–2023). The concept explores the use of play as a process to be used by artistic researchers; more generally, it challenges research methods, experimental rules, artificial settings, and technologies. Finally, the ludic neuro-performances elaborate new forms of play related to emerging technologies such as neurointerfaces and AI.*

Introduction

In this article, I propose the use of the ludic method as an experimental system in research. In an interdisciplinary practice, this method was developed over the last decade, involving various formats of play and art. As an artistic research method, it builds on dynamic game mechanics, arts, and science. It results in the creation of artworks which aim to connect the human and non- human, the cognitive and the emotional, the political and societal with a new form of artistic games to reflect and intervene in contemporary conditions of the world based on technologies.

Using the ludic method, we developed neuro-performances in the *Neuromatic Game Art: Critical Play with Neurointerfaces* research project.[1] This approach aims to develop games as experiments and to use neuro-interfaces in performances. The experimental setup becomes a subject of research; insight is gained through the collection of brain data during performances and via reflection on the experimental setting in combination with the experiences undergone during a performance. It constitutes a playful 'ludic' version of an epistemic thing[2] in the sense of Hans Jörg Rheinberger (2006). Here the experimental apparatus is at the centre and is an element of the performance.

The term 'ludic method': Explanation and definition

In my artistic doctoral dissertation submitted at the University of Plymouth, *Ludics for a Ludic Society. The Art and Politics of Play* (2011)[3] , I elaborated the ludic method. In an effort to establish the ludic method, with the aim of integrating play mechanisms and research, I founded the Ludic Society. The projects of the 'Ludic Society'[4] were a series of urban and exhibition games, shown at international venues, such as Piksel

---

1   https://neuromatic.uni-ak.ac.at. See also: A Dobrosovestnova, M Coeckelbergh, M Jahrmann, 2021. 'Critical Art with Brain-Computer Interfaces: Philosophical Reflections from Neuromatic Game Art Project.' In: *HCI International 2021-Late Breaking Papers*, Springer International Publishing.

2   In the research process, the 'epistemic thing' is the object of investigation, which can develop into a 'technical object' in the course of the investigation, i.e. into something that can be used as an instrument in the investigation of further 'epistemic things'. However, this boundary is not static and the identification as either an 'epistemic thing' or a 'technical object' is not necessarily permanent. Cognition is therefore neither inevitable nor complete. Rheinberger's experience as a molecular biologist has brought the 'materiality of the natural sciences' into the focus of the history of science. Extracted from Wikipedia, referring to the book: *Experimentalsysteme und epistemische Dinge. Eine Geschichte der Proteinsynthese im Reagenzglas*. Frankfurt am Main 2006.

3   This dissertation provides an analysis of, and critical commentary on, the practice of playfulness as a persistent phenomenon in the arts, technology, and theory. Its aim is to introduce political reflections on agency through the study of playful technological artefacts, which have largely been ignored in recent discussions on games and play. Following the critical analysis of historical discourses and studies of concrete play under differing auspices, seeking to understand play as an inherently political form of agency, this thesis's research question addresses the immersive effects of playful agency in symbolic exchange systems and in the material consciousness of the player. https://pearl.plymouth.ac.uk/handle/10026.1/4 53

4   http://ludic-society.net.

Fest Bergen, Laboral Gijon, and ars electronica Linz. With 45 international members from various disciplines – both researchers and artists – we were able to examine the effect of the use of new technologies and game mechanics in the context of art (Objects of Desire, 2008).[5] On stage, we also reflected the human condition of the player by using new technologies such as the internet of things ('The evening of the Ludic Society', Ro Theatre Rotterdam, 2006).[6]

By means of playful exchange in various fields of expertise, the ludic method allows transdisciplinary teams of artists, performers, researchers, and early adopters of technologies to critically examine how a certain research question is shaped and what effect the topic has on the audiences. To grasp the method in greater depth, we need to understand play in relation to technologies and arts as based on an open set of rules, which puts a focus on self-reflexivity. A central aspect of the ludic method is experiencing the essence of technologies as a subject. Following the ludic method introduces a new trope to artistic research via public play with emerging technologies. In ludic method settings, an element of play is applied to demonstrate and sometimes also invert the role of technologies and the artistic researcher.

The ludic neuro-performances

In the ludic neuro-performances, we applied a ludic method and used neurointerfaces to measure and analyse brainwaves during public play and performance. Often in ludic neuro-performances, only minimal action was required from the performers as players and from audiences as observers of a public play. As we found out, the ludic neuro-performances correspond very well with studies of idle games,[7] which is a common term for very simple incremental games that only require minimal action. In the Ludic Soirée Series 2022, Larissa Wild describes the increasingly present passivity in some art games (think about the games of David O´Reilly, such as 'Mountain' or 'Everything') as a mirror of the world as we know it. In these idle games the player can do very little, mostly only one action to trigger the process of the gameplay. In her presentation Wild gives numerous examples of consumer games:

> The new genre of low-interaction games challenges the definition of games, their limits, and their rules. Low-interaction games take away an integral part of games and thus propose a new range of definitions. They develop a new type of relationship with the player – almost a dominant one – and are still widely enjoyed and played by thousands. Through analysing low-interaction

---

5   http://ludic-society.net/desire/.

6   https://v2.nl/events/the-evening-of-the-ludic-society.

7   Idle games are often called 'click and tap' games. On many gaming forums, they are defined as simple incremental games.

games we can find and compare patterns in other game genres as well as in our society. [8]

In the ludic neuro-performances, artists and researchers used such low-interaction game principles. The use of neurointerfaces does not allow a lot of physical action in performances.

An alarming consequence of these tendencies is self-optimisation as a digital imperative in everyday life. Sensitive personal data is increasingly capitalised and becomes part of a social scoring system. Neurointerfaces, currently on the cusp of becoming consumer articles (for example, as EEG headsets), provide direct access to brain activity, thus enabling the user for the first time in history to control devices by pure thought. Scientific investigations are using the possibilities of neurointerfaces to improve understanding of brain functions, or to help people with disabilities to regain better quality of life. However, the devices also breach the privacy of our thoughts, recording and measuring very personal data on brain activity; this raises major ethical issues.

Neurofeedback installations are increasingly present in the arts. Investigating perception was always also an artistic endeavour. From the first experiments that turned psychophysiological research into experiential formats, such as Marcel Duchamp's optical apparatuses, via Gysin and Burroughs's Dream Machines, to the Ganzfeld installations of James Turrell or Olafur Eliasson's perceptual experiments, the analysis and manipulation of human brain function has often been a site of strong intersection between the arts and the sciences. A database of artworks using brain-computer interfaces,[9] though probably incomplete, lists over 40 works, starting with Alvin Lucier's seminal *Music for Solo Performer* in 1965, which used electroencephalography (EEG) to generate music. More recent examples include pieces with multiple participants exploring brainwave synchronization[10] or questions of intimacy,[11] a film that can be controlled via a brain-computer interface,[12] complex interactive multi-media installations,[13] and an opera influenced by the actor's brain waves.[14] These examples show the increasing overlap with other media, such as wearable technologies, and also reflect the growing mutual interest of neuroscience

---

8   https://www.dieangewandte.at/aktuell/aktuell_detail?artikel_id=1644244159247.

9   Prpa M, Pasquier P: https://bci-art.tumblr.com (School of Interactive Arts+Technology, Simon Fraser University, Canada).

10 Dikker S, Oostrik M, *The Mutual Wave Machine* (2013), supported by the Marina Abramovic Institute at the EYE Amsterdam.

11 Lancel K, Maat H (2016) *The E.E.G. Kiss* (http://www.lancelmaat.nl/work/e.e.g-kiss/).

12 Richard Ramchurn [firstpost.com]. source: http://braincontrolledmovie.co.uk/trailer/.

13 ::vtol:: (2014) Solaris. http://vtol.cc/filter/works/solaris.

14 Pearlman E (2017) *Brain Opera: Exploring Surveillance in 360-degree Immersive Theatre*. PAJ 116: 79–85.

and art.[15] While the performative quality of these works can serve as an inspiration, most of them miss a participatory aspect (an exception is an artistic neuro-feedback game)[16] and barely address critical aspects of neurointerfaces.

By contrast, in the Austrian Science Fund's artistic research project *Neuromatic Game Art: Critical Play with Neurointerfaces* (National Research ID AR 581) from 2020 to 2023, our aim was to critically reflect upon the potential of neurointerfaces for arts and artistic research. Mobile brain-computer interfaces are now capable of linking body, brain, and electronic networks. In the *Neuromatic Game Art* project, we wanted to use neurointerfaces as functioning scientific apparatuses that were props for performances. We combined the experimental measuring and collecting of data using neurointerfaces on stage with a *mise en scène* featuring the visualisation of brain data and the use of AI in performances. Because of the sensitive technology machinery of brainwave analysis and the difficulty to distinguish data noise caused by muscle movements, in short artifacts from brain data, we had to reduce activity caused by play on these interfaces. The rules of play in the ludic neuro-performances were thus very limited. To enact research during live situations, we also used the process of artistic writing as a performative act during our research. In an act of hacking the discourse, this was thus an experimental means to examine the subjective experience of alternative research possibilities. We developed experiments, analogous to scientific experiments, on cognition, behaviours and performance.

The series of performances developed in the *Neuromatic Game Art* project feature a combination of experimental settings from neuroscience, where the audience is both participant and player; the application of game design principles for the performance score; and the use of electroencephalograms, transforming brainwaves into sound and visuals. The personal data of artists, researchers, and participants in experiments was merged into installations, which served as a stage for public play with audience participation in the experiment. The participants own insights into how the measurements of their brain activity reflected their internal perceptions were also displayed as part of the stage design.

Two ludic neuro-performances

In the following section, I will use two performance examples that were conceived using the ludic method and explain what happened in these two performances with

---

15   Public event with Jahrmann, Glasauer, and others (https://www.bernstein-network.de/de/bernsteinconference/past-conferences/2018/insights-in-art-and-science-exploring-the-boundaries).

16   Stober JM (2015) *Ride Your Mind.* http://rideyourmind.com.

respect to the performers, the audience, and the technology, as well as what was achieved as a result.

Example one: *Brain Machine Dérive*, 2020

figure 1: Margarete Jahrmann engaging visitors in a Tarot-game conversation. Photo: Martina Lajczak.

Brain machine dérive (2020) is an example of an elastic writing performance with neurointerfaces.[17] It was performed at the Colloquium on *Artistic Research in Performing Arts* (CARPA7).[18] Following current tendencies in the arts to incorporate gameplay and technologies in theatre performances, four performers gave a staged public philosophical reading on the 'philosophy of the interface'. The readings followed game rules and showcased the brain activities of the reader measured by electroencephalography in real-time. Poetical references, for example dealing with expectations and superstitions regarding neuro-interfaces as brain reading devices and a means for telepathy, were factored into the texts to empower the audience to take a critical stance towards neurointerfaces.

---

17   https://neuromatic.uni-ak.ac.at/blog/derive-performance-critical-philosophy-play/.
18   Performance documentation on Carpa Website: https://nivel.teak.fi/carpa7/brain-machine-derive/.

The choreographer and artistic researcher Charlotta Ruth developed a score for this neurointerface performance. Its aim was to record brainwaves with a consumer neurointerface headband and to record the data while playing a card game and live writing. We wanted to measure and indicate arousal levels in reaction to certain playing cards displayed. During the performance, we then invited the audience to ask questions about the future. As part of the ludic method we used a game rule: to react to each question with a card. For that purpose, we used a self-designed set of cards for telling the future. At the same time, another performer undertook an act of automatic writing, typing the same questions into an early version of Chat GPT. We read out the answers produced by Chat GPT to the audience. Then we concentrated on the playing cards and displayed the visualisation of our brainwaves using the *Mind Monitor* software tool, running on our mobile phones. During the whole performance we measured and recorded the brainwaves of the four performers. Finally, we analysed the brainwave data to interpret the feelings we had while performing.[19]

Our aim was to demonstrate a new form of technological writing in artistic research, in which the audience and AI both contribute to producing the text of the performance. A key outcome of the performance was that the performers found the interaction with the audience in text production to be highly motivating. The live visualisation of our brain activity influenced the focus of questions from the audience during the performance and, in a feedback loop, also our own behaviour as performers. The use of a self-designed set of fortune-telling cards was the stimulus in the experiment. The technological setting with neurointerfaces, visualising brain activity, was key to the performance.

The performance allowed discursive reflection with the audience in a live situation. It triggered a discourse about mind reading, neuroscience, and ethical questions around public data harvesting. In a live research process during the performance, we were able to use neurointerfaces to investigate the application of technologies of quantification of the self and surveillance. This neuro-performance constituted an interplay of performance and neurointerfaces. As an experimental research game, it connected art and science.

---

19   https://www.uniarts.fi/en/documents/margarete-jahrman-and-charlotta-ruth-brain-deriv
      e-detournement-a-neuro-philosophical-situated-gpt-3-writing-game/.

Example two: *Zero Action in the Savings Bank*, 2022

Figure 2: Performance view, hyperscan with two players in Zero Action, *Margarete Jahrmann, Zarko Aleksic, Stefan Glasauer. AIL Angewandte Interdisciplinary Lab Wien, 2022. Photo: Stefan Glasauer.*

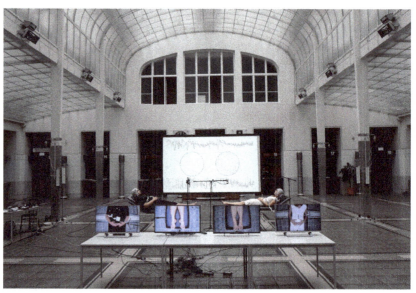

In the performance *Zero Action in the Savings Bank* we wanted to demonstrate how the brain activity of performers involuntarily synchronizes during a performance and how we can play a kind of idle game, as described by Wild (2022). The performance involved two performers, Žarko Aleksić and Margarete Jahrmann, lying on examination beds, looking at each other. Four cameras monitored each performer's body, filming the unintentional micro movements of the two performers and displaying these videos publicly. Unintentional muscle contractions were blown up on the screens in front of the performers and displayed to the audience. Each noise or other indicator of the presence of the audience influenced the measured brainwave activity of the performers – as displayed on a huge, game-like projection behind the performers. Both performers' brain waves were recorded using a 32-channel EEG (electroencephalogram) in a simultaneous hyperscan. Because the brain activity of the two performers was recorded at exactly at the same moment, it was possible to store comparable valid datasets. The brain activity was interpreted and visualised using a custom-made software, developed by Stefan Glasauer, the chair of Computational Neurosciences, from the Brandenburg Technical University Cottbus.[20] The visualisation of the brain activity of the two performers was represented in two circles. The moment the neurointerfaces registered synchronization, lines appeared inside the circles, representing the activity in certain brain areas. The audience watching noticed that it was possible to influence the intensity of connections between the two 'brain' circles on the screen via noise or other indicators of their presence.

This setting was presented as a *zero-action game*. The game mechanic was divided between the audience and the performers: The performers on the examination beds, equipped with neurointerfaces, played a 'passive' game. The playing activity was unintentional, in other words 'idle': muscle movement and brain activity. The audience took part in the experiment through its also largely 'idle' presence. It acted as a stimulus to the performers, who tried not to react, but who of course reacted involuntarily.

The outcome of this ludic neuro-performance was to integrate the neuro-interface with a new orientation in artistic play that is opposed to capitalist logic because it refuses to actively play. In this inter-passive micro performance, we entered into a dialogue without words with the audience. The topic was mutual unintentional interplay between performers and audience. In that sense the audience was passive/idle in the conventional understanding of play, but active in terms of its presence as part of the performance.

Afterword

The ludic neuro-performances use idle game principles of minimal action. They demonstrate how the increasingly available neuro-interfaces are not just tools for self-optimization but can be used as vehicles for a new form of passive play. In this way, neurointerfaces can be turned into tools of artistic expression. This approach critically addresses via performances the non-consensual play by technological systems with human entities that directly capitalises biometric data.

The ludic neuro-performances use ludic methods to reflect upon the social significance of neurointerfaces. The connection to science is underscored by the use of repeatable experiments and experimental design. We see how scientific tools become part of artistic research and then contribute again to the performance research process. The ludic neuro-performance as an artistically exploratory approach, relates performative practice to playful but rule-governed procedures. The performative play allows the testing of a new genre of performance using neurointerfaces – between science and art, where subjective experience is at the centre.

---

20   https://neuromatic.uni-ak.ac.at/blog/zero-action-in-the-savings-bank/.

One of the future possibilities for ludic neuro-performances will be to contribute to experiments in our partner research field of behavioural neuroscience that can be carried out under more natural conditions. Experiments are usually conducted in restricted and unnatural laboratory situations, which makes generalization to everyday life questionable. The ludic neuro-performances demonstrate how this situation can be amended by means of publicly accessible art.

The emergence of mobile and consumer interfaces for the measurement of brain activity promise a new genre and research field in performance that includes hybrid spaces between interfaces, technologies, and the body.

References

Coeckelbergh, Mark. 2021. 'Time Machines: Artificial Intelligence, Process, and Narrative.' *Philosophy & Technology* 34, 1623–1628. https://doi.org/10.1007/s13347-021-00479-y

Dobrosovestnova, A., Mark Coeckelbergh, and Margarete Jahrmann. 2021. 'Critical Art with Brain-Computer Interfaces: Philosophical Reflections from Neuromatic Game Art Project.' In *HCI International 2021-Late Breaking Papers*, edited by Constantine Stephanidis et.al., 558–574. New York: Springer International Publishing.

Jahrmann, Margarete. 2021. 'Ludics: The Art of Play and Societal Impact,' in *Not at Your Service. Manifestos for Design*, edited by Björn Franke and Hansuli Matter, 319–329. Berlin: Birkhäuser.

———. 2011. 'Ludics for a Ludic Society. The Art and Politics of Play.' Ph.D. Thesis, University of Plymouth.

Ruth, Charlotta, Margarete Jahrmann, and Georg Luif. 2022. 'Brain machine dérive.: Neuromatic Research Group' in *Proceedings of Carpa7: Elastic Writing in Artistic Research*. Theatre Academy University of the Arts Helsinki. https://nivel.teak.fi/carpa7/brain-machinederive.

Rheinberger, Hans-Jörg. 2006. *Experimentalsysteme und epistemische Dinge. Eine Geschichte der Proteinsynthese im Reagenzglas.* Frankfurt: Wallstein Publishing.

Biography

Margarete Jahrmann is an artist and artistic researcher, full university professor, and has been head of the department and master's programme in Experimental Game Cultures at the University of Applied Arts Vienna since its establishment in 2021. As an experienced researcher and pioneering game artist, she led the research project 'Neuromatic Game Art: Critical Play with Neurointerfaces'[21] from 2020 to 2023. Since 2024, she has been principal investigator of the interdisciplinary research project 'The Psycho-Ludic Approach: Exploring Play for a Viable Future'. Both projects have been funded by the Austrian Science Fund (FWF). Her art and research projects focus on play as an experimental system. Jahrmann publishes and exhibits internationally (e.g. 2024: featured AI artist Spike Magazine; 2023: AI Institute Nagoya; 2021–2023: Re:publica Berlin Art Show; 2021–2023: AMAZE Playful Media Festival Berlin; 2022: Havana Biennale; 2017: ars electronica Linz; 2004: transmediale, Haus der Kulturen der Welt Berlin.

---

21   https://scilog.fwf.ac.at/magazin/das-spiel-mit-den-gehirndaten.

New (Game) Technologies for the Theatre

Directing Avatars in Live Performances – An Autonomy Simulacrum of Virtual Actors

Georges Gagneré

Abstract *We propose to review the main stages in the history of computer-based virtual actors, with a view to exploring virtual reality and discussing various approaches to human simulation. The notion of autonomy emerges as a key issue for the virtual entities. We then explore one way of building elements of autonomy and conclude with an example of avatar stage direction leading to a simulacrum of autonomy in a live performance.*

Introduction

Artificial beings have fascinated natural humans ever since they discovered they could transform nature using tools. In his latest book *Automates, robots et humains virtuels dans les arts vivants (Automata, robots, and virtual humans in the performing arts)* Edmond Couchot recalls that Homer in the *Illiad* evoked 'mechanical maids, made of gold, having the appearance of young girls and created by [Hephaestus] to help him in his work, all endowed with speech, reflective thought (*noos*) and a certain physical strength' (Couchot 2022, 16)[1]. The divine blacksmith had thus invented creatures intelligent enough to assist him. Three millennia later, the project is being carried out by humans themselves, thanks to the recently invented science of computing and the sub-discipline of artificial intelligence, a complex field that aims to completely externalize our cognitive processes.

In the first part of this chapter, we propose to review the main stages in the history of computer-based virtual actors, with a view to the emergence and exploration of virtual reality. This will enable us to discuss the various approaches that have been taken to human simulation, i.e. to the dynamic reproduction of complex human behaviours and appearances in the form of models, algorithms, and programs. The notion of autonomy emerges as a key issue in the creation of virtual entities. The second part is then devoted to exploring one way of building elements of autonomy

---

1   Unless otherwise indicated, this and all other citations from non-English sources have been translated by the author.

88 New (Game) Technologies for the Theatre

by explaining how the virtual actors used in video games and performing arts can be moved. We break down the various techniques used to control them and to simulate elements of autonomy in virtual worlds. Finally, we focus on an example of avatar stage direction leading to a simulacrum of autonomy in a live performance.

The simulation of the virtual actor

The first realistic virtual humans were the result of an artistic commission to a couple of computer science researchers, Nadia and Daniel Thalmann, originally from Switzerland, who began their career in Canada in 1977. After developing the MIRA-3D computer language for computer-generated images, with which the short film *Dream Flight*, directed by Philippe Bergeron, won international scientific acclaim in 1982 (Thalmann, Magnenat-Thalmann and Bergeron 1982), they made the film *Rendez-vous à Montréal* (Magnenat-Thalmann and Thalmann 1987). This film, whose subject matter is a meating between a virtual Marylin Monroe and Humphrey Bogart at Montreal's Bon Secours market, was screened in 1987 for the 100th anniversary of the Canadian Order of Engineers. The realism of Virtual Marilyn, representing the culmination of ten years of research in computer graphics, made a lasting impression. This type of work was the first concrete evidence of the possibilities that digital technology and computer language offer for the simulation of reality.

Inhabiting the new virtual reality

The late 1980s saw the emergence of what Jaron Lannier called Virtual Reality (Heim 1994, xvii), which offers natural humans sensory access to a 3D simulation of physical reality *via* a virtual reality headset and data gloves. Before the term was coined, Myron Krueger had used the term Artificial Reality to refer to the artistic experiments he carried out in the 1970s (Krueger 1983), particularly the experiment *Videoplace* (1974), which allowed viewers to inhabit a computer-generated image with their digital silhouette and to interact with artificial creatures. It became possible to immerse oneself in a digital pixel matrix, manipulate it in real time, and tame the entities inhabiting it.

Virtual reality turned on its head the bold proposals Brenda Laurel had made to the developer community in *Computers as Theatre*, to use Aristotle's reflections on Greek tragedy in his book *Poetics* as a model for building efficient interfaces (Laurel 1993, 50). Drawing inspiration from the process of *mimesis*, and its dramaturgical mechanisms for describing actions in the form of tragedy triggering *catharsis*, she proposed the development of effective, stimulating interactions of a user with the actions proposed by a program. However, this controlled, vertical approach to an interaction scenario soon appeared limiting to Laurel, not least because of the immeasurable, unpredictable richness offered by emergent virtual reality. The key notions of interactivity and simulation allow users to explore new realities by inhabiting the envelopes of artificial creatures. Inspired by *Videoplace*, Brenda Laurel conceived and realized *Placeholder* in 1992, one of the first performative art installations in virtual reality, in which two spectator-performers project themselves into the image of a raven, a spider, or a snake to experience new bodily sensations.

Simulating the natural human

Nadia and Daniel Thalmann returned to Switzerland after their successful experiments in Canada and founded respectively the MIRALab at the University of Geneva and the Computer Graphics Laboratory at the Ecole Polytechnique Fédérale de Lausanne (EPFL) in the late 80s, where they focused on 3D simulation of the human being. Two possible approaches soon became clear: on the one hand, enabling users to project themselves into cyberspace with an appearance that resembled them, connecting with other virtual human beings; and, on the other, populating the virtual world with artificial humans who would possess their own autonomy, thanks to research into artificial intelligence. In the late 1990s, their work led to the first classificatory schema for virtual humans.[2] In this schema, the avatar serves as a simple artificial vehicle for a human user, enabling him or her to immerse and exist in a manner close to his or her natural bodily vehicle in the new reality simulated by computers and their peripherals. Jean-Claude Heudin also notes a reversal of polarities in relation to the etymology of the notion, which comes from the Sanskrit *Avatāra*, and which in the Hindu religious tradition designates the incarnation of an extra-human entity in a living earthly body. But in the context of virtual reality, 'instead of a deity incarnating in a material body, it's a material body that 'disincarnates' into a virtual representation.' (Heudin 2008, 210).

The Thalmanns' project enables a participant to inhabit his or her own synthesized body envelope with the aid of a motion capture system, and to visualise the result directly in the virtual environment using a 3D head-mounted display. The goal is not necessarily for the participant to see themselves, but rather to appear as their expressive digital double to another participant. 'Disembodiment' in the avatar is then achieved by means of control peripherals akin to the bars used to move the wires of a marionette, although guidance is generally very different from that of a puppet, as we shall see later. In a further, logical step, guidance can then be automated using algorithms, giving the virtual characters elements of autonomy. As Daniel Thalmann

---

2   This classification contains four categories, avatars, guided actors, autonomous actors, and interactive-perceptive actors (Cavazza et al., 1998), which we detail in the section *Describing the autonomy of a virtual actor*.

puts it: 'Our ultimate goal is to create credible, realistic synthetic actors – intelligent, autonomous virtual humans with adaptability, perception, and memory. These actors should be able to act freely and emotionally. Ideally, they should be conscious and unpredictable' (Thalmann 1998, 65). To achieve this, the project needs to draw on the computer science discipline of artificial intelligence, which has seen regular ups and downs in institutional funding since the 1960s. The avatar's virtual body is no longer inhabited; it must exist on its own, and, to do this, it must be equipped with mechanisms that enable it to move, perceive the virtual world and other virtual entities, feel emotions, and enter into social relations. At the 1997 Interactive Telecom conference, this research project gave rise to a tennis match in which a player in Geneva at MIRALab played with his avatar against the avatar of another player at EPFL in Lausanne, while the Virtual Marilyn from the 1987 project refereed the match autonomously.

Different approaches to simulation

There is as yet no standard for simulating virtual humans, and every laboratory, video game engine, and cyberspace platform, every researcher and every artist has their own simulation model or approach. Simulation based on the natural laws of physics and biology led Jeffrey Ventrella to propose a model (Ventrella 2000) that could evolve according to the laws of genetics, and which was subsequently used to develop the online virtual world *Second Life* from 2003 (Linden Lab 2003). Ken Perlin's work led him to combine technology with an artistic approach to create virtual characters capable of improvisation (Perlin 2000). This enabled him to generate real-time theatrical performances in which the characters could interact with physical participants, lasting up to a week without interruption.

Ventrella and Perlin's work was inspired by Norman Badler's 1980s research on the human simulation project *Jack*, which was used, in particular, to prototype NASA's Space Shuttle. *Jack* generalized the principle of inverse kinematics, enabling the joints of a virtual human to be manipulated in a way that is plausible for contact with the virtual environment (Badler, Barsky, and Zeltzer 1991). It was under Badler's direction that Catherine Pelachaud submitted her PhD thesis (Pelachaud 1992), before pursuing her research into socio-emotional conversational agents. This scientific discipline works on giving a human appearance to entities endowed with artificial intelligence, enabling them to interact with natural humans in a wide range of social activities. Catherine Pelachaud has worked, in particular, on the simulation of emotions and non-verbal expressions and created the GRETA virtual agent model (Grimaldi and Pelachaud 2021).

In parallel to these approaches, which were all based on the implementation of a pre-existing model endowed with behavioural skills that enable it to simulate social interactions, another approach inspired by what the history of cognitive sciences describes as the fourth wave of cybernetics, starting with the work of Humberto Maturana and Francisco Varela (Maturana and Varela 1987), has led researchers to develop autonomy in virtual humans based on the concept of emergence. In the early 2000s, the mathematician and artist Michel Bret built virtual dancers who learn to dance on their own using neural networks (Bret 2000). This has enabled him to create choreographic performances with the artistic collaboration of Marie-Hélène Tramus at the Digital Image and Virtual Reality (Image Numérique et Réalité Virtuelle) laboratory at Paris 8 University (Bret, Tramus and Berthoz 2005). These experiments involve what they call 'second interactivity' (Couchot, Tramus and Bret 2003). They depart from the action-reaction processes typical of early cybernetic theories to rather approach presence and interaction in line with the concept of enaction developed by Varela, which is based on 'the enactment of a world and a mind on the basis of a history of the variety of actions that a being in the world performs.' (Varela, Thompson and Rosch 1981, 9)

This approach to autonomy in artificial intelligence was formalized by Jacques Tisseau at the Centre Européen de Réalité Virtuelle (CERV) in Brest. It combines the reciprocal influence of the notions of prediction, action, and adaptation (Tisseau, Parenthoen and Harrouet 2006). This led CERV to develop the Atelier de Réalité Virtuelle (ARéVi) programming library, which was later used by researcher Pierre de Loor to create an experimental dialogue between an autonomous entity and an actress. Conducted as part of the ANR INGREDIBLE (Bevacqua et al. 2016) project in 2010, in collaboration with a theatre company, the experiment led the researcher to conclude that 'the user's engagement can be improved if the virtual actor has behavioural characteristics defined through enaction' (De Loor et al. 2014).

At the same time, the fifth and final volume of the *Traité de réalité virtuelle* launched in 2003 by Ecole des Mines researcher Philippe Fuchs is entirely devoted to virtual humans and offers a panorama of advances within several scientific disciplines that are brought together to collaborate on interdisciplinary research projects (Fuchs, Moreau and Donikian 2009). Production of this volume was coordinated by Stéphane Donikian, whose research into interactions in crowds is the basis of the Goalem tools used to simulate complex autonomous behaviours in many fields, including video games and animated films (Goalem 2023). This research is continuing and benefiting from continuous advances, with the 2020s marking the rise of approaches based on deep learning and new algorithms whose results in the recognition and simulation of language and images maintain the fascination of natural humans for the subject.[3]

---

3   The publication *Actor & Avatar* (Mersch et al. 2023) gives references providing an overview of many research projects, results, and topics related to virtual actors and the future of AI.

Describing the autonomy of a virtual actor

We will now return to Daniel Thalmann's classificatory schema (see note 1) and its reinterpretation by artist-researcher Cédric Plessiet to question the relationship between the avatar and the autonomous virtual human. In the fields of video games, digital art installations, and the performing arts, Plessiet assumes that the movements of virtual entities can be analysed along two axes: that of the origin of movement, i.e. the principle that leads the entity to carry out gestures and actions in the virtual world with its virtual body; and that of the decision to move, i.e. the choice and intention to carry out a movement, and which corresponds to the possession, or not, of free will (Plessiet et al. 2019). He then deduces four types, depending on whether the origin and decision belong to the virtual entity or not (are internal or external), and which he names after theatrical or mythological notions. For the Virtual Puppet, the origin and decision of its movements lie outside itself. It corresponds to what Thalmann called the Avatar. By contrast, the Virtual Actor generates and decides on movements, corresponding to Thalmann's Interactive-Perceptive Actor. The entity that decides on its movements but does not generate them is a Virtual Mask, in reference to the theatrical tradition of masks, in which the performer must adapt his performance to the personality of the mask he wears and which 'controls' him. Finally, the last type is the Virtual Golem, who is at the origin of his movements but a slave to external decisions.[4] Thalmann's Guided Actor and Autonomous Actor fall into this category in the sense that they must possess their own means of movement to respond to instructions from an external human guide or from environment detection algorithms, which we can then consider, following Plessiet, as an internal stratum of movement animation.

Thalmann's classification was influenced by the discovery and exploration of virtual reality, which at the end of the 90s was still confined to those research laboratories that possessed powerful graphics workstations and access peripherals that were still very expensive: motion capture systems, data gloves, HMD or CAVEs (rooms where 3D images are projected onto the walls and the user wears special glasses) (Cruz-Neira et al. 1993). The challenge of virtual reality is to enable a human being to access this new reality via an Avatar in an environment that can simulate social activities with the other three types of Actors. The ultimate goal of the research is to simulate all human complexity in the digital matrix to achieve the figure of the Interactive-Perceptive Actor. Plessiet's classification focuses on the virtual entity from the point of view of its computer construction and enables us to recognize and an-

---

4   The Golem refers to the mythological figure from Jewish folklore that is formed from earth, brought to life by a magical incantation, and who blindly obeys its master, without free will.

ticipate the constraints that appear depending on the situation in which the entity is immersed, in the field of cultural and artistic uses.

In both cases, we observe a common strategy of describing a simulation or simulacrum of the Actor (Perceptive and Interactive) by making the Puppet (the Avatar) climb all the stages of a progressive emancipation on the way to the Golem (the Guided or Autonomous Actor). This is radically different from the enactive approach taken by Bret, Tisseau, and De Loor. However, it is widely used in the fields of animation, video games, and the performing arts, and will allow us to describe several steps in the construction of Golems aimed at approaching a simulacrum of the Virtual Actor.

From the Puppet to the Actor via the Golem

Sculpture-matrix and real time

Our starting point is Plessiet's notion of the sculpture-matrix (Plessiet 2019, 28) as a minimal computer representation of an anthropomorphic figure, which can be seen as an echo of the notion of the image-matrix proposed by Edmond Couchot in the late 1980s to describe the revolution that was about to overturn artistic and cultural practices (Couchot 1988, 189–219). The image-matrix implied abandoning the analogue concept of the optical image in favour of the expressive possibilities inherent in the nascent digital order, which made an image the association of a new technology of perception of the real/physical and a computer language with precisely established rules. The sculpture-matrix proposes an even more precise appropriation of all the potential offered by computer simulation.

Figure 1 (A and B) shows two sculpture-matrices of me: on the left (1A), a 3D representation of my body and face created by Cédric Plessiet. It is attached by the process of skinning to a virtual armature of joints and sticks, the union of the two being called bones and forming the skeleton of the sculpture-matrix. Describing the positions and rotations of the skeleton's bones animates the entity. The image on the right (1B) shows the same skeleton dressed by another skeletal mesh, which has the shape of an almost flat silhouette, except for the feet, of a previous version of my avatar. The field of possibilities is infinite, as is the range of positions the sculpture-matrix can take in 3D space.

Animation and video games use two main techniques to animate a sculpture-matrix. The oldest involves equipping the bones of the skeleton with controllers to form a rig and creating the movement curves of each bone from successive poses (see figure 1C). The artist-animator uses the rig to achieve the desired poses. The other technique is to use a motion capture system to calculate the positions and rotations of the physical limbs of the person performing the movement. This is a complex operation, as it involves reconstructing an intermediate skeleton from the capture data, and then matching this skeleton with the skeleton of the sculpture-matrix, while respecting the proportions, using a motion-retargeting process. Both techniques make it possible to save interpolation data between animation poses or successive motion sensor positions and replay them at will. Motion curves can then be edited and modified to adjust motion quality.

Figure 1: Two sculpture-matrices with their skeleton in Unreal Engine (A and B) (Epic Games 2023) and the motion curves in Motion Builder (Autodesk 2023) (C). Screenshot by Georges Gagneré

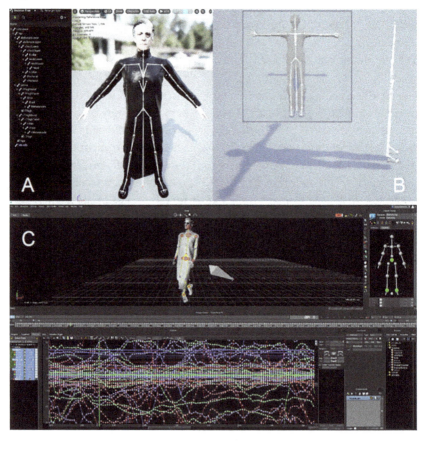

At this stage, we make a distinction between the field of animation, which uses precalculated computer techniques, and that of video games, which uses real-time techniques to obtain the final images that are presented to the viewer/player. In precalculated mode, each image is calculated separately, with computing times depending on the complexity of the VFX and the rendering quality of the sculpture-matrix movements. The result is put in a file and transmitted linearly to the viewer during the broadcast. What we're interested in here is the real-time mode of using motion information to deploy interactions with the recipient of the images – whether a player, actor, or active spectator. Our starting point is the control of an avatar by an actress wearing a motion capture suit, whom we'll call a mocaptress. We are in the mixed-reality scenic environment proposed by the AvatarStaging setup (cf. figure 2) (Gagneré and Plessiet 2018).

Figure 2: AvatarStaging setup showing a mocaptor controlling his avatar by motion capture. Image by Georges Gagneré

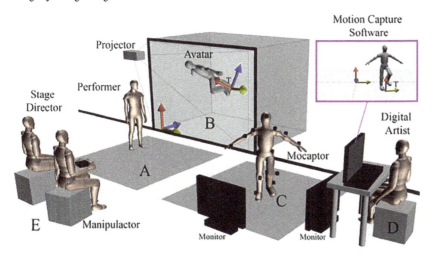

The mocaptress moves in her own acting space C, surrounded by monitors that allow her to adapt the position of her avatar in space B to its physical partner in space A. She keeps eye contact with the avatar in every position to fine-tune the staging situation. We propose to imagine that there are no monitors and that the mocaptress must remain oriented towards the video rendering screen of virtual space B to control its image. This scenario has already been encountered in artistic productions and introduces the concept of guiding an avatar (Gagneré and Plessiet 2019). Since we are in real time, we can also modify the avatar's position without the mocaptress moving.

Game development tools

We can also use a method that consists of placing the avatar in a capsule, transforming its movement to make it walk on the spot and simultaneously moving the capsule along the trajectory that corresponds to the root of the avatar (cf. figure 3A.). This root corresponds to the projection of the skeleton's main bone, in relation to which all other bones are referenced using the parentage method. This technique of using real-time motion from a motion capture system or from playing a pre-recorded animation is called root motion. Figure 3A shows two states of movement in which we can recognize the character in an idle position on the left, and the character walking in place in front of the white door. Combining these two movements in a black wireframe capsule allows the character to walk by, orienting the capsule in space. With this technique, to achieve the avatar's previous orientation according to the actor's movement, all you must do is turn the capsule on the spot at the right angle.

Figure 3: Avatar root motion using a capsule (A). Finite State Machine (B). Behaviour Tree (C) (Epic Games 2023b). A: Image by Georges Gagneré; B and C: Images by Epic Games© public online tutorial.

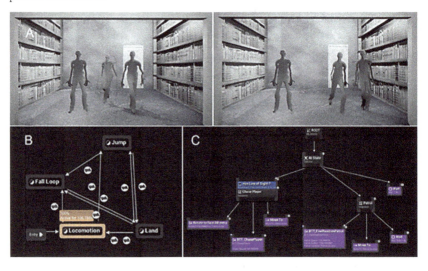

In a live-performance setting, when working with a mocaptress, these techniques aren't necessary, as you can rely on her skill to perform the avatar's desired movements. By contrast, they are necessary in a video game context. Apart from the non-interactive moments of the cinematics, which are animations and mobilize pre-recorded files, it is not possible to use an animation that moves a player's avatar from a given point to another along a trajectory. Instead, you need to use of a Virtual

Golem/Guided Actor. The player is free to move and orientate the capsule at any speed in 3D space, and the avatar walks in place, adjusting its speed. This technique gives correct visual results, as long as no attention is paid to the position of the feet, which glide lightly over the ground before stabilizing when they reach the right speed. The algorithm used to control the movements is a Finite State Machine (FSM), which allows different movements to be chained together according to precise rules that correspond to the movement possibilities offered to the player (see figure 3B).

In what way can we consider an entity that uses a walking animation combined with an idle animation to be a Golem, since it has been transmitted animations produced by a mocaptor or animator, i.e. an outside person? Precisely because, unlike a Puppet, the entity is equipped with a mechanism that it activates with relative autonomy according to instructions transmitted to it by an external player. It could be argued that the FSM is also programmed by a developer outside the entity. We would then have to consider the Golem as a kind of pre-programmed automaton. The assessment is subjective and linked to the evaluation of the complexity of the algorithms associated with the entity. An example often used is the pathfinding mechanism, which consists of analysing the environment via a NavMesh (navigation mesh) and applying an algorithm to move from one point to another, avoiding any obstacles in 3D space. In this case, we consider that the start and end points are given by external instructions, but that the organization of the movement based on the pathfinding algorithm and the NavMesh enables the entity to use its walking capsule to generate a movement that will bypass the obstacles encountered without external guidance. The entity is thus the originator of its own movements.

The next step is to increase the Golem's degree of autonomy by equipping it with a Behaviour Tree (BT) mechanism, which consists of assembling FSMs that react to changes in parameters describing the 3D environment (see figure 3C). The Golem's behavioural skills progress in the direction of those imagined for the interactive-perceptive actor. FSM, pathfinding, NavMesh, and BT are video game engine tools that can be used to endow an entity with elements of artificial intelligence. Will the increasing complexity of these tools lead to conscious autonomy? Proponents of the enactive approach would say no, and video game developers or artists are not seeking to achieve this goal. Rather, they aim to materialize simulacra of autonomy that elicit a 'willing suspension of disbelief' (Coleridge 1817, 145) from players and viewers alike, so that they can immerse themselves in a game or interactive installation.

Autonomous actor simulacrum: The Shadow

We conclude this exploration of virtual actors by describing a simulacrum of autonomy used in a work combining sculpture-matrix, video game tools, theatre, and virtual reality on a mixed stage. *The Shadow* (cf. figure 4) is a theatrical performance

I conceived and produced in 2019 involving a physical actor and five virtual entities that I call shadow avatars, in reference to their nature as flat silhouettes that can be inhabited by a mocaptor (cf. figure 1B). My approach to the avatar was initially based exclusively on the use of real-time motion capture using AKN_Regie software, which I developed as a plugin in the Unreal Engine video game engine environment (Gagneré 2023). This software combines the engine's resources to apply them to what I call avatar direction to achieve a simulacrum of autonomy. In broad terms, avatar direction applies theatrical actor direction methods to a mocaptor controlling an avatar in such a way that it performs replayable and modifiable scenic gestures according to the acting of its physical partner.

Figure 4: The Shadow (2019), *after Andersen, direction Georges Gagneré with Eric Jakobiak. Image by Georges Gagneré*

I imagined the presence of shadow avatars in relation to a physical actor who tells Andersen's fairy tale *The Shadow*, in which a scientist abandons his shadow after sending it to explore a house inhabited by a mysterious musician, who turns out to be Poetry. In contact with her, the scholar's shadow becomes almost human and grows rich, using its shadow powers to sneak into the homes of the wealthy and blackmail those with secrets to hide. After several years, the shadow returns to torment its former owner. I imagined that an actor would tell the tale to both spectators and shadow avatars on stage in a virtual small theatre. As the story unfolded, the shadow avatars, captivated by it, start miming the protagonists, reliving the various episodes over the course of the 50-minute show (Gagneré 2020).

Each shadow avatar's journey consists of a series of cues triggered directly by the physical actor reading the story, seated at a small table to the left of the virtual theatre, using a midi controller (see figure 4). There is no stage manager standing between the actor and the avatars. The paths of the avatars form a kind of visual score of pre-recorded animations, with the performer as narrator. Each animation was carefully recorded by a mocaptor listening to the tale's narration under my stage direction, according to the following acting protocol: We systematically alternated stage gestures that I call salient, followed by non-salient gestures. This intuitive approach to stage salience is inspired by the principle of idle loops, used in video game animation. This salience is the opposite of an idle gesture, which can be looped back on itself without creating a conspicuous repetition effect. An example is the resting position prior to walking, represented in figure 1B by the character on the left. He assumes a waiting position on the spot, not very active but not immobile, curled in on himself while waiting to receive the order to walk, still on the spot but in the capsule set-in motion. A salient gesture, on the other hand, is expressive and cannot be looped without the spectator immediately detecting the repetition. The threshold of salience is an empirical fact, and a very attentive observer could detect a looping process, even with a non-salient idle animation.

Based on this principle of systematic alternation between salient and non-salient stage gestures for all recorded animations, I developed the Salient-Idle Player feature in AKN_Regie, which equips each shadow avatar and allows the actor to successively trigger the acting animation, ending in a loop where the avatar listens and waits for further instructions. Does this feature transform the shadow avatar from puppet to 'basic' golem? Probably not. But it's a puppet guided by an internal mechanism specific to the nature of its movements, and which receives its acting instructions from the external actor. The end result, from the spectator's point of view, is to trigger the suspension of disbelief that makes him feel that the five shadow avatars are performing the show autonomously in relation to the physical narrator.

Prospects

> The human lineage exists only insofar as it stakes its own existence on a kind of headlong rush with no horizon – other than the one it draws for itself – for some, or towards an end that transcends it for others. Hence the impossibility of defining it in an absolute manner. Hominization never ends. Artificial living arts take part in this debate and suggest, by tinkering, a possible way of living together with these newcomers. (Couchot 2022, 205)

From the first stylized simulations of *Dream Flight* to the tinkering with shadow avatars in *The Shadow*, it's clear that the field of virtual actor simulation offers an infinite territory of exploration for artists. For scientists, it's a question of simulating human beings and offering them new ways of inhabiting virtual reality. In the wake of Georges Simondon, who demonstrated that culture and the arts must appropriate technical objects as bearers of humanity, to actively accompany the evolution of our societies (Simondon 1958), I continue to explore new avenues of autonomy for shadow avatars, gradually integrating FSM and BT into AKN_Regie. I wish to build performative experiences that will enable spectators and mocaptors to meet these new creatures immersed in virtual reality. Instead of remaining a mere spectator of shadow avatars, I wish to experiment with the possibility of one's own shadow escaping out of control and improvising with other shadows that have also managed to elude their owners. This could lead the dispossessed owners to make strange discoveries. To extend Couchot's vision of virtual newcomers living with natural humans, it would then be a matter of exploring new potentialities of presence and relationship to others.

References

Autodesk. 2023. *Motion Builder*. Accessed 28 May 2023. https://www.autodesk.eu/products/motionbuilder
Badler, Norman, Brian I. Barsky, and David Zeltzer. 1991. *Making Them Move*. Burlington: Morgan Kaufmann.
Bevacqua, Elisabetta, Romain Richard, Julien Soler, and Pierre De Loor. 2016. 'INGREDIBLE: A platform for full body interaction between human and virtual agent that improves co-presence.' *Proceedings of ACM MOCO Conference*, Thessaloniki.
Bret, Michel, and Jean-Claude Heudin, eds. 2000. 'Virtual Living Beings.' *Virtual Worlds. VW 2000. Lecture Notes in Computer Science*, vol 1834, Springer, Berlin, Heidelberg. https://doi.org/10.1007/3-540-45016-5_12
Cavazza, Marc, Rae A. Earnshaw, Nadia Magnenat-Thalmann and Daniel Thalmann. 1998. 'Motion Control of Virtual Humans'. *IEEE Computer Graphics and Applications* 18, no. 5 (Autumn): 24–31. https://doi.org/10.1109/38.708558
Coleridge, Samuel T. 1817. *Biographia literaria*. Books on Demand, 2018.
Couchot, Edmond. 1988. *Images. De l'optique au numérique*. Paris: Hermès.
———.2022. *Automates, robots et humains virtuels dans les arts vivants*. Paris: Presses Universitaires de Vincennes.
Couchot, Edmond, Marie-Hélène Tramus, Michel Bret, and Diana Domingues, eds. 2003. 'A segunda interatividade. Em direção a novas práticas artísticas'. In *Arte e vida no século XXI. Tecnologia, ciência criatividade*. São Paulo: Unesp.
Cruz-Neira, Carolina, Daniel J. Sandin and Thomas A. DeFanti. 1993. 'Surround-Screen Projection-based Virtual Reality: The Design and Implementation of the

CAVE', SIGGRAPH'93: Proceedings of the 20th Annual Conference on Computer Graphics and Interactive Techniques, 135–142.

De Loor, Pierre, Kristen Manac'H, Charlie Windelschmidt and Frédéric Devillers. 2014. 'Connecting Interactive Arts and Virtual Reality with Enaction.' Journal of Virtual Reality and Broadcasting, 11, no. 2 (February). https://doi.org/10.20385/186 0-2037/11.2014.2

Epic Games. 2023. 'Unreal Engine' Accessed 28 May 2023. https://www.unrealengin e.com.

———. 2023b. 'Unreal Engine Documentation' Accessed 28 May 2023. https://docs. unrealengine.com

Fuchs, Philippe, Guillaume Moreau, and Stéphane Donikian. 2009. Le traité de la réalité virtuelle. Volume 5: les humains virtuels. Paris: Presses des MINES.

Gagneré, Georges. 2020. 'The Shadow.' Proceedings of the 7th International Conference on Movement and Computing (MOCO '20), Association for Computing Machinery, New York, NY, USA, 2020, Article 31, 1–2. https://doi.org/10.1145/3401956.34042 50

———. 2023. 'AKN_Regie, un plugin dans Unreal Engine pour la direction d'avatar sur une scène mixte.' Journées d'Informatique Théâtrale – JIT22, October, Lyon.

Gagneré, Georges, and Cédric Plessiet. 2018. 'Experiencing avatar direction in low cost theatrical mixed reality setup.' Proceedings of the 5th International Conference on Movement and Computing (MOCO '18), Association for Computing Machinery, New York, NY, USA, Article 55, 1–6. https://doi.org/10.1145/3212721.3212892.

———. 2019. 'Espace virtuel interconnecté et Théâtre (2). Influences sur le jeu scénique.' Revue: Internet des objets 3, no. 1 (February). https://doi.org/10.21494/iste.o p.2019.0322.

Gagneré, Georges, Tom Mays, and Anastasiia Ternova. 2020. 'How a Hyper-actor directs Avatars in Virtual Shadow Theater.' Proceedings of the 7th International Conference on Movement and Computing (MOCO '20), Association for Computing Machinery, New York, NY, USA, 2020, Article 15, 1–9. https://doi.org/10.1145/3401956.34 04234

Goalem. 2023. 'Goalem tools' Accessed 28 May 2023. https://golaem.com/.

Grimaldi, Michele, and Catherine Pelachaud C. 2021. 'Generation of Multimodal Behaviors in the Greta platform.' 21st ACM International Conference on Intelligent Virtual Agents, Sep 2021, Kyoto (virtual), Japan. htpps://doi.org/10.1145/3472306.347 8368

Heim, Michael. 1994. The Metaphysics of Virtual Reality. New York: Oxford University Press.

Heudin, Jean-Claude. 2008. Les créatures artificielles. Des automates aux mondes virtuels. Paris: Odile Jacob.

Krueger, Myron W. 1983. Artificial Reality. Boston: Addison-Wesley.

Laurel, Brenda. 1993. Computers as Theater. Boston: Addison-Wesley.

Linden Lab. 2023. 'Second Life' Accessed 28 May 2023. https://secondlife.com/.

Magnenat-Thalmann, Nadia, and Daniel Thalmann. 1987. 'The Direction of Synthetic Actors in the Film Rendez-Vous a Montreal.' *IEEE Computer Graphics and Applications7*, no. 12 (December): 9–19.

Maturana, Humberto, and Francisco Varela. 1987. *The Tree of Knowledge: The Biological Roots of Human Understanding*. 1st ed. Boston: New Science Library.

Mersch, Dieter, Anton Rey, Thomas Grunwald, Jörg Sternagel, Lorena Kegel, and Miriam Laura Loertscher (eds.). 2023. *Actor & Avatar – A Scientific and Artistic Catalog*, Bielefeld: transcript.

Pelachaud, Catherine. 1992. *Communication and coarticulation in facial animation*. Ph.D. Dissertation. University of Pennsylvania, USA. Order Number: UMI Order No. GAX92-11983.

Perlin, Ken, and Jean-Claude Heudin, eds. 2000. 'Creating Emotive Responsive Characters Within Virtual Worlds.' *Virtual Worlds. VW 2000. Lecture Notes in Computer Science*, vol 1834, Springer, Berlin, Heidelberg. https://doi.org/10.1007/3-54 0-45016-5_10.

Plessiet, Cédric. 2019. *Quand la marionnette coupe ses fils. Recherches sur l'acteur virtuel*. Habilitation à diriger les recherches, Université Paris 8 Vincennes Saint-Denis. https://hal.archives-ouvertes.fr/tel-03555676.

Plessiet, Cédric, Georges Gagneré, and Rémy Sohier. 2019. 'A Proposal for the Classification of Virtual Character.' *Proceedings of the 14th International Joint Conference on Computer Vision, Imaging and Computer Graphics Theory and Applications* – Volume 2: HUCAPP, Prague, Czech Republic:168-174. https://doi.org/10.5220/00075694 01680174.

Simondon, Gilbert. 1958. *Du mode d'existence des objets techniques*. Paris: Éditions Aubier.

Thalmann, Daniel. 1998. 'Des avatars aux humains autonomes et perceptifs.' *Flash informatique*, École polytechnique fédérale de Lausanne.

Thalmann, Daniel, Nadia Magnenat-Thalmann, and Philippe Bergeron. 1982. 'Dream Flight: A Fictional Film Produced by 3-D Computer Animation.' *Proceedings Computer Graphics '82*, Online Publications: 352–367.

Tisseau, Jacques, Marc Parenthoen, Fabrice Harrouet, and Philippe Fuchs, eds. 2006. 'Modèle pour l'autonomie.' *Le Traité de la réalité virtuelle. Volume III. Outils et modèles informatiques des environnements virtuels*. Paris: Presses des Mines.

Varela, Francisco, Evan Thompson, and Eleanor Rosch. 1991. *The Embodied Mind: Cognitive Science and Human Experience*. Cambridge: MIT Press.

Ventrella, Jeffrey, and Jean-Claude Heudin, eds. 2000. 'Avatar Physics and Genetics.' *Virtual Worlds. VW 2000. Lecture Notes in Computer Science*, vol. 1834, Springer, Berlin, Heidelberg. https://doi.org/10.1007/3-540-45016-5_1.

Biography

Georges Gagneré is digital artist, stage director, and member of the collaborative platform didascalie.net, which focuses on performing arts in mixed realities. Since 2014, he has been developing AvatarStaging, a framework allowing real-time avatar direction in 3D. He has staged many productions in French national theatres and organized numerous workshops on the impact of new real-time technologies on theatre and scenic writing. He is associate professor in digital arts at the University Paris 8 and a member of the ATI-INREV team. http://gagnere.fr

Unreal Engine in the Theater: New Challenges for the Lighting Designer

Victor Inisan

Abstract *While visualisation software has transformed the profession of lighting designer, these tools are neither complete nor photorealistic. So why not turn to video game engines, which provide better capacities? Unreal Engine has recently taken this step by creating a plugin that allows control of lights from the game engine: What potentials do such programs offer to reshape the work of the lighting designer?*

Introduction

The last four decades have seen considerable changes in the field of stage lighting. First of all, this period has witnessed the popularization of motorized projectors: If 'it seems that the idea of using remote control of the pan, tilt and the focus (PTF) of a spotlight came into the collective consciousness of the lighting industry in the early 1960s' (Cadena 2010, 12), they have become dominant since the 1980s and 90s. More recently, luminescent sources (discharge lamps at first, then light-emitting diodes) have become dominant in the marketplace at the expense of incandescent lamps: In a way, 'we're at the start of a revolution in home, commercial, and public lighting that will be the biggest shift in the sector since the development of the tungsten filament over 100 years ago', as Sal Cangeloso wrote ten years ago (Cangeloso 2012, 6–7). Indeed, LED lighting is beginning to change the way we understand light and is part of a much larger transformation: 'the digital age seems to have taken hold and become a permanent fixture in our civilization, and LED technology is part of that logic' (Massol 2012, 1). In fact, it is becoming obvious that 'light is more and more electronic and less and less physical' in the words of the light designer and collaborator of Claude Régy, Rémi Godfroy (interview with the author, 14 December 2017).[1] This is true equally of the way designers use light and of the kind of light emitted, which is flatter and smoother than the light of incandescent bulbs.

---

1 Unless otherwise indicated, this and all further translations from non-English-language sources are by the author.

The new techniques logically require new means of control: LEDs and motorised lights require more powerful and capable lighting desks to exploit all the features inherent to them (colour changers, zoom, pan & tilt, etc.) in an intuitive and efficient way. In this regard, if we were to draw inspiration from the field of video, we could say that lighting consoles have progressively gone from analogue to digital. Moreover, the digital revolution has also allowed visualisation software to play a major role in the creation of light shows. Indeed, in the event industry, which mobilizes large budgets (high number of projectors; advanced equipment) in a short period of time, lighting designers model their lights in 3D before the show, both to help to conceive them and to facilitate the flow of information to the teams during the tour. Consequently, the software is now at the heart of both the logistical and the artistic aspects of a light show. This is the case of software such as VectorWorks or wysiwyg,[2] whose name is based on the acronym 'What you see is what you get'. It is only in a second step that digital consoles connected to visualisation software, such as Eos[3] or GrandMa,[4] allow the running of live light plots that perform what the designer had previously modelled.

In live performance, however, the spread of new lighting technologies is much more limited than in the case of events, for at least three related reasons: first, it is a smaller industry, which attracts less interest from the international lighting companies. Second, live performance lighting designers are often wary of these new technologies and still use a lot of incandescent halogen lamps. In fact, they often perceive these transformations as a 'takeover of the industry' to the detriment of the artistic, as Marie-Christine Soma, a great French lighting designer put it (interview with the author, 9 December 2017). Third, there are also artistic reasons why new technologies may not be taken up, relating to the quality of luminescent light, which is inferior to the rendering of incandescent colours (Inisan 2021, 95–108). For these reasons, the need to replace the tools used for lighting design and control is not felt so strongly. Moreover, since the time available for light creation on set is far longer than in the event industry, with lighting designers on live shows often having the opportunity to work for several weeks in the theatre, this further reduces interest in computer modelling. Thus, most of the entry-level consoles for live shows integrate fairly basic software (e.g., Cobalt) which makes handling some new technologies awkward while favouring the control of older sources.

---

2   VectorWorks (www.vectorworks.net) and wysiwyg (www.cast-soft.com/wysiwyg-lighting-d esign) are complex 3D design software suites that can be used in a range of fields, such as live events and architecture.

3   Eos (www.etcconnect.com/Products/Consoles/Eos-Consoles/) is a series of lighting desks designed by ETC that became very popular among the lighting designers, especially for live performances that don't require GrandMa.

4   GrandMa lighting desks (www.malighting.com) are the most popular devices used to control lights in major live events (concerts, TV shows, conferences, etc).

Some lighting designers have also ventured into the field of simple virtual consoles (e.g., DLight,[5] QLC +[6]). With an ENTTEC box, for example, they can transmit a single DMX[7] universe via a USB cable. A yet smaller number are starting to be interested in software with integrated visualisation functions. The simplest are virtual consoles with 2D schematics (Lightkey, Millumin, Sunlite, and DasLight 4), or even with basic 3D (Chamsys[8]): In fact, these are not even lighting plans but merely contain sets of reference points. But as Yragaël Gervais, lighting and video designer, notes, the very tension that currently exists around control tools in live performance is perhaps a sign of a transformation to come:

> The new generations are completely different. In theatres, we live with people who still have classic consoles, classic programming, and who are stuck in this. Afterwards, they will be very good at adjusting a projector, making a beautiful front light. These people can place and adjust everything well, and then I can program the way I want, but they can't, because they are stuck with their tools. There is really a difference between two schools of lighting; the teams in theatres seeing us arriving can be a bit lost: the first thing we tell them is to put away the console… (interview with the author, 10 January 2018).

As for Marie-Christine Soma, she explains:

> There are people who think it's great, like any novelty, the geeks in fact. As soon as there's something new, they think it's great. And others who have a form of reticence: There are technical directors who find it very bad, while some are very enthusiastic (interview with the author, 9 December 2017).

In this regard, Christine Richier, director of the lighting section of the École Nationale Supérieure des Arts et Techniques du Théâtre (ENSATT) distinguishes two types of lighting designers among her students: the traditionalists and the geeks,

---

5   DLight (www.getdlight.com) was been the most popular simple virtual console at the beginning of the 'digital era' of lighting. It is not really used anymore at this time.

6   QLC+ (www.qlcplus.org) is an open-source virtual console that looks a lot like DLight. Even if it has more or less the same specifications, it remained less popular. As with DLight, it now looks quite outdated.

7   DMX is the principal computer protocol used for lighting since the end of the 1980s that allows the transmission of various kinds of light information from the console. Thus, the operation of the lights differs according to the variation of the DMX signal. DMX contains 512 channels – 512 different pieces of information are possible: The whole is referred to as a 'universe', and it is possible to multiply universes when more information is needed.

8   Though all the lighting controllers named here are more complex than DLight and QLC+, they remain very accessible options for the beginner.

3D visualisation in live performance

It is not surprising that some lighting designers are starting to use 3D visualisers from the event industry to design their theatre lights – even if these software packages require the use of digital consoles that are often still lacking theatres. In fact, we anticipate that, alongside the generational shift, another factor that will boost the uptake of visualisation software is its ability to compensate for the lack of access to theatres or rehearsal spaces. Many productions are confronted with this problem, especially emerging productions which struggle to obtain stage time. Indeed, the use of 3D software allows for significant progress on the visual design of a show outside of a theatre, much better than with schematic or 2D lighting design software. Moreover, since it is possible to experiment with proposals and effects in a virtual environment that also integrates movement, the use of a video game engine can lead to savings in the number of necessary technical purchases.

That said, this kind of usage can also be found in larger theatre productions: In this case, it is rather that they allow the exploitation of certain lighting technologies to the fullest. This is for example the case of Antoine Travert, lighting designer for Thomas Jolly, user of wysiwyg and GrandMa consoles. As he attests:

> I'm a geek. Afterwards, I have the console between my legs. Philippe Berthomé, for example, with whom I work on *Thyeste*, he must know how to manage a console, but he always has someone with him, he doesn't climb either. My job is mostly encoding machines. The more I have, the better (interview with the author, 4 April 2018).

However, it must be recognized that while most of these software programs are of excellent quality for the visualisation of light, they remain rather basic when it comes to designing materials and spaces: They model the scenes of shows, certainly, but not really detailed sets. In fact, in live shows, the modelling is very often done by the scenographer using different software (such as Sketchup[9]), and the stage design file is then imported into the lighting software. Wysiwyg and VectorWorks, which are also used in architecture, are more complex, but they struggle to be photorealistic. Moreover, it goes without saying that none of the software is capable of rendering the movement of the sets and actors, though it is possible to build different scenes,

---

9   Sketchup (www.sketchup.com) is a very popular software for 3D visualisation and modelling.

i.e., different placements, without seeing the movement itself. In short, light visualisation, even where it has been adopted, is still usually unable to model what a show will look like as a whole. It is an advanced technical tool, sometimes useful for artistic purposes, but it remains mostly alien to the staging process.

Where some more or less successful attempts have been made to create visualisation and control tools that are as artistic as they are technical (Bardiot 2016, 431), it seems that video game engines have been particularly interesting for live performance teams: Indeed, they are the only tools capable of creating integrated environments that aggregate movement (sets, characters) – so that it is possible for a designer to obtain a more or less complete visualisation of a performance in advance. Of course, the use of game engines for theatre design does not seem to be inevitable: First, visualising an entire show in advance is almost fundamentally opposed to the definition of a live performance, which occurs in the moment and depends on actions that may occur spontaneously. Second, these game engines are made for … producing games: In other words, they are not optimised for this kind of visualisation. Very often, they require training in coding, which almost no director or lighting designer has.

The case of Unreal Engine

In this context, Unreal Engine, developed by the American studio and video game distributor Epic Games, seems particularly interesting. Unreal Engine, which has gone through five versions since its release in 1991, makes it possible, like most other game engines, to create photorealistic environments of great quality that are incomparably superior to those made using any classic visualisation software. Furthermore, unlike all the visualisation software mentioned above, Unreal Engine is totally free, since it works on a system of royalties that must only be paid to the license holder when profits exceed a million euros – something that remains very rare in live shows. By way of comparison, wisywyg costs 3,000 euros per year, and while Capture[10] offers a free student version, to access the full range of features, you'll need to pay between 400 and 2,000 euros, depending on which DMX universes are to be unlocked. In addition, Unreal probably has two advantages over its competitors in the live performance field:

- Entirely coded in C++, Unreal has long been inaccessible for artists, and even sometimes for programmers compared, for example, to Unity. However, thanks to a system of associating nodes called Blueprint, it is now possible to create

---

10   Capture (www.capture.se) is a 3D visualisation software that has been optimized for live performance. Contrary to VectorWorks for instance, it is not dedicated to architecture.

scenarios without coding, making the design of environments quite accessible for someone who does not know how to code.

- Officially released in April 2022, the latest version of the software, Unreal Engine 5, has greatly improved photorealism. It immediately became the default system for creating triple-A games, i.e., video game blockbusters. This improvement comes in particular from the processing of lights via Lumen, a tool that allows much more detail in the environments and greatly accelerates design work.

This is why Unreal, perhaps more than any other engine, seems appropriate to accommodate live performance visualisation. A first DMX plugin was released in Unreal Engine 4 in early 2022: It allows live show visualisation with theatre projectors and the electronic patching of the projectors. However, the virtual console function is still very limited, and is only useful for testing lights. As is often the case in visualisation, it is necessary to use an external console (virtual or real) to create sequential effects. So, what does this plugin actually offer lighting designers, and more generally to a live performance team? Since it is recent and has been designed more for events, asking what the plugin will achieve, both in terms of work organization and transformation of show aesthetics, remains a matter for speculation. I have tried to put forward two sets of assumptions – the first concerning changes in the division of responsibilities in theatrical projects that use Unreal; the second about the interest of the use of Unreal itself.

First set of assumptions

1. Certain software tools are already successfully unifying the sequencing of light, sound, and video (e.g., QLab[11]): 'a more stable relationship between the control of light and the control of the other elements of the show – music, midi elements, video – becomes possible' (Toeplitz 2010, 27), writes composer and musician Kasper T. Toeplitz about the modernisation of technologies. Nevertheless, this is still rare in the field of visualisation: It is therefore safe to say that Unreal brings greater unity not only to control, but also to the design of the aesthetics of a performance. Unreal, which is quite easy to use, would even allow a director to be involved in the construction of the 3D visualisation. If the lighting visualisation belongs to the lighting designer, the visualisation of materials and spaces to the set designer, then, for instance, the director can intervene in the file by determining in advance what the movements of the actors are. The director is thus encouraged to be the technician-creator of his or her own work. Thus, a team

---

11 QLab is a multimedia control software that allows light, sound, and video to be controlled from the same interface (https://qlab.app).

gathered around the same Unreal environment could create a show whose set would be the artistic result of a virtual design.

2. Since the lighting designer can start the visualisation before the rehearsals and continue the design outside of the work sessions in the theatre, it seems that he or she could more easily be invited to participate in dramaturgical considerations. In a way, integrating lighting visualisation into the creative process of a show solidifies the role of the lighting designer as an artist in his or her own right.[12] In fact, as the DMX plugin is prepared by programmers who have no real affinity with live performance, we can distinguish between the lighting designer – who until recently was considered a pure technician – and pure programmers, who can access the source code and prepare the interfaces without knowing the works they allow to be produced.

3. As the director can intervene in the file and the lighting designer himself becomes an artist, one could imagine a convergence between the two professions. Frédéric Poullain, former assistant of François-Éric Valentin, even imagines, in the long term:

F.P.: A computer scientist will create a network with a small team and then the lighting designer, who will not be entirely unfamiliar with the technology – but who will primarily be a representative of artistic and literary culture – will make visuals.

V.I : So you think that there will be a valorisation of the work of conception ?

F.P.: Yes. It could even become a training course for directors, we could almost make the lighting designer's job disappear (interview with the author, 1 February 2018).

Second set of assumptions

4. In his book *L'Éclairage des spectacles* published in 1982, Yves Bonnat imagined a lighting system where 'all the modular elements of information processing will be grouped together in a room and will receive orders by radio or telephone cable from a removable console barely larger than a pocket calculator'! (Bonnat 1982, 69) In fact, control by smartphone, although still rather unreliable, is not far from realizing this dream. In this context, one can speculate about the nature of a lighting plot: At what point does the lighting concept stop being technical and

---

12   The term 'lighting designer' only arrived in France in the 1950s: it was Pierre Saveron who, along with Jean Vilar, was the first to be named as such – and no longer 'chief electrician".

start being artistic? It is no longer 'the set and sequence of indications of effect and directives for change consigned in a transmissible document [...] to ensure the proper unfolding of a performance and the service of a staging' (Freydefont 1995, 212), to use Marcel Freydefont's definition: the technical plan becomes almost the performance itself in germ, encapsulating all the aesthetic aspects of a production. The use of Unreal cements this direction: What is the nature of the file that contains all the potentialities of visualisation of a spectacle? The software, which was considered a simple technical tool, becomes not only the vector of the work that it foresees, but perhaps even a part of the work itself, or even an alternative version of it. In a way, the artistic nature of Unreal – since it is first and foremost a video game creation tool – can be considered to have deeply infused the field of live performance.

5. If we give artistic credit to the Unreal visualisation, we could consider that in a way a visualisation file – just like a recording – can act as a memory of a performance, since it is a virtual version of what happened. This would make it possible to preserve valuable traces of performances, especially when the theatricality does not place the text at the centre, and it is therefore more difficult to archive. In this case, could we imagine that the document that comes closest to the performance is a visualisation file? Would it be possible to study these visualisation files in the same way as we do with a musical score or even a theatrical text?

The limitations of Unreal

If the use of Unreal augurs a transformation of the organization and the nature of artistic work, it must be recognised that it is for the moment only a thought projected on the future. Indeed, Unreal currently has a series of central drawbacks that still block the possible realization of these assumptions – namely:

1. Up to now, the plugin's DMX addressing system is rather rudimentary: It doesn't yet rival that of most of the software developed specifically for events and live shows. Moreover, some elements of the plugin, which is inspired more by video games than by live shows, still show a lack of porosity between the two domains.

2. Live control of the projectors is almost non-existent and the coupling with the consoles is less evident than with other software and consoles: It would therefore be necessary to pair Unreal and consoles and/or to develop a virtual console within Unreal (as is the case with software such as L8 for example).

3. The fact that USB-DMX boxes are excluded from the plugin is quite contrary to Unreal's interests, since these are the cheapest hardware devices and therefore precisely the ones that emerging companies are more likely to have available. Indeed, like many other modern systems, the DMX signal is not transported

by an XLR cable but by an RJ45, via two specific protocols, Artnet and sACN,[13] which, if they are gradually taking the place of DMX as modernisation of technologies proceeds, remain marginal in precarious economies and often absent from small theatres. Thus, the need to acquire ArtNet and sACN nodes makes it slightly more complex to use for a simple installation.

4. Unreal does not have a projector library, which is the key to visualisation. As a result, it is often necessary to manually create the machine you want to control. In the case of complex projectors, this wastes precious time.

In other words, perhaps the most significant aspect of the use of Unreal is the application of the virtual environment itself to live performance. This establishes a kind of paradoxical digitalization of live performance through a medium whose origins are found in videogames and architecture and which is completely alien to the traditional working protocols of most theatre teams. Anticipating the movements of the actors in a performance, Unreal appears to be a delicate matter, as these are far more random than those in a virtual file. One can also ask the question of the influence of Unreal on a theatrical work: Can one detect that a show has relied on a visualisation software to exist? Is it worth noting this or not? If questioning theatrical lighting 'allows us to question the very imaginary of the theatre' (Chaouche, Vialleton 2017, 6–7), as Sabine Chaouche and Jean-Yves Vialleton explain in the introduction to the 273rd issue of the *Revue d'histoire du théâtre*, which was devoted to performance lighting, maybe we could extend the interrogation to the various lighting tools that the lighting designer tends to use. At this point, one could reasonably say that Unreal is appropriate in some artistic proposals, and that it is not so much relevant in itself as in accordance with dramaturgies where visualisation is a determining tool for the realization of a work that justifies taking the necessary time. To date, it is still too difficult to know if it remains a niche tool or if it will really impose itself in the sector by radically transforming the way theatrical creation works.

---

13 Artnet and sACN are network protocols allowing to send DMX data over ethernet. Artnet allows sending 32,768 universes down a single network cable. sACN (streaming architecture for control networks), allows to run 63,999 universes of DMX data down a single network cable.

References

Bardiot, Clarisse. 2016. 'Les partitions numériques des digital performances', In *Partition(s), Objet et concept des pratiques scéniques (20e-21e siècles)*, edited by Julie Sermon and Yvane Chapuis. Dijon: Les Presses du réel, Manufacture – Haute école des arts de la scène de Suisse romande, 429–441.

Bonnat, Yves. 1982. *L'Éclairage des spectacles*. Paris: Librairie Théâtrale.

Cadena, Richard. 2002. *Focus on lighting technology*. Cambridge: Entertainment Technology Press.

Cadena, Richard. 2010. *Automated Lighting, The Art and science of moving light in theatre, live performance and entertainment*. Waltham: Focal Press.

Cangeloso, Sal. 2012. *LED Lighting. A Primer to Lighting the Future*. Sebastopol: O'Reilly.

Chaouche Sabine, Vialleton Jean-Yves (*et al.*). 2017. *L'Éclairage au théâtre, XVIIe-XXIe siècle, Revue d'histoire du théâtre* n°273.

Freydefont, Marcel. 1995. 'Conduite', edited by Corvin, Michel, *Dictionnaire encyclopédique du théâtre*. Paris: Bordas.

Guinebault-Szlamowicz, Chantal, et al. 2007. *Faire la lumière, Théâtre Public*, n°185.

Inisan, Victor. 2021. *L'Adieu au soleil. Imaginaires de la luminescence dans le spectacle contemporain*, PhD diss. University of Lille.

Keller, Max. 2010. *Light fantastic. The Art and Design of Stage Lighting*. Bonn: Prestel.

Massol, Laurent. 2012. *Les LED pour l'éclairage. Fonctionnement et performances, critères de choix et mise en œuvre*. Paris: Dunod.

Reid, Francis. 2001 [1976]. *Lighting Stage Handbook*. New York: Routledge,

Toeplitz. Kaspar T. 2010. 'LEDS et contrôleurs DMX : à la croisée de la lumière et de la musique', *in Patch* n°11. Paris: Centre des Écritures Contemporaines et Numériques.

Biography

Victor Inisan has a PhD in theatre studies and is currently employed as an ATER (non-tenured teaching and research associate) at the University of Rennes 2. He graduated from the ENS of Lyon and the University of Lille and has spoken at several events in France and abroad (University of Padova, Fondazione Cini, University of Tartu) about the dramaturgy of light and the cinema of David Lynch. He has also written for specialized magazines (*Supernatural Studies, Horizon/Théâtre, Opium Philosophie*) and intervenes regularly as a critic of live performance in various media (France Culture, *I/O Gazette, AOC, Détectives Sauvages*).

At the same time, Victor Inisan is a playwright, director, and lighting designer. Author of *C'est moi Guy* and *Papa congèle*, and director of two shows with the Groupe Le Sycomore (*Au revoir mon amour, Éclairage Public*), he founded his art company, UltraComète, in 2021. As a lighting designer, he assists Emmanuel Sauldubois and Jérémie Papin, and creates lights for the shows of Lawrence Williams, Julien Avril, and Louise Dupuis.

Combining Layers of Reality. Video Game Elements in Live Performance

Christophe Burgess

Abstract *In this text, the Swiss theatre director Christophe Burgess recounts his experience in the theatrical project that ultimately became the immersive performance entitled Brainwaves, led by the company RGB Project. It was presented for the first time on 6 November 2021 at the Théâtre les Halles in Sierre, Switzerland. Burgess discusses this interdisciplinary project, which explored artistic research and collaboration between artists and 3D designers. He deals with the question of directing, working with actresses and avatars, collaborating with multiple designers and the connection between performance and game. He also talks about the technological apparatus that enabled the nine spectators to wear VR headsets and immerse themselves in a virtual world that becomes the universe of the paraplegic protagonist, Ivy.*

Figure 1: Brainwaves (2021), direction: Christoph Burgess. Photo: Céline Ribordy

118 New (Game) Technologies for the Theatre

The performance: *Brainwaves*

In 2021, I directed the immersive performance *Brainwaves* (Théâtre les Halles, Sierre, Switzerland), realized by RGB Project (the theatre company), with the collaboration of ZEROTERA (an interactive media and design Lab), Estelle Bridet (actress), Lisa Courvallet (actress), Lucy Meier (the stage designer), Ana Carina Romero (the costume designer), Djamel Cencio (the composer and sound designer), Cyprien Rausis (the stage control collaborator) and Izabella Pluta (the scientific expert).[1] Ivy, the only character in the performance, is suffering from *locked-in syndrome*[2], and has spent most of her life unable to communicate except through her eyelids and eyes. She grew up in a body that didn't allow her to set her thoughts in motion, as if enclosed in a shell. In this performance, thanks to a neural interface that gives her access to a virtual body in a computer program, she experiments with a new way of being, beyond her bodily constraints. The spectators are invited to immerse themselves in Ivy's story and in this original artistic experience. The immersive performance combines live performance and virtual reality (VR). Seated in a circle, in the presence of actress playing the virtual character and equipped with a VR headset, the audience members have access to a previously unimagined world. In a staging that blends several layers of reality, they follow Ivy's virtually reincarnated journey through the twists and turns of her digitized life. *Brainwaves* evokes and reflects on our relationship to identity, the construction of our memories, and the spiritual symbolism that animates us.

The origins of the project: VR, body/mind and interaction

The three of us are childhood friends who belong to a collective called the RGB Project, which is interested in creating immersive scenic realities. We are all active in different fields: I work in live performance and theatre, Michael Goodchild is more into contemporary art and the visual arts, and Emilien Rossier, whose back-

---

1 The original, longer version of this text was published as: Christophe Burgess, 'Orchestrer une mise en scène d'un projet interdisciplinaire', In *Ici et ailleurs. Corps aux frontières du réel et du virtuel*, Cahier de création *Brainwaves*, edited by Izabella Pluta. Lausanne: Ed. Association Theatre in Progress, in print.

2 *Locked-in syndrome* 'consists of almost complete paralysis. Consciousness and cognitive function are not affected. People cannot express themselves with their face, cannot move, speak, or communicate on their own, but they can move their eyes up and down and blink'. https://www.msdmanuals.com/fr/accueil/troubles-du-cerveau,-de-la-moelle-%C3% A9pini%C3%A8re-et-des-nerfs/coma-et-%C3%A9tat-de-conscience-alt%C3%A9r%C3%A9 e/syndrome-d-enfermement [author's translation, accessed 29 July 2023].

ground is in music, works in the field of production. We wanted to do a project together.

Emilien Rossier, producer:
Michael Goodchild and Christophe Burgess are very interested in video games, and this aspect has accelerated the creation of sets to support this kind of project. The trigger was a call for projects from Cinéforom, the Romandy foundation for the cinema, which supports cinema in French-speaking Switzerland. We saw this as an opportunity [...] [1]

Our artistic common ground for this project was *immersion*. The question of how to completely immerse a spectator in a show was our first objective. Understanding what could be told by this means was our second objective. We wanted to explore the notion of immersion at every level: visual, aural, narrative, and physical. We spent two years looking for an idea we could develop together, and then we came across Gilles Jobin's performance *VR_I*.[3] It is a dance performance in virtual reality where the audience wears VR headsets that locates their artificial bodies in a virtual world. That artistic work was the catalyst for us. We realised that virtual reality was the digital tool we wanted to use.

From a narrative point of view, we wanted to tell the story of what goes on in the mind of a person suffering from *locked-in syndrome*. *Brainwaves* was born of these two stimuli: the digital tool to be used and the topic to be explored. At the start of our research, the performance was about a person who was in a coma and our aim was for the audience to connect directly to this person's mind.

However, moral questions arose, such as whether you really have the right to enter someone's thoughts without their permission. In the end, we chose a person who was locked in their body for neurological reasons. Quite quickly, the notion of the relationship between body and mind came to the fore. I had read reviews of the French film *The Diving Bell and the Butterfly* (*Le scaphandre et le papillon*, Julien Schnabel, 2007), which made me want to read the book on which this film is based (Jean-Dominique Bauby, *Le scaphandre et le papillon*, 1997). In this autobiographical book, Jean-Dominique Bauby recounts his life before his stroke and his experience of *locked-in syndrome*, which confined him to a body that no longer responded to his mind.

With this performance, we really wanted to allow the audience to intervene directly in the narrative, as they do in video games. With video games, we're used to following the narrative thread while remaining active, because the story can only

---

3   *VR_I*, choreographic conception: Gilles Jobin, technological realisation: Artanim, premiered: 2017.

move forward if you activate the controller. I think it's important not to always be a passive spectator... and that goes for everyday life too.

Ivy, the character

Figure 2: Brainwaves *(2021), direction: Christophe Burgess, Estelle Bridet as Ivy. Photo: Céline Ribordy*

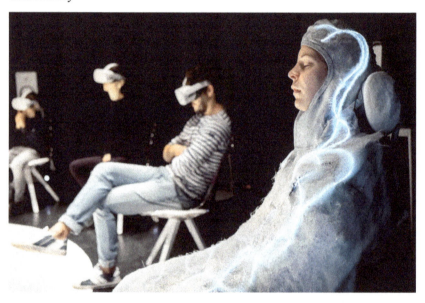

Ivy, the character of the play, appears to the audience in form of an avatar in virtual space that they perceive through VR headsets. Physically, we didn't want her to look like a human, but rather to have the appearance of a humanoid. We didn't want to portray a realistic world, so we didn't want Ivy to have a realistic female appearance. This was primarily for aesthetic reasons. I find that representing existing worlds is too difficult to achieve and, as a result, it's rarely successful; virtual reality simply doesn't yet allow us to do that. So, I wanted to go for something more poetic. At the start, we imagined Ivy to be smaller because she had remained paralysed in a child's body. Over time, she obviously grew up and became a teenager, but she grew up lying in a bed or sitting, so her notion of the body was different. She doesn't necessarily have a woman's body. But in the end, Ana Carina Romero, the costume designer who drew the first avatars, imagined her directly as a woman, and that worked too.

Working with the two actresses who played or controlled the avatar

In April 2021, I gave the first version of the script to the actress Estelle Bridet and to Michael Goodchild, who augmented it with texts from Ivy's childhood diaries, from her stays in hospital and at MOTUM, the fictional medical centre that looks after patients suffering from *locked-in syndrome*. Quite quickly, I invited Lisa Courvallet, the second actress, to take part in the project and take on the role of Ivy.[4] Lisa was very fond of video games but had never really studied the question of virtual reality on stage. The immersive performance was then played by either Lisa or Estelle, alternating in the role, which was also important because of the physical effort required of the actresses. We then started work on the stage, that was a playing area defined in the Lab at the Théâtre les Halles in Sierre. I started directing the actresses without a virtual reality headset, so that we could be perfectly clear with each other and then defuse any VR-related concerns that might arise.

Estelle Bridet, actress:
Lisa and I watched videos of people who really have this illness. For example, to find out what kind of faces they have. At one point, I leave the cocoon that provides the character with the cables and other connections they need to survive, and I transform into an actress. I wear a device consisting of a bicycle helmet and an iPhone, which captures my facial movements, and I stand in the middle of the circle formed by the spectators. After that, it's my real movements that animate the avatar. [2]

At first, the actresses had some trouble understanding what I was getting at, because they didn't have any images or visual feedback, which gradually came later. I initially had to make them imagine what the virtual setting looked like, as there was nothing to show them yet. At first, we worked on the scenes set in the rather simple places that I called 'non-places', which are fairly neutral virtual environments. This meant they could focus on their interpretation without having to also take the virtual aspects into account. This was the first step into performing in VR for them. During these rehearsals, the actresses could observe each other. Seeing the other performer using the VR headset made it much easier to understand and imagine the virtual space. The play thus took shape on the physical space, but it wasn't until the entire virtual setting was ready that the performance really took off, because the actresses could see where they were placed and understood the relations between the virtual and the physical space.

---

4   We had already collaborated on my project *Homo Solaris*, a performance conceived in 2019 and presented at les Teintureries drama school in Lausanne (Switzerland).

The next step was to be able to have the actresses perform in the physical world as if they were performing within the virtual world so that there was no glitch in the audience's perception of their virtual presence. They had to share the same environment as the audience. I was lucky to have two actresses because each had a different way of interpreting the character. As each actress had their particular way of interpreting the role, I tried to work with them in a way that encouraged their intuitions. This meant there were effectively two different Ivys for the play. I directed Estelle first, then Lisa took over and brought in new elements which Estelle then took over. It was collective work of a circular nature. Knowing what acting to apply to the virtual avatar was a real challenge, because it's still a rare experience in the theatre.[5] Nobody talks about acting methods for a virtual character in a live performance.[6]

Basil Denereaz (ZEROTERA), avatar designer:
[...] The avatar is the central element of the performance, as the spectators will see it virtually from start to finish, and it's the element to which we, the 3D designers, have paid most attention. Apart from the back-and-forth between the different members of the design team, we had to be logical about using the right connection techniques. These were necessary to avoid any of the production stages failing, since everything is interconnected by a series of closely linked software programs, the result of which is the final avatar. A lot of knowledge and techniques from cinema and video games were used to create this avatar, and a great deal of research went into bringing it to life. Our immersive performance uses a lot of live motion capture, based on sensors in the suit that the actress is wearing. [...] We, the 3D design team, were responsible for the whole complex technical set-up. The big challenge for us was to ensure that the avatar of Ivy didn't 'slide' sideways (her body isn't straight) and always remained right at the centre of the stage. [3]

The avatar and the technical challenges of motion capture

There are obviously some acting methods suitable for motion capture for cinema, but it's not quite the same thing for theatre. Cinema isn't live action, and the body isn't always present in its entirety. In the end, our intuition led us to look for inspiration in masks and the puppet theatre. The mask is an important reference to the *commedia dell'arte* where several characters wear this theatrical prop. It is about very physical theatre in which the main focus of expression is shifted to the actor's body. In addition, the relationship between puppet and puppeteer due to manipulation

---

5   Research on this subject has been carried out by Georges Gagneré and Cédric Plessiet at the University of Paris 8 since around 2014 [editor's note].

6   A few experimental projects have been carried out: For instance, the *Masque and avatar* project (2015–2017) at the University of Paris 8, and *Actor and avatar* (2016–2020) at the Zurich University of the Arts [editors' note].

through strings is the same as between the actresses and the avatar they bring to life.

Paul Lëon (ZEROTERA), 3D designer:
These days, VR headsets, are getting cheaper and the one we chose was quite affordable. What's special about it is that it can be used as a stand-alone technology, meaning that it doesn't need to be connected to a computer on which the video game or other application is running, as did most of the old headsets, such as Oculus Rift or HTC Vive. Above all, this gave us flexibility, as we only had to plug in one cable. Most VR headsets have three or four inputs, which can be quite heavy on the head and so on. Ours was light enough for a play that lasted about thirty minutes, and that was a factor we had to consider as well, apart from the price. We thought of the video headset used in the Quest 2 video game, which requires hand tracking. It is equipped with small cameras that track space. The condition we were looking for was that the VR headset should be as autonomous as possible and as accessible as possible to the public. [4]

At first, we separated work with the actress's face from work with her body. Spectators don't see Ivy's face in much detail – only when the avatar is very close. This is a simple matter of pixels: close up, the resolution is rather poor, and you can only make out broad details, such as whether the avatar is speaking. We therefore worked mainly on the body rather than the face. However, sometimes the body alone wasn't enough. For example, at one point, Ivy laughs at her own joke, but her giggle wasn't enough, she also had to move her head a little, and that was a problem. One could say that there's a cartoon-like relationship to the body, due to the exaggerations. The actresses had to be able to balance the exaggerations so that the viewer continues to believe in them.

Not every technology we used was originally intended for live performance purposes, especially the VR system, so we had to do a bit of DIY. The use of Oculus Rift VR headsets is more familiar now, so we integrated features from that system into the VR headset technology that we were appling. We used *rococo* motion capture suits that the actress wears, to which we added an extra sensor from Vive, another type of VR headset.

The motion capture was recorded at the Lausanne Cantonal School of Art (Ecole Cantonale d'Arts de Lausanne), and the rest of the work was done at the Théâtre Les Halles in Sierre, during the rehearsal period.

Unifying performing arts, game culture, and digital technology

Within the *Brainwaves* team, I am the theatre director who manages the interdisciplinary high-tech project. My role goes beyond the classic skills of directing. I see myself as an orchestra conductor because I had to combine the music with the colours of the image and the acting to give the impression of unity. I'm happy to have been able to forge a link between my lifelong love of video games and the performing arts. There's a whole generation of us who have these two passions and manage to bridge the gap between the two.

However, I trained as a traditional actor at les Teintureries drama school (Ecole supérieure de théâtre – les Teintureries). The basic curriculum focused on questions like how to work with classical texts or how to pronounce Molière or Shakespeare. But as well as the more 'classical classes', there were also all sorts of other courses on offer, including improvisation and the use of video by people with an interest in film and new technologies. There are more and more artists who are attracted by this hybrid aesthetic, such as the British pioneers Blast Theory, machina eX (Germany), Extralaben (Switzerland), and Madame Lupin (France).

Working with ZEROTERA was a great experience. We gradually realised that the group of people we had brought together was very diverse and had a range of very different backgrounds: I spoke to them in my theatre language, they spoke to me in their computer language. We didn't have the same concerns. In spite of everything, we realised that there were a lot of things we could do together, and we developed a certain *modus operandi*. Overall, *Brainwaves* functioned as a kind of visit card for our company. We had little money and little time, but we still managed to achieve what we wanted.

The use of sound in the performance

I wanted to create an entire world of sound for *Brainwaves*. I invited Djamel Cencio, who creates ambient music and whose work I've always appreciated. I'd talk to him about a scene, tell him what I wanted it to feel like and explain the broad outlines, then he'd compose something, show it to me and I would give him new directions. That's how we worked for the entire play in terms of music. As I'm not a musician, my wishes concerned colours, feelings and form. He would then write appropriate melodies and the results were always perfect. He often came up with things that I hadn't thought of, but which worked well. He really brings something extra to the performance with his music, and we realised that it did fifty per cent of the work. What's more, he created the environment for the sound effects. Sometimes they go unnoticed, but it still affects our perception.

Djamel Cencio, composer and sound designer:
For a while, I was concentrating on the sound design and the technical problems, and even the installation of the system, which is complicated. The control room was complex, with the triggering of the sounds, because every time Ivy made a move, a technician had to press the button to generate the sounds. There were a lot of technical things to sort out. For the sound design I worked with ZEROTERA who triggered the visuals. Another technician, Cyprien [Rausis], was the sound manager. He had a screen in front of him and was able to get a visual on the actress to trigger the sounds at the right moments so that they could be sent to all the headsets. [5]

Sounds are omnipresent, except for one moment when Ivy speaks. Sometimes the music is used to cover up the noise Ivy makes when she comes out of the cocoon, so that the audience hears nothing of it and their immersion is maintained.

Sometimes it helps to explain things. It adds an atmosphere that you don't necessarily hear, but which you sense, and which puts you in a different state. It can also be used to dress up the image and make it much more realistic.

The role of the audience

The big surprise during the *Brainwaves* presentations was the reaction of the audience. I didn't think that both a child and an elderly person could enjoy our performance. The younger generations are used to using these digital tools and have no problem with virtual worlds, but there are people who are more resistant and who denigrate video games. I grew up with adults who thought video games were destructive. I looked at the figures in terms of revenue in billions worldwide in 2020; cinema made 12 billion, music 20 billion and video games 175 billion, which is six times more than the other two media combined. We are often told that theatre is the mirror of society. Today, society is evolving and becoming technological. That's why it's important to take these digital tools, to engage with them, and thus to take an interest in the people whose world they belong to and who aren't used to coming to the theatre. It was quite wonderful to see families coming to the show, which brings generations and interests together. I didn't think it would be so intergenerational.

Figure 3: Brainwaves *(2021), direction: Christophe Burgess. Photo: Céline Ribordy*

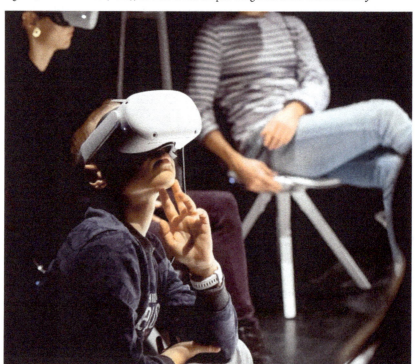

In the first version of *Brainwaves*, we wanted to allow the audience to see their virtual hands in the virtual world. People were supposed to physically participate at the end of the story. Unfortunately, for technical reasons, this proved impossible. It was very frustrating at the time. However, we intend to remedy this frustration regarding interaction during our next play, *Les enfants du Rhône*. We also want to move towards the use of artificial intelligence as an interactive tool. We are still working on this project, which will take place in the Théâtre Les Halles, Sierre in 2025.

Quotations

[1] Izabella Pluta, 'Plus loin que le rêve... Entretien avec Michael Goodchild et Emilien Rossier', In *Ici et ailleurs. Corps aux frontières du réel et du virtuel*, Cahiers de création *Brainwaves*, edited by Izabella Pluta. Lausanne: Association Theatre in Progress, in print.
[2] Doris Naclerio et Anne-Sophie Zuber, 'Jeu d'acteur et performance du double virtuel. Découvertes et contraintes. Entretien réalisé avec Estelle Bridet et Lisa

Courvallet', In *Ici et ailleurs. Corps aux frontières du réel et du virtuel*, Cahier de création *Brainwaves*, edited by Izabella Pluta. Lausanne : Association Theatre in Progress, in print.

[3] Basil Denereaz (ZEROTERA), 'Avatar, enjeux de conception', In *Ici et ailleurs. Corps aux frontières du réel et du virtuel*, Cahier de création *Brainwaves*, edited by Izabella Pluta. Lausanne: Association Theatre in Progress, in print.

[4] Léonard Guyot, Evan Kelly, Paul Lëon, Kylan Luginbühl, Valerio Meschi et Yaël Sidler (ZEROTERA), 'Corps actoriel à l'épreuve du design 3D. Entretien réalisé par Izabella Pluta', In *Ici et ailleurs. Corps aux frontières du réel et du virtuel*, Cahier de création *Brainwaves*, edited by Izabella Pluta. Lausanne: Association Theatre in Progress, in print.

[5] Djamel Cencio, 'Personnage et univers sonore : intrications', In *Ici et ailleurs. Corps aux frontières du réel et du virtuel*, Cahier de création *Brainwaves*, edited by Izabella Pluta. Lausanne: Association Theatre in Progress, in print.

References

Denereaz, Basil (ZEROTERA). 2024. 'Avatar, enjeux de conception', In *Ici et ailleurs. Corps aux frontières du réel et du virtuel*, Cahier de création *Brainwaves*, edited by Izabella Pluta. Lausanne: Ed. Association Theatre in Progress, in print.

Cencio, Djamel. 2024. 'Personnage et univers sonore : intrications', In *Ici et ailleurs. Corps aux frontières du réel et du virtuel*, Cahier de création *Brainwaves*, edited by Izabella Pluta. Lausanne: Ed. Association Theatre in Progress, in print.

Guyot, Léonard, Kelly, Evan, Lëon, Paul, Luginbühl, Kylan, Valerio, Meschi, Sidler, Yaël (ZEROTERA). 2024. 'Corps actoriel à l'épreuve du design 3D. Entretien réalisé par Izabella Pluta', In *Ici et ailleurs. Corps aux frontières du réel et du virtuel*, Cahier de création *Brainwaves*, edited by Izabella Pluta. Lausanne: Ed. Association Theatre in Progress, in print.

Naclerio, Doris, Zuber, Anne-Sophie. 2024. 'Jeu d'acteur et performance du double virtuel. Découvertes et contraintes.Entretien réalisé avec Estelle Bridet et Lisa Courvallet', In *Ici et ailleurs. Corps aux frontières du réel et du virtuel*, Cahier de création *Brainwaves*, edited by Izabella Pluta. Lausanne: Ed. Association Theatre in Progress, in print.

Pluta, Izabella (ed.). 2024. *Ici et ailleurs. Corps aux frontières du réel et du virtuel*, Cahiers de Création *Brainwaves*, Lausanne: Ed. Association Theatre in Progress, in print.

Pluta, Izabella. 2024. 'Plus loin que le rêve… Entretien avec Michael Goodchild et Emilien Rossier', In *Ici et ailleurs. Corps aux frontières du réel et du virtuel*, Cahiers de création *Brainwaves*, edited by Izabella Pluta. Lausanne: Ed. Association Theatre in Progress, in print.

Biography

Originally from the Valais region of Switzerland, **Christophe Burgess** graduated from les Teintureries drama school in Lausanne (Switzerland) in 2019. He is currently working on immersive theatrical forms and/or those incorporating new technologies. In 2021, he obtained Certificates of Advanced Studies in theatrical animation and mediation at La Manufacture (Switzerland). In autumn 2023, he co-organised the third edition of meetings of emerging artists from the Valais *FAIS COMME CHEZ TOI – les rencontres des artistes émergent.e.s valaisan.ne.s*, at the theatre hub SPOT in Sion (Switzerland). At the end of 2024, he will finish a Master of Arts in Public Spheres at the School of Design and College of Art (EDHEA) in Sierre.

Working at the Interface of Games and Performance

Gaming in Performance. Between Research and Artistry

Matt Adams, Blast Theory, interviewed by Helen W. Kennedy

Abstract *This interview with Matt Adams explores some of the key influences and trajectories underpinning the work of Blast Theory, an internationally renowned arts organisation at the forefront of innovative interactive storytelling. Here the focus is on how the artistic practices of Blast Theory make use of and advance the possibilities of play, games, and live performance.*

Introduction

Founded in England in 1991 and led by Matt Adams and Nick Tandavanitj, Blast Theory[1] has been at the forefront of experimentation in multi-media performance and interactive storytelling. Collaborating with the Nottingham University's Mixed Reality Lab,[2] the group often uses cutting-edge technology to design immersive experiences through which players confront complex themes of morality, ideology, and complicity, while engaging with a mediated storyworld designed with their own unique exploration of its boundaries in mind. Their work has been featured at numerous festivals, including: Tribeca Film Festival, Sundance Film Festival, the Venice Biennale, the Dutch Electronic Arts Festival, the Sonar Festival in Barcelona, and the Palestine International Video Festival. Their work with the researchers and scientists of Mixed Reality Lab has led to their co-authorship of over 45 research papers, and the artists of Blast Theory continue to contribute to and expand public awareness of interactivity and performance by means of residencies, institutional curation, teaching, and contributions to major research projects.

Helen Kennedy: *Welcome! This is an interview for a special collection that's inspired by a conference that explored the intersection between live performance and video games. So let's start by thinking about where Blast Theory might fit into that. If we think of it as a continuum or an intersection, how would you describe Blast Theory's work within that broad framework?*

---

1   https://www.blasttheory.co.uk/.
2   https://www.nottingham.ac.uk/research/groups/mixedrealitylab/.

Matt Adams: We were always interested in making interactive work from the very first project we made: *Gunmen Kill Three* in 1991.[3] And we tended to use quite avant-garde techniques and structures. We were influenced by performances and happenings, and techniques from visual art and experimental theatre in the way in which we made interactive work. And then in the late 90s we discovered – through beginning to work with VR – just how far computer games design had developed. And that moment – suddenly thinking about our work as a game, rather than as interactive art – was transformative for our practice. It helped us unlock a different way of making work, and of finding an audience. Thinking about the public as *players* meant that suddenly we could talk to a five-year-old or a ten-year-old about what we did and they were like, 'Oh cool, it's a game, how do I play?' Not 'It's an avant-garde art performance at the Institute of Contemporary Arts (ICA) in London? Please tell me more!' Which, of course, is a sentence no one has ever said...

From that moment on, we have made work that is both performative and live, and either a game or in some way driven by ludic design principles. I see those principles as running through all of the work, even if some work that we've made that doesn't at first blush look like a game according to any sort of meaningful definition.

Helen Kennedy: *OK, fantastic. There's two follow up questions I want to ask, one which goes back into those early influences – can you say a little bit about the works that inspired you? Just a couple of key examples that were inspiring you in those early 90s.*

Matt Adams: Our immediate imperative to make work was UK club culture in the late 1980s where the rave scene and an underground scene of club culture was happening. That felt era-defining and that is what many of the people around us were doing with their weekends. We felt that there was an opportunity to do something that had a club energy, with ideas and politics built into that. My background is in theatre and that was my love and that's what I thought that I was going to be – a theatre director – when I was at UCL (University College London). But I was also really influenced by the Russian constructivists and Piscator and Brecht and those first multimedia experiments in the 1920s and 30s. When Piscator was designing theatres with cinema screens built in, and there was this enormously fertile period of new media photography and film that happened in the 1920s and 30s. So that was a big influence. And then, Allan Kaprow and Judson Church, those experimental practitioners in New York in the 50s, 60s, 70s, had a really big impact. Robert Wilson was a massive influence on us, ironically, when none of us had ever seen any piece of Robert Wilson. It was all through photos, text descriptions and Philip Glass recordings.

---

3   https://www.blasttheory.co.uk/projects/gunmen-kill-three/

Helen Kennedy: *A second question that came out of what you were just saying there was around that discovery of computer games and what they were now doing, the innovations that had happened there and what the possibilities were and the way in which that shift in games impacted upon how you understood your work, your audience, your relationship with them as players. Can you explain what it is about games? What do they afford? What do they allow/enable from a creative design perspective? What is it that excited you about what computer games could do?*

Matt Adams: That's a very big question.... Games are uniquely audience-focused – a game dies in a nanosecond if the player of the game does not know why they are playing or what they can do or why they should do it. So it's a rigid discipline of focus on the public who are engaging with your work. And for us coming out of avant-garde/live art/performance arts/YBA-era stuff[4] – plenty of that has a unique level of disdain for the public and has no interest in whether they can or cannot engage with their art. So what it meant for me, for us, was to provide a framework for the development of our work.

It requires addressing micro-design questions such as: 'What am I doing', 'What can I do', 'What should I do next', 'Where am I going', 'What am I trying to achieve'? Those questions are all activated constantly, and then you have this macro level, which is across the arc of a work: Can you then make that language take you to interesting places?

It's worth remembering that in the 90s it was still axiomatic that video games were childish and puerile, and strictly for adolescent males and that they only involved violence, car chases, or silly cartoons. That they were inherently unserious, and there was not really an indie scene yet – it was beginning, but it was very nascent at the time.

Of course, there have been interesting people doing interesting things with games right the way back to the early 60s, but the cultural framework was very different.

So I was very excited about a question such as 'Can you make a game about the Gulf War that deals with virtuality and brings in Baudrillard's ideas about virtuality, and ideas from Debord's *The Society of the Spectacle*?'(Baudrillard 1983; Debord 1967). 'Can you make a war game set in the Gulf War, that in some way deals with questions of epistemology?' And, in retrospect you can see that in *Desert Rain*[5] we were engaged in trying to make a war game that could talk about warfare, and to me, that fact seemed a very intoxicating intersection.

---

4   According to Tate.org.uk, the label Young British Artists (YBAs) is applied to a loose group of British artists who began to exhibit together in 1988 and who became known for their openness to materials and processes, shock tactics, and entrepreneurial attitudes.

5   https://www.blasttheory.co.uk/projects/desert-rain/.

Helen Kennedy: *That's really fascinating, and I like that conception about the 'micro level' you describe: how games stand or fall, don't they, on how well they are communicating what you as a player need to do, rapidly enough, teaching you how to do it and making it interesting enough to keep you there?*

Matt Adams: And where games are like theatre is, the thing needs to get up on its feet at the first possible opportunity. And any draft or document or script can collapse instantly as soon as you try to do it.

For a piece of theatre, you can think, 'ohh yes, I've written a really great scene.' You try to act out that scene, it can be terrible. Games are exactly the same. You can spend ages refining your rules, until you give it to a couple of people and say, 'Alright just play this will you?' You can find all of your smart ideas instantly falling to ash in your hands. They're both practice-based disciplines and we've always felt that is our focus – it has always been about practice. We're not called Blast Theory for no reason!

Helen Kennedy: *And they live, don't they, in the moment of the play? So, the lines or the rules might be written down and the game designed but all of that is a dead form, if you like, until that moment, just as you said, when two actors inhabit a performance, or a player picks up and starts to play. Really interesting.*

You've talked about how your practice weaves together performance and game, and you've talked about the early roots.... Are there other switch points in the journey where the emphasis changed again? So, you talked about, suddenly there was this possibility of gameness and ludic design principles and then you really exploited that. So how did that go? How did that progress in terms of your aesthetics or your adoption of new technology?

Matt Adams: Yes, so by 2000, 2001, we're playing with GPS receivers, which at that time were still standalone, expensive devices that just spat out latitude and longitude. We were working with the Mixed Reality Lab at the University of Nottingham, so we started to make location-based games, starting with *You See Me Now?* (2003)[6] and thinking about the city as a space for play.

We made a number of works that do that. I think the other thing that I would mention in that respect is that when we were commissioned to make Ulrike and Ea mon *Compliant*[7] for the Venice Biennale in 2009, I came across Philippa Foot's work, and the trolley dilemma, and the branch of philosophical enquiry around setting ethical problems as questions that could potentially have binary outcomes.[8] And to

---

6   https://www.blasttheory.co.uk/projects/can-you-see-me-now/.

7   https://www.blasttheory.co.uk/projects/dial-ulrike-and-eamon-compliant/.

8   Phillipa Foot was a moral philosopher who posed the 'Trolley Problem' which invites you to consider a hypothetical situation in which you as the driver of a tram must, through

me, that was an amazing overlay onto games language because it's a form of play; the trolley dilemma is a hypothetical question for you to inhabit. There is something about the subjectivity of theatre, where you watch a character, and you're invited to empathise with them, or see the world with their perspective. There's something about games language where you are inserted into a situation as the protagonist (with some degree of fictional overlay) and then Philippa Foot's idea of thinking about a hypothetical question as a way of unpacking something that is ethically complex. Each of those aspects has been folded in on one another in terms of how I think about the work that we make.

Helen Kennedy: *Have the ethical dilemmas that you've chosen to put within the work, has that responded, to at different times, different kinds of cultural or political events, or propensities that you've seen? Has that been important, or have they been more, I don't know, universal if you like, or ahistorical?*

Matt Adams: Yeah, I mean thematically we're very heterogeneous. We're really drawn in all kinds of strange directions. For me they are often politically driven or recurrent. Ulrike and Eamon *Compliant* (2009) is about Ulrike Meinhof of the Red Army faction and Eamon Collins, who was a member of the IRA, and both of them made a journey towards political violence. I was interested in how people made that transition. *Operation Black Antler*,[9], which we made in 2016, is inspired by the undercover policing scandal in the UK. [In Operation Black Antler you are given a new identity as part of a small team; you are briefed and then sent into an undercover operation. Most of the game takes place in a public house; there you must meet, build empathy with, and ultimately try to win the trust of someone whose political and moral views may be the polar opposite of your own.] Some of our works are very clearly refractions on particular events but, more typically, it's about how we as individuals make sense of the world around us, and what obligation we have to act politically. I'm very interested in the fact that we're all slightly called to account for our complicity in the world, and to make a difference in the world, especially if we think that we're somehow progressive or left-of-centre, and yet almost all of us are quite bad at it – and I put myself at the front of that queue. Why is it that we find it so difficult to actually activate change in the world? Our work explores that space between passivity and action, or the space between: simplification so that you can act, versus acknowledging the complexity and diminishing your ability to act.

---

your own actions, choose between running down and potentially killing five people on the tracks ahead or diverting the trolley and killing just one person on a different section of track (Foot 1967).

9 https://www.blasttheory.co.uk/projects/operation-black-antler/.

Those sorts of threads to me, they repeat, because it's a problem I can't get out from under.

Helen Kennedy: *That is really present in* Operation Black Antler. *That simplification versus complexity and the inability to operate in a condition of complexity. How do you make decisions when it's all a bit confusing and indeterminate... really fascinating.*

I wonder. You used the word complicity there, and I was thinking about some of your works that positions your player in a way as complicit. Can you tell me a little bit about the design process, where you're thinking about that player inhabiting that complicity and the potential uncomfortableness of that? How do you conceptualise that and the aesthetics of discomfort that exists within that mode of complicity?

Matt Adams: It's very common in our work for the participants to be uncomfortable and to head on a journey where the destination is literally unknown in every sense: geographically unknown; conceptually unknown; socially, not clear. Even the edges of the work are often unclear. In *Operation Black Antler*, you don't really know what is the limit of this world, if a police car goes past, is that part of it? Could that be part of it? You know, that porous nature between the work and the outside is very important.

In terms of the design process, the work often starts from an insight about behaviour, or perception. There is that kernel of something we think is interesting.

We were commissioned by the Sundance Film Festival and two other festivals in the States and in Canada to make a piece of 'locative cinema'.[10] As research for that work, we did experiments here in sunny Portslade where we walked up the High Street in pairs with one person on the phone talking to the other person maybe 10/20 metres in front and telling them what to do. Saying 'Sit down here' or 'Look there'. At one point, in this improvisation, one person said: 'Look at that bank; you see the bank? If you were running from there with two holdalls filled with heavy things, which way would you go to get away the quickest?' The person on the phone was like: 'I'd definitely go down that alley. I would be away quite quickly.' Then that gradually unspooled into: 'And the police, where is the nearest police station to here? If they were called, where would they be coming from?'

'If you had to choose a window that you were going to break into that bank, which window would you choose? Have a look and see which one you think.' 'Well, actually there is a skylight up on that roof there... That looks like a good one.'

We each experienced a sense of enormous guilt and we realised that we are on the line between playing a game and planning a crime. We all felt implicated. *A Machine*

---

10   Sundance Film Festival, 01 San Jose Biennial and the Banff New Media Institute 2010.

to See With (2010)[11] was made in the aftermath of the financial crisis. So we were all thinking about banks: who gets robbed by banks, and who robs banks.

Helen Kennedy: *It seems like maybe those questions come back to the fore over and over again because some of those early works and experiences feel like they'd be useful things to be playing with again, A Machine to See With feels like something you could be easily working on right now.*

Matt Adams: Yeah, we always joke about *Desert Rain* (2000),[12], which is the work we made about the Gulf War, that if you make a work about the horrors of American foreign policy, you have a perennially evergreen piece of work, because American foreign policy will always be there to remind you…

Helen Kennedy: *Exactly. So where did we get to? Is there more you could say about liveness and how important that is? That sense of maybe the precarity of liveness, which is slightly different to the precarity of 'Will it work or won't it' of a game?*

Matt Adams: The really big difference is that, when you're in a live performance, there is some kind of contract between audience and performer that is consensual at that moment, which is that we, together, are going to make this thing happen. And I, as an audience member, I'm sitting watching you on stage and I know that you could trip over and fall flat on your face, quite literally, and ruin the pretence that you are the King of Denmark – but hopefully you won't. We both accept that this risk is present. That in itself is thrilling aesthetically, but I think, more profoundly, it's a political thing. Of course you know in England, censorship of theatre only stopped in the 60s, prior to that, your script had to be approved by the government before it could be performed. Which is partly to do with the fact that there's quite a long history of riotous behaviour in theatres, these were unmarshalled spaces where all sorts could go on. It goes all the way back to Shakespeare and before.

So, I think that's not just a sort of historical curiosity. That's also to do with a sense of being here, in this place at this moment, and this thing is happening right now. And the very best live work I've seen, you have that sense that you are *entirely* in this moment and that anything could happen next. Really good shows do not feel like comfortable things.

I was a witness/participant in the poll tax riot in 1990. On that day all sorts of rules in life were suspended because 200,000 people took control of central London for several hours, and the police could do nothing about it. That's been an incredibly transformative thing in my life because it was a moment where something that is

---

11   https://www.blasttheory.co.uk/projects/a-machine-to-see-with/.

12   https://www.blasttheory.co.uk/projects/desert-rain/.

performative, a march with banners and some speeches, turns in a split second into something that was much, much more serious, and much more challenging. And in 1989 my partner at the time was living in Berlin as the wall came down, and I was there the week after that and so I experienced that sense of: All the things that you thought were completely here forever can change overnight, quite literally. We forget at our peril that things can shift quickly.

Helen Kennedy: *Yes, lovely. And so beautiful. A way of describing the sort of potential that anything could happen, everything could happen, change could happen. It's immanent, isn't it, in a really interesting way. By going back to the poll tax riots and thinking about your early work, you've reminded me that they were, in a way, transforming city spaces and transforming public spaces through play. Is it still possible to do things on that kind of scale now? Have the infrastructural demands in terms of getting commissions, permissions etc., have they made that harder now than it was, or is it still possible to really turn the city into a play space in the way that you could back then?*

Matt Adams: I think it is possible. I think those works came about because we were in the generation where the mass privatisation of public space was one of the driving ideological moves. The Thatcher-Reagan period really was about destroying these common spaces and public spaces. It's worth remembering that no land was private at some point and at various points throughout history, people have taken that land and said 'I own this now and I have a sword in my hand – or a deed in my hand – and you can lump it', and working people have been pushed off the common land over and over again and of course the early Internet was a form of common space that has slowly been privatised. I think you can still make those works. I think ironically, the culture of care and safety around the public is a more challenging thing to work with now. It's important, I understand that, but I also think that we all should be able to take some fucking risks! I feel for a generation of younger people who are not talked to all the time as strong, powerful, resilient people who can take on the world, but are talked to in terms of their care, and their fragility and how they need to be looked after.... And these are not binary opposites where you have to have one or the other – but I just think that there is something about risk-taking that is really important and obviously in a number of our works that risk-taking has really manifested.

Helen Kennedy: *It is very empowering, potentially, isn't it? It has the potential to empower you: taking those risks and surviving them, and learning through them, and experimenting through them, which I think is another thing that I didn't frame a question around but, a number of your works do invite people to inhabit a different persona.*

Can you say a little bit about how you've enjoyed creating these characters to play? Because it's on the same lines as getting them to inhabit ethical dilemmas, but often it's through personas, isn't it?

Matt Adams: I think you can see that in terms of my theatre background, obviously. One of the things that I think is notable about our work is that we're playing a lot with those fictional languages. You are an undercover cop. You are Ulrike Meinhof. You are going on a mission in a desert in the Gulf War, but nearly always in your own clothes with your own voice to a level that you feel comfortable to do. So you are not called on stage to impersonate someone or to perform. It's an invitation to think about yourself in a different way, to act otherwise. Often that's through tasks. In *Operation Black Antler*, we say, 'You're going to a pub. There is a far-right group meeting there. You will go and engage them in conversation and find out what they're doing'. And then it's for you to decide what that might mean for the persona that you're invited to inhabit.

I think we all do that all the time. Our 'fun self' who turns up to a party is something that we work with. Why is Glastonbury Festival so transformative? Because when you go through the gate you can more or less do whatever you want. If you want to wear wellies and a feather boa off you go, you know, no one will stop you. It's all good. We aim to create spaces where in a relatively unpressured way there is a gentle onramp from your ordinary self who's just bought a ticket for a show, through to: I am now undercover trying to engage this far-right person and I'm going to have to sympathise with their anti-immigrant views if I want to get the information I need. That transition can be done along a gentle graceful slope where you can both move up into that fictional position, and withdraw from it, at will. You've often got quite a lot of agency around that. For me, that's a freeing political thing because it's a sense of how you can inhabit different subject positions; you can inhabit different points of view.

Part of *Operation Black Antler* is to learn some degree of sympathy for undercover police officers. It's not really a work about the evil state and how terrible they are. It's really about the work they do: Once you start lying to someone at a party, how the hell do you keep a grip on what's going on? It's really hard, you know? And we did endless amounts of research about the work, including speaking to undercover police officers. And it's very challenging but also inherently theatrical. They act a role, all day long. I return to that sense of theatricality, again and again.

Helen Kennedy: *I think that in a way you've captured something that I've noticed about your work in the past where you're negotiating the sort of technomanic/technophobic binaries that emerge around surveillance technologies or the internet or mobile phones and those sorts of binaries and extremes that are once more in play around artificial intelligence. On the one hand, there are proclamations of the transformative and liberational potential of AI, offering up new kinds of freedom, new kinds of creative opportunity. On the other hand, there are those who foresee a Terminator 'singularity' moment, when AI suddenly eradicates us all as swiftly as* *possible. Say a little bit for me about what Cat Royale (2023)[13] is exploring in relation to our attitude towards AI, because I think the work is asking some interesting questions.*

Matt Adams: There's a whole range of great artwork about how AI is problematic, about ethics, and when we began to look at it, I felt that there's something else that we could look at which is to do with: 'Can we make AI visible?'

Can you see something learning in front of you? In *Cat Royale*, over the 70-odd hours that the piece was running, the AI offers 500 different games to the cats, and is learning each time which game is liked best by which cat. You can see a system gradually learning.

This is a machine-mammal interaction with no human ostensibly present. It was interesting that most of the negative comments that we had – and of course there was an army of those people on Facebook – said it's unfair on the cats because there are no humans. They haven't got any human contact: a classically solipsistic human thing, because obviously what cats need are humans!

Cat Royale is delightful and playful and slightly funny and almost silly and also dystopian. There were moments when I was watching it where you can see the robot playing with the cat and I'm thinking, 'That cat is having a ball. They're having a really nice time. They're loving pulling on that feather toy, and the robot is pulling back'. And that feels like a glimpse into some sort of future, which of course is: The cats in *Cat Royale* are us. It's a work about 'Human Royale', really. What do we do when we outsource our happiness to algorithms? Where does that leave us?

Helen Kennedy: *I heard there briefly that obviously you've had positive and negative feedback on Cat Royale. What has this negative feedback been largely about? Is it the absence of a human factor for the cats?*

Matt Adams: Yes, people have hated that. We prepared for over a year for hostility for that project. I undertook hostile media training. Because it's very easy to frame *Cat Royale* as 'artists shut cats in box with robot'.

Helen Kennedy: *So just because we probably are getting to the end of our time, there's two things that I wanted to talk to you about again, which is about the cyclical nature of how things happen, and it feels like the Uncle Roy All Around You[14] work and the Can You See Me Now[15] work has a new relevance now as people are starting to do these kind of digital twin/hybrid experiences. I wondered what your thoughts were about, you know, how pioneering you'd been*

---

13   https://www.blasttheory.co.uk/projects/cat-royale/.
14   https://www.blasttheory.co.uk/projects/uncle-roy-all-around-you/.
15   https://www.blasttheory.co.uk/projects/can-you-see-me-now/.

then, 20 years ago? But what's your perspective on the potential aesthetic around those hybrid works?

Matt Adams: I don't know. All I can really say is I am always interested in making work that stems from a degree of ignorance and uncertainty on my part. At times we have made work which seems eerily prescient, for example, we made *Spit Spreads Death*[16] about pandemics in September 2019, just three months before COVID was first present in Wuhan.

Sometimes that's coincidence, but I think some of the time that happens because Ju, Nick, and I are all interested to go into territory where we feel a little bit ignorant and a little bit out of our depth. That enables me to follow a hunch or something that is poorly understood and that enables me to stretch myself.

I've sometimes thought about creativity like this: How far will you swim off the beach before you feel like you really should head back now. The most creative people I know are people who are very happy to keep going away from shore for a long, long way. Where other people are a bit like: 'But we can't even see the beach now, I really think we should turn back.'

Helen Kennedy: *Curiosity seems to me like a driving force there, maybe part of that ignorance, maybe a more positive way of framing that is curiosity about what you don't know. And so very quickly then: the Metaverse. It feels like the Metaverse probably has delivered on some of your worst fears around the internet in terms of its commercialisation and commodification. There is a games and performance drive happening there with more and more performances taking place in the Metaverse and building audiences. There is also a renewed sense of possibility within that space in terms of creating greater democracy, or finding new ways of inhabiting those spaces, with work that isn't already commercialised or commodified.*

Matt Adams: Yes, maybe. Lots of the things that you just said could apply to earlier phases of VR or to Second Life, for example. I don't believe that aesthetics creates new power relationships. I think power relationships create aesthetics. And if the aesthetics have not already succumbed to the power relationships, the power relationships turn up to make sure that they do. It was said with a straight face at conferences for over a decade that the internet was an inherently democratising thing. *Inherently*. It makes everything horizontal and flat and normal hierarchies will not exist. In the Metaverse, the fundamental laws of power will exist as ever. That still means that there is potential for utopian things to happen, and transformative things to happen. I believe in fighting for that, and the good artists can posit things that enter into the cultural bloodstream, and become new ideas, and those ideas can be transformative.

---

16   https://www.blasttheory.co.uk/projects/spit-spreads-death/.

Helen Kennedy: *I had a question ... one of my final questions ... about audience engagement and implication or involvement in your work. How have you sought to advance audience engagement and, in some ways, audience implication or involvement in your work?*

Matt Adams: I suppose, what I perhaps haven't said in quite this way is that: In designing games, we're giving you as a participant *agency*. Agency and control is inherently an interesting thing because it enables you to *act* as a consumer of a cultural work, to become a participant. To make decisions, and most decisions that you make are quite narrowly defined in games, but of course games are legion with examples of emergent behaviour: little hacks, cheats, cheat codes, people working out ways to get round things, subverting things.

This is, in itself, replete with possibility: to go into a piece of work where you can make a decision, or you can act in a certain way.

Helen Kennedy: *Sometimes – so you talked about agency there – but sometimes, there's also playing with how passive they might be, how suddenly things take control. So that also feels like something you've got in play in that...*

Matt Adams: Yes, that says a lot about me. You see these distinct power relationships in our work so often. One of the things that often exists in our work is a sense of isolation and loneliness – a sort of sadness. Because that's often my experience of the busiest, most social spaces on the internet. I always feel like I'm a slightly uncool kid on the edge of the party, and that doesn't feel great. I came off Facebook about seven or eight years ago and one of the enormous weights that was lifted from me was the sense of being permanently at some sort of school mixer, which I was *not* well suited for!

Helen Kennedy: *We're more or less at the end now. We talked about what you've been up to recently – What's up next?*

Matt Adams: We are making a work called *The Unstruck Sound* in Estonia next year, as part of Tartu, Capital of Culture, which is where we are going to train some young people to go out and interview people who remember life in 1974 in Estonia. And we're going to collect stories about Estonia in 1974 and then write a science fiction film, set in 2074, using those stories.

I've been really interested for a while in how in the 50s and 60s, where progressive politics was at its height, the hard-right cadre all retreated, to the universities especially. So, you know, Milton Friedman and all those guys, the University of Chicago, and they did the intellectual and cultural work to think about what a privatised, neoliberal world would look like. And for ten or 15 years, they just wrote papers and had little seminars and conferences and stroked themselves against copies of Ayn Rand novels...

But what that meant is that when Pinochet, then Reagan, then Thatcher came, when that moment came, where the progressive ideal in the mid late 70s looked tarnished, they had all of the thinking in place to say: This is what you do – privatise the trains, privatise the buses, privatise the water, privatise the gas. All the thinking had been done. I'm interested in whether, in a moment of sort of right-wing, nationalist resurgence, whether there's a way of trying to keep our eyes on that past and to use it to think about utopian ideals and to try and articulate: What would a utopia look like?

Can we think of that? And so I think, yeah, 1974 in Estonia, I don't know anything about it really, but I imagine it was a moment where the Soviet ideal was just about still alive. You know, there was still a moment in which communism could be the panacea. Maybe it was already gone by then – I don't know, I'm interested to find out.

We did a project in Hull [England] called *2097: We Made Ourselves Over*,[17] and we did interviews there with people. One of the things that came out was older people talking about their euphoria when they moved into the new housing estates in the 60s and 70s – how they were amazing things with plumbing, and central heating, and communal spaces. And they were all brand-new, they had gardens, they could drive easily, where previously it had been hard. It was a time where working people were being given things that were of real value to them, you know? And that really stayed with me because, of course, we're so used to the idea that all of these tower blocks were terrible to start with. And that's not quite how it worked. So, I think there's just something in there about those kinds of utopian moments that I'm interested in exploring.

Helen Kennedy: *Fascinating, I'm excited to see what happens! So it's going to be a utopian science fiction and well, where will it go? Is it going to be part of a festival?*

Matt Adams: It will be a film. We're going to make a short film, shot in Estonia. Estonian cast and crew and probably in the Estonian language – we haven't quite worked that out yet. And then, yeah, it'll be showing at film festivals, shown online.

Helen Kennedy: *Interesting. It feels like you are continuing to explore a more political, critical role for the artwork. The artwork is holding open the idea that, like you said, we want to remind ourselves that things weren't always as they are now.*

---

17   https://www.blasttheory.co.uk/projects/we-made-ourselves-over/.

Matt Adams: Time will tell as to how that exists, and it may be that actually what it does is open up different forms of imaginative space at a much more modest level, just like how we might live in 2074 in a way that is responsible.

Helen Kennedy: *Have things like climate change started to leak into your work, has it become an important thing for you to think about through your aesthetic practice?*

Matt Adams: Not really through aesthetics. I mean, the project we did in Hull was also a science fiction. And in that, we made a future world where you just never see vehicles. Everyone's on foot everywhere, and it's not explaining what happened, but you just assume vehicles are either non-functional or not required. What I am interested in is a kind of imaginary, new forms of imaginary about the future that might be things that we aspire to, or can invest in. I do think that there is a real danger in the dystopian sci-fi trope that actually what you're doing is implanting normativity, *future* normativity, which is like: 'Yes, of course there will be massive surveillance in the future. It's in every film I've ever seen!' Individually, all of those science fiction projects are to *warn* us of surveillance in the future, but there is also a counterfactual going on there...

Helen Kennedy: *Exactly, a sort of a dominant oppressive technological imagining that conditions an acceptance of these things as our very near future reality. Which I think is also really interesting around the way that AI is being talked about and why it's so important to challenge that in whatever way you can. Which is why, yeah, I guess* Cat Royale *is an interesting work in that regard.*

Matt Adams: Yes! Because some of those forms of dystopia are essentially just disempowering, aren't they? It's like: well, if crime is going to be exponentially growing to the point where the police have lost all control and people will shoot you in the head and the police will do nothing about it. It's like, what are you supposed to do with that vision of the future? And that is a surprisingly common vision, where the state is only an oppressive force.

From my point of view, the state is actually where we collectively come together and agree things about how we want to live. It is not an 'Other' thing. It is *us*. And that imaginary of: What is the state, what is government, what is it there for, and who is it? Neoliberalism has almost entirely excavated the metaphors for the idea that we come together as a society to set rules for how we all want to live together and to look after each other, and so yes, that is an act of imagination.

Helen Kennedy: *I think that is a great place to end Matt, with that counter image that holds open the space for that act of imagination. Thank you so much for your time and we all look forward to what happens next.*

References

Baudrillard, Jean, 1983. *Simulations*, translated by Phil Beitchman, Foss Paul, and Paul Patton, New York: Semiotext (e).

Debord, Guy, 1967. *Society of the Spectacle*, Detroit. MI: Black and Red.

Foot, Phillipa. 1967. 'The Problem of Abortion and the Doctrine of the Double Effect', *Oxford Review*. 1967, 5:5–15.

Biographies

Matt Adams co-founded Blast Theory in 1991. The group makes interactive art to explore social and political questions. Matt has curated at Tate Modern and at the ICA in London. He has lectured at Stanford University, the Royal College of Art, and the Sorbonne.
Blast Theory has shown work at the Venice Biennale, Sundance Film Festival, and Tate Britain. The group collaborates frequently with the Mixed Reality Lab at the University of Nottingham and Matt has co-authored forty-five academic papers. Blast Theory has won the Golden Nica at Prix Ars Electronica, the Nam June Paik Art Center Award, and has received four BAFTA nominations.

Helen W. Kennedy is Professor of Creative and Cultural Industries at the University of Nottingham. Her research interests are feminist games culture and the wider diversification of access to creative practice; the ludification of cultural participation, innovations in experience design and the cultural evaluation of immersive experiences. Kennedy has published widely in game studies and the emergent field of live cinema, where her work focuses on the intersections between performance, play, and narrative in the experience design. She has led a number of national and international projects seeking to improve women's access to and experience within spaces of creative production – across screens, VR, and immersive technology more broadly.

Machina eX: Working Collectively at the Interface of Theatre and Video Games. In Conversation with Clara Ehrenwerth and Anton Krause

Réjane Dreifuss and Simon Hagemann

Abstract *This interview with two current members of the German artist collective machina eX, pioneers of game theatre, looks back at some of their work from the last thirteen years and addresses various questions about the interplay between games and theatre. The discussion touches upon topics including the role of the audience, aesthetic aspects of games, different kinds of venue, the role of technology, and the political dimension of games.*

Interview

Machina eX has been researching the interface between theatre and computer games since 2010. The Berlin-based theatre collective was formed by a group of students from the University of Hildesheim and has been producing participatory game theatre ever since. Machina eX combines modern technologies and spatial arrangements inspired by computer games with the means of classical theatre to create immersive, playable theatre plays that are also walk-in computer games, as the collective calls its performances[1]. Since its inception, machina eX has produced around thirty game theatre shows in German-speaking countries and internationally.

Réjane Dreifuss: *More than ten years ago, a few Cultural Studies students from the University of Hildesheim founded the theatre collective machina eX and developed interactive theatre shows inspired by point-and-click adventure games. How has the team changed over time?*

Clara Ehrenwerth: The machina eX collective[2] has existed for 13 years. The team has changed a lot over time. There used to be nine of us at the beginning. Since then,

---

1   See https://machinaex.org/en/
2   Information on the machina eX collective can be found at https://machinaex.org.

some have joined, and others have left. The independent theatre scene and the Berlin location don't suit everyone's life plans, at least not in the long term. People want to move on to other things at some point. There are currently four of us in the core team, but we have a large circle of associates around us who are not involved with machina eX on a daily basis but join us for specific projects. Some 15 to 20 people are typically involved in our projects (in areas such as scenography, sound design, dramaturgy, game design, programming, interaction design, etc.).

Simon Hagemann: *With this high fluctuation of members, is it still possible to speak of a fixed artistic label or identity?*

Clara Ehrenwerth: Absolutely. I think there are enough things that characterise us as a collective that have been incorporated into our artistic style and that have remained constant. Which is not to say that we always use the same handwriting. In its different variations, this combination of theatre and game, or other forms of expression and games, has remained what connects all our projects. In recent years, we have experimented more than before due to the pandemic and have changed the format relatively significantly as a result.

Anton Krause: Machina eX is characterised not only by the people who take part, but also by a certain aesthetic approach to the topics and problems that we are artistically dealing with. There is always a great fascination with the kindred spirit, the way in which we feel like looking at certain issues and then moulding them into a form in which the performers then work with them.

Simon Hagemann: *Adventure games have characterised machina eX performances. How has this aspect developed over time?*

Anton Krause: I saw the first play by machina eX at the University of Hildesheim in 2010. At the time, I had the feeling that while other theatre groups might have found their way to games, here it was the other way round: It was gamers who found their way to theatre. They took point-and-click adventure games seriously very early on. They saw them as a cultural form of expression, as a cultural practice, and then transferred them into a theatre. Which is normal for theatre. The great power of theatre is that you appropriate the cultural practices that take place in society and bring them to the stage. Games have always been inherent to our collective. This can also be seen in our logo, both the former and the new version. The central motif is and remains the mouse pointer, and not without reason, but because games are a central element in our work.

Simon Hagemann: *How has the relationship to games developed? Are the collective members still gamers? Are there still so many artistic influences coming from this side?*

Anton Krause: We are still a very game-affine collective. We think out of the game. Interestingly, this game theatre[3] format has become much bigger in the last 13 years. So have digitalisation and interaction. We mostly use digital tools to involve and move the audience. We don't use digitalisation as a topic, but as a means of participation. We use digital feedback and tools to enable this agency, participation, and decision-making. A performance would be otherwise too difficult to moderate if everyone could simply do everything. With computer games, the player has a certain range of options that they can explore. It's the same with our projects. There are many different formats of computer games. We don't try to work our way through all of them. Some computer game formats don't interest us at all, and some others interest us very much, which you can see again and again in the gameplay of the performers. They play like so-called NPCs, non-player characters, and the audience member sees and feels it because they don't have an actor in front of them, but an NPC.

Clara Ehrenwerth: In recent years, we have also been strongly inspired by board games. In the production *Life Goes On* (premiere HAU Hebbel am Ufer, Berlin, 2022),[4] we developed a cooperative multimedia board game that first took place in the theatre and could then be played at home as an online version. During the preparation and the research phases, we played a lot of board games to understand how mechanisms of cooperation, storytelling, and puzzles work in this context and how analogue and digital tools can be combined. Many board games now have digital extensions or supplementary tools. So, over the last few years, we've also played a lot of board games and didn't just have controllers in our hands.

Réjane Dreifuss: *The founders of machina eX were all enthusiastic video gamers and theatre makers. How does that fit together? How did you come up with the idea of combining theatre and video games?*

Clara Ehrenwerth: I think they go together wonderfully. I don't see the big gap in between. There are so many parallels between theatre and videogames. It's still a

---

3   Among those involved in the development of the concept of game theatre was the German critic Christian Rakow in 2013. https://nachtkritik.de/index.php//index.php?optio n=com_content&view=article&id=8728:a-presentation-about-the-new-game-theatre-and-its-political-relevance-at-the-conference-replayce-thecity-in-zuerich&catid=53:portraet-a-profil&Itemid=83.

4   https://machinaex.org/en/life-goes-on-2022/.

bit of a relic from the separation between highbrow culture and light entertainment that you think there are two completely different worlds, but it's the same as between literature and theatre, music and theatre, or film and theatre. There is a lot of overlap between theatre and videogames, and one has often grown into the other. It's productive to throw the characteristics of games and theatre together and see what happens when you bring strategies from videogames onto the theatre stage or into the theatre space. That was the basic idea behind machina eX. Back then, there were already action-based games that could also be played in physical spaces, such as paintball. In other words, there were already games which were more physical, dealing with speed and skill, but not so much with storytelling, and the idea at the time was to see what would happen if you transferred a format like a point-and-click adventures game into a theatre space. The point-and-click adventure has the great advantage that it is also story-based and therefore a lot of content is dealt with there, and we found the way this content is conveyed, namely interactively, so interesting that we also wanted to try it out in the theatre.

Simon Hagemann: *At the same time, escape rooms have also become increasingly popular in recent years. What distinguishes your work from this format?*

Anton Krause: In the German Wikipedia article on *Escape Games* (in German *Escape Game* refers to both physical escape rooms and the related genre of point-and-click videogames), there is even a reference to machina eX as one of the first theatre companies dealing with this topic in Germany.[5] The organisers of escape room games have different problems than we do. They must make a living from the people who take part in their games. We don't have to do that. Our job is to look at society and make something exciting out of it. We deal with social issues, and we get money for that. As theatre makers, we do projects for fewer audience members and in that way, we can create much more complex narratives than those who are economically dependent on them. We can also afford for a project to be a flop. The mechanics we use are partly those used in escape rooms and escape games. The idea that time stands still until one acts, for example. Escape rooms are about finding the solution. In our projects, the puzzle may look like it's been solved, but players quickly realise that there's always another solution, and they can discuss these other solutions with the others audience members they are playing with. Machina eX makes socially critical escape games, so to speak. Escape rooms are created under different parameters. The development of an escape room game can take up to 2 years, compared to a time of 6 weeks for a theatre production, for example.

---

5   https://de.wikipedia.org/wiki/Escape_Game.

Réjane Dreifuss: *Are your projects intended exclusively for the theatre or also for other venues?*

Clara Ehrenwerth: We mostly do projects with theatres, but they often take place outside the theatre space. However, we also collaborate with museums from time to time. In 2018, for example, we developed a web-app based game at the Natural History Museum in Bern, which can still be played in the exhibition.[6] We work for schools, in urban spaces, in Berlin on Tempelhof Feld, or in a medieval bastion. Since 2020, in the wake of the coronavirus pandemic, we have also created living room adventures and online board games.

Réjane Dreifuss: *You often make plays for very few people. Do you ever plan to expand your projects and work with more performers and audience members, like Punchdrunk does, for example?*

Clara Ehrenwerth: This is something that would really appeal to us. But the apparatus you would need would be much bigger. It's not just done with a few more performers, you also need a much larger space, or several spaces and a correspondingly larger team to build it. Tickets for Punchdrunk's current show in London cost around £110. They are set up differently to us, who live from cultural funding. Punchdrunk has a machine in the background like a musical. We can't afford that; we simply can't afford such a large ensemble. But we are trying to expand anyway. We haven't done a play for 12 audience members for a long time now. Most of the recent projects have been designed for about 30 people. These 12 audience members came from our observation at the time that 12 is a size of a group of people where you can still get to know each other in a 90-minute performance. I might have come with one or two other people, and I got to know the others. Not in the sense of everyone introducing themselves, but I know that it's the person who said that before or something. Once the group reaches a certain size, that no longer works. You have a peer group within the group. We don't want that. We want the group to function as a group. That's why we've always made sure that the plays we've done for 30, 40, or 50 audience members are divided into smaller groups. To be able to make plays for a larger audience is a topic that keeps us busy, because we want to make our plays accessible to as many people as possible.

Réjane Dreifuss: *Who are the audience members that take part in your plays? Are they interested in theatre or rather in games?*

---

6   Expedition Fieberwahn – Ein mobiles Spiel durchs Museum: https://www.nmbe.ch/de/mus eumsangebot/expedition-fieberwahn.

Clara Ehrenwerth: It depends on where we play. If we are a guest of a theatre in a smaller town, then the theatre audience of that town will come. Often the younger ones, but not always. Sometimes there is a mix of a theatre audience and people who play games and are coming to the theatre for the first time. We have a mix of people, the ones who are more into theatre and the others who are more into games. There are still mutual prejudices, not among everyone of course, but it does happen. When you see that the puzzling and tinkering also has a quality, when you see the other way round that a story that is complex – following, listening, observing, getting to know the characters – is also interesting, there is a mutual respect, and we are happy when it works.

Anton Krause: In recent years, this audience has been growing together. There are many younger people, aged 25–35, who both go to the theatre and play video games. For the younger generation, there is no clear line between theatre and games that you can draw. Some of the performers we work with are also passionate gamers. When they're not on stage or learning lines, they're playing games. Video games are growing into society. My friends' children are growing up with consoles and computer games and for them, it's not a novelty, it's just always been there. You also must bear that in mind.

Simon Hagemann: *What role does the audience play in your projects? Are your audience members both players and spectators?*

Anton Krause: Every now and then we have one or two audience members who initially only accept the role of spectator and are lured into gaming over time. Very rarely, we have people who completely refuse to become active. We generally think that's a pity. It's nice when everyone plays and takes part. We design the games in a way that makes you want to take part and we usually have a good turnout. If you want to watch from the outside all the time, that's a pity because you lose a quality of the performative act. The performative act that you carry out yourself is part of the action and is important because it also tells a story. If I refuse to participate, then I miss out on a large part of the complexity of the experience, and we try to avoid that. Anyone who comes to our plays wants to take part, that's how we want to announce our projects; we don't hide anything. This is a specific format: I know what this format offers me, and I want to take part. We have been offering this format for 13 years and it has its own audience. There are people waiting for the next machina eX production to come out here in Berlin or in Düsseldorf, and they go there. They want to see it. Those are our fans.

Simon Hagemann: *In theatre studies, there is a debate in relation to immersive theatre about the extent to which audience participation can be understood as emancipatory or, on the con-*

trary, as a practice of neoliberal patterns, as the audience itself must become entrepreneurial to get the most out of a performance.[7] How do you deal with this question of participation?

Clara Ehrenwerth: I don't think that participation and being invited to join in is neoliberal, but rather democratic. We are experiencing a turn; stories are not only told in a representative way. Audience members no longer want to sit exclusively in front of a stage and watch how characters on the stage in front of them experience stories, act, and make decisions. Nowadays the audience members often want to be the ones who press the button, who must make the decisions, not necessarily alone, but as a group. I think this way of playing is an interesting way of playing a democratic society before I think of entrepreneurship and neoliberalism. It doesn't mean that the other [form of theatre] can no longer exist. We didn't start to make theatre with the desire to abolish representative theatre, but rather to invent a subspecies of this genre.

Simon Hagemann: *Are there also possibilities for counterplay in machina eX performances? Can the players also do something that is not intended by you?*

Clara Ehrenwerth: That works to a certain extent. People always find solutions or ways to play the game that we didn't even plan for. A good example is the project *Right of Passage*, which we did in 2014.[8] The setting was an abstract refugee camp in a fictitious region, and it was about playing a kind of bureaucratic hell simulator to get enough documents together to be allowed to cross the border. It wasn't about portraying the fate of refugees, but about making bureaucratic hell tangible. One evening, 30 audience members decided to storm the border during the performance. They decided to no longer stand in front of the customs officer (performer) and have their documents stamped or not, but that they would simply run over the border. No scene was planned for this. They won in a way, but the situation couldn't really be anticipated by the game. If you compare this to a computer game metaphor, it's like this: We designed the console, of course, if you press the A button, you can press it. If you'd rather press Y, then maybe it's not here, you can press an empty space, but nothing happens. The button assignments are designed by us and within this framework we try to build the story, the game, as big as possible, so that if you somehow turn off somewhere, you can still find something left and not just a wall. It is a question of time, how much can I enrich the story with side scenes, how many

---

7   See the article by Olivia Levet in this volume or Alston, Adam. 2016. *Beyond Immersive Theatre: Aesthetics, Politics and Productive Participation.* London: Palgrave Macmillan.

8   See https://machinaex.org/en/right-of-passage-2014/ or https://www.srf.ch/play/tv/kulturplatz/video/ohnmacht-erleben---die-fluechtlingstragoedie-als-mitmachtheater?urn=urn:s rf:video:98a51fad-5f84-4ffe-b631-454685f007e2.

other props or rooms can I design. There is a time and an economic limit to this. In any case, we always try to offer different endings that are triggered either by decisions or by gameplay. In a *Telegram* game, for example, which are mainly chat adventures, it's not even that time-consuming to have lots of different answers ready or to prepare different side quests, because it's just texts, photos, and audio material at first, but not a new door that opens a new sub-game.

Réjane Dreifuss: *This leads me to the next question: What kind of theatre do you make? Should theatre be entertaining or political? What are the issues regarding your work?*

Clara Ehrenwerth: We are quite broadly based. We've just done a play about geo-engineering, weather manipulation, and various strategies to combat the climate crisis (*Wenn der Regen kommt*, Stadtraum Moabit, Berlin, 2023).[9] In recent years, we've dealt twice with the *Treuhandanstalt (trust agency)*,[10] which privatised the German Democratic Republic companies in Germany after 1990 during reunification.[11] We have also done a lot of science fiction, or rather we always like to go into 'near future' scenarios, in a manageable time[frame], e.g., five years, or in parallel worlds.[12] A certain entertainment aspect is always important to us. We are not interested in a reference theatre where the audience can come and understand everything if they have mastered certain educational canons. We want anyone and everyone to be able to come to our shows and play with us. Of course, there are still barriers. The current play, for example, is not suitable if you have mobility restrictions.[13] There are language barriers and technical barriers. If you play with a smartphone, a certain level of technical expertise is required. I would say that our projects focus on immersion and entertainment; we want people to have a kind of flow experience where they can completely immerse themselves in the game for the time being. The reflection is more something that happens in the follow-up discussion, at best also as a group, where topics can be deepened or taken up again. There is often no time for such discussions in the short duration of the game.

Anton Krause: Our approach is political. But the political doesn't take place in a discourse. We are not part of a train of thought that *sophisticated* people have been elabo-

---

9   *Wenn der Regen kommt* (2023): https://machinaex.org/en/wenn-der-regen-kommt-2023/.

10 The Treuhandanstalt was a public institution founded in the late phase of the German Democratic Republic with the task of privatising the state-owned enterprises of the GDR according to the principles of the social market economy and ensuring the performance and competitiveness of the companies after reunification. A series of scandals and social protests arose in connection with the privatisation.

11 *Layers of Life* (2021) and *Life Goes On* (2022).

12 *Like Caretaker* (2019).

13 *Wenn der Regen kommt* (2023).

rating for the duration of rehearsals. Well, yes, but not mainly. As an audience member, I can reflect in retrospect on the possibilities for action that I had, my own behaviour in the game, and the opportunities that the game offered me. I can draw metaphors for the world I live in, and then I can decide again whether I enjoyed it, how I decided, whether I would have wanted more freedom of action in one place or another, or would do again what I just did. Through this reflection, you can sometimes describe much more complex systems that are difficult to describe in words, such as climate change, for example, it suddenly becomes tangible, and that is the great quality of gaming. I enter a system, I have to understand it and then I can also criticise it. I am involved in understanding it, and that's also my role in it, and I find that interesting. Hopefully, the audience members who do it will get this added value from it, this greater understanding. That's why we often have problems with theatre critics who look at our plays and see them as a discourse, completely as a discourse, as if we were chewing the discourse for them. That sometimes gives the feeling that it's only entertaining or too shallow or discussed by too few people. But I think it's precisely this gaming experience and this cultural practice of gaming that has a huge impact on it.

Réjane Dreifuss: *Could you give us an example of a project where the audience members/players are confronted with those ethical questions and decisions to make?*

Clara Ehrenwerth: A good example is the play *Lesson of Leaking* that we did in 2016.[14] It was set in 2021, in a near future that is now in the past. It was before Brexit and before the massive rise of the AfD[15] in Germany and the right-wing populist movements in Europe. The story was about a fictitious scenario of a referendum on Germany leaving the European Union and a right-wing populist Chancellor, who had initiated the referendum. During the play, it emerged that the vote was to be manipulated, which was also information that the group of players discovered. At the end of the evening, the audience, consisting of 12 to 15 people, had the option of making public that this election was to be manipulated or destroying this data and allowing the manipulation so that Germany would remained in the EU. That was a dilemma. Of course, you don't want to manipulate anything, but you also don't want to play along with the right-wing populist chancellor. The play was 'gamey', with real game scenes and puzzle scenes, you had to crack a safe and commit a hack together. There was a lot of play and suspense and at the end someone was standing there with this CD, and you had to decide: destroy it or make it public. There were strong discussions between the audience members. The question was: What do we do with

---

14   https://machinaex.org/en/lessons-of-leaking-2016/.

15   AfD. Alternative für Deutschland: Alternative for Germany. A right-wing populist political party in Germany.

this CD? The audience members sometimes spent 20 minutes discussing what to do. There was no more game in it. We played *Lesson of Leaking* for a long time, three to four years, in various European countries. We were in England or Greece, for example, and it was interesting to see how these discussions changed depending on where you were. Sometimes, there was also an international festival audience, people from different countries coming together and meeting the local audience. So we had a lot of exciting discussions that were no longer about the subject matter of the game, but about issues that are happening in the world right now, that the political world brings with it.

Simon Hagemann: *How do you use the technology for your plays? Is the approach rather: We want to tell this story and need those tools to be able to realise it? Or is it the other way round: It's a kind of laboratory; here's an exciting tool and we want to do something with it, how can we use it and confront the audience with it?*

Anton Krause: In the beginning, there were some interesting tools that we used. In the meantime, we have acquired a certain amount of expertise over the years, and we have created our own framework[16] in which we are no longer dependent on certain tools. We mainly think about interfaces, what do we want to do, what format would be good for this, and what do we need for it. Then we acquire the knowledge and can then blend it with our storytelling machine, I would say. We have no pressure to innovate and don't have to do VR or anything like that. But we could work with VR if it's artistically appropriate.

Clara Ehrenwerth: Yes, exactly. *Adaptor: ex*, as the framework is called, is really a great relief. We've been using it for almost three years now. It's currently helping us to develop our plays. It's open source if other people want to do something with it.

Réjane Dreifuss: *machina eX works with game designers, for example with Martin Ganteföhr.[17] How does the collaboration work?*

Clara Ehrenwerth: It's difficult to generalise. Martin was the only one who worked with us as a game designer and a computer game author.[18] Otherwise, we tend to

---

16 https://machinaex.org/adaptorex-seit-2021/.
17 Martin Ganteföhr is an interactive writer and designer and Professor for Game Art and Design at HBK Essen, Germany. Website: http://gantefoehr.com.
18 Martin Ganteföhr has worked with machina eX twice: on the projects *Toxik* (Hau Hebbel am Ufer, Berlin, 2015) https://machinaex.org/en/toxik-2015/ and *End Game* (Hau Hebbel am Ufer, Berlin, 2015) https://machinaex.org/en/endgame-2017/.

work with technology teams that make computer games, among other things. It was interesting to develop a play with Martin because he normally works for a different format. We talked a lot about what works and doesn't work in theatre. One thing is the length. A computer game has a completely different running time. The duration of our plays is between 60 and 120 minutes, which would be a very short production in an adventure game. Martin thought the story in terms of a big arc, which then had to be accommodated in a much shorter narrative time. He always thought about computer characters, who can do pretty much anything graphically, while our performers are flesh and blood creatures and therefore can't suddenly start bleeding. In the beginning, Martin didn't always have the output graphics of our characters on his screen. In any case, it was a productive collaboration. We learnt a lot from each other. It was exciting to see what he could bring to the table and what he might have picked up from us.

Simon Hagemann: *The gaming industry is booming. The public is becoming more and more gamey, as Anton said. Are golden times ahead for machina eX? What are your projects for the future?*

Clara Ehrenwerth: We'll see how golden the times become. As in many other countries, Germany is cutting back quite a bit on cultural funding. This will also affect us, although we are in a luxurious situation. We have already received concept funding from the city of Berlin, which we will receive again for the next four years. During this period of time, we want to expand our network and become more international. We are currently interested in how we can co-produce and tour internationally without the CO2 emissions that would otherwise be caused by such a guest performance – if we were to fly to Korea with a team of six people, for example. We want to further develop and think about the methods of working together that started during the pandemic. Not to leave these methods in a suitcase as an emergency crisis tool, but to see what we can do with them on an international level.

We now know a few performance companies with whom we have a lot of overlap, who also make digital theatre in their countries and work with games. They are from South Korea, Singapore, New Zealand, India, Great Britain, and elsewhere and do similar things to us. We would like to develop a play with them or show our plays to each other and go beyond the current guest performance mode. In 2024, we will co-operate with a group from Wellington. We will not fly there with our play and they're not coming to Germany with their play, but we're going to swap productions; they're going to cover a machina eX play, and we're going to cover a Binge Culture play.[19] We'll see how it works out. We're all excited because we've never staged someone

---

19   Binge Culture is a collective of artists living and working in Wellington, Aotearoa New Zealand. https://www.bingeculture.co.nz/.

else's material before. From an artistic perspective, I see the golden age for us now primarily in this exchange movement. We'll have to see what the funding situation will be like. In general, we're happy if we can continue to reach an audience that either has no connection to games or spends half their free time playing games.

Biographies

Clara Ehrenwerth started working with machina eX 10 years ago. She has been a permanent member of the collective since 2018 and is responsible as managing director and writer.

Anton Krause has accompanied the collective several times, but only recently joined machina eX as a director and mediator. He is interested in the interfaces between analogue spaces and digital worlds.

What Even Is Video Game Performance?

A conversation between Marleena Huuhka and Harold Hejazi

Abstract *The following text is a conversation between performance scholar Marleena Huuhka and live artist Harold Hejazi about video games as a medium of performance. Through examples from their work, they discuss video game performances and gameplay as performance today and the possible futures of these intermedial forms of performing arts.*

Conversation

In the summer of 2023, performance scholar Marleena Huuhka invited live artist Harold Hejazi to discuss the nature of video games as a form of performance. Harold Hejazi has been working at the intersection of games and performance since 2015 and performing with video games since 2020. Marleena Huuhka has been researching video games through performance theory since 2016. The two had just co-curated an exhibition about games as art at Poikilo Museums in Kouvola, Finland,[1] where they led exhibition tours through the lens of gameplay as performance.

Marleena Huuhka: Hi Harold! Do you think the practice of playing is art?

Harold Hejazi: Hey Marleena! Well, I do think so, especially when the player intends it to be. Perhaps you could say I have a Duchampian view on the matter, where playing is art if the player says it is. What do you think?

Marleena Huuhka: I think it also depends on the definition of art in general, but I do think playing can be defined as art. Who defines it is another question. I think that playing can also be framed as art – or, maybe more specifically, as performance – by the people looking at it. In some cases, the player might not even know their involvement in that process. I think the discussion on games as art[2] has long been focusing

---

1   https://www.poikilo.fi/nayttelyt/nayttelyarkisto/pelipoikilo/

2   See for example, Smuts 2005; Kirkpatrick 2011; Sharp 2015; Deardorff 2015; Bourgonjon et al. 2017; Bosman and Wieringen 2022.

on the actual games as visual, narrative, or cinematic art, and play as practice has been a bit absent.

Harold Hejazi: Well, performance and games have both always been on the periphery of the art world, so the combination of games and performance is quite vulnerable to misrepresentation and reductionist critique. Also, performances are typically expected to be reserved for the stage or film, and games are often expected to be experienced behind a screen or shared around a table, so perhaps it's difficult to imagine a creative playing field where these worlds collide and combine.

Marleena Huuhka: I think there are also some underlying prejudices about both fields generally. Performance, especially performance art, might have been considered as elitist, while games and gameplay have had a reputation of being a sort of childish or, at best, juvenile pastime. I feel that, especially in the field of theatre and other performing arts, games have often only been seen as something to use in performance, although exceptions to this are popping up increasingly.[3]

I have also encountered a lot of people in the performing arts field that deny knowing anything about games or refuse to accept their cultural importance. While I don't necessarily think of games as the ultimate medium, I find it hard to understand such dismissive thinking.

Harold Hejazi: Do you mean that games have usually been 'something to use in performance' as in props or themes rather than the gameplay being the performance itself? Certainly, game performance is a medium that is still slowly gaining awareness of itself. And just so we're on the same page, by 'game performance' I am referring quite loosely to a combination of a game and a performance.

Marleena Huuhka: Exactly. There is a significant difference between games as aesthetic tropes and gameplay as performative action. I think, as the field is pretty new, these things get easily scrambled. For readers interested in these categorical differences, I have written an article about the matter. In the article I suggest five approaches to understanding video games as/with performance: video games as an aesthetic resource, video games as a structural category, performances staged inside video games, performances made with video games, and gameplay as performance (Huuhka 2020).

Harold Hejazi: I'm curious what you see in the future of video games/gameplay as performance. Do you have any predictions for the form?

---

3   Since the 2000s, performance companies have increasingly been using game elements, as, for example, described in Benford and Giannachi 2011.

Marleena Huuhka: I think in the future there will be more emphasis on virtual reality, and theatres will surely expand their repertoire to the virtual. When it comes to gameplay as performance, I don't know if it will ever be popular,[4] as it seems to be a bit hard to swallow in both fields. But I do believe games, and especially game technologies and aesthetics, will be increasingly appropriated in theatre practices in the future.

Harold Hejazi: I fully agree that game technologies and aesthetics will only increase in prevalence in theatre and performance. By virtue of existing on the digital plane, video game performances allow for new horizons of possibility. However, I disagree that gameplay as performance is unlikely to become popular. Aren't gaming videos already a massive form of entertainment? It's safe to assume that there are more people watching video game performers online than there are people attending theatre performances.

Marleena Huuhka: In my experience, there has been reluctance to accept video games, or rather the gameplay experience, into the traditional canon of what is considered art. What I mean by 'gameplay as performance' is actual acts of gameplay being framed as performance, and I don't really see those sorts of deliberate acts as being so popular. Maybe it is a phenomenon that exists mostly in my conceptual horizon and not in the actual practices of players or performers.

I agree gaming videos are a significant form of entertainment already, and I do believe their impact will be visible in other types of entertainment and performance in the future.

Harold Hejazi: I predict that the passive theatre spectator will evolve into that of an active multiplayer audience member. Perhaps people won't pile into theatres to just watch a performer play a game, but I do think audiences will go to theatres to participate as active players of games led by main performers[5]. Multiplayer game performance will allow audiences greater levels of immersion in the narrative or conceptual framework of a game, allowing them to experience multiple structures and viewpoints.

In some formulations, audiences might sit at a proscenium stage all with their own game controllers in their hand,[6] or they might be in a black box moving freely in an immersive VR piece.[7] These performance formats are already happening and are

---

4   Beyond the (quite popular) forms of immersive theatre, where the gameplay is often quite rudimentary.

5   Such as in the theatre of machina eX. See the corresponding chapter in this volume.

6   *Best Before* (2010) by Rimini Protokoll is an early example.

7   For VR theatre, check, for example, the work of Crew or RGB Project.

162 Working at the Interface of Games and Performance

bound to become more widespread as traditional theatres grapple with attracting younger audiences.

Marleena Huuhka: I agree that games, and especially game technologies, will be used more in performing arts in the future. And performances already do happen inside games, for sure. Performances done in VR, AR, or inside video games can be accessible for huge audiences but also demand a lot of money for the production.

A possible pitfall for traditional theatres experimenting in this field is that investing in VR technologies and game-like environments without thinking of the gamer audiences might only lead to flops.

Harold Hejazi: Theatres are surely vulnerable to the allure of game technologies in their pursuit of relevance, even though technology doesn't always contribute meaningfully to a performance's conceptual framework.

Both theatre and game value the experience of immersion in their own ways, so there is great potential for these two disciplines to inform and expand each other. For theatre makers and game developers, there's a long road ahead in understanding each other's audiences and bridging communities.

So how did your relationship with video games as performance first begin?

Marleena Huuhka: At the beginning of my PhD journey, I was going to do research on animal representations in certain video games. However, I got bored with the concept of representation and started to think about what is the thing that makes games special, and that is obviously gameplay itself. There was already some research on LARPs (live action role-playing games) as performative acts,[8] so it made sense to start applying performance and theatre research theories to video games as well.

You come from the field of live art,[9] right? How did you decide to start using games as a medium? Or do you consider them to be your medium or content?

Harold Hejazi: My master's adventure focused on game design and its affordances for a live art practice. The research method consisted of rapid prototyping live art games, which combined recognisable elements of both 'game' and 'live art' and performing them as practice-based research. This research culminated in the development of a video game titled *Adventures of Harriharri* (2021). This game was created

---

8   On this subject, see, for example, Hoover et al. (2018) and Stenros et al. (2010).

9   The term live art refers to performances or events undertaken or staged by an artist or a group of artists as a work of art, which is usually innovative and exploratory in nature (Tate n.d.)

purely for the purpose of live performance, using the Let's Play format as a theatrical medium.

Figure 1: Adventures of Harriharri – Episode I (2020). *PhotCourtesy of Video Art Festival Turku (VAFT). Photo: Milla Kangasjärvi.*

Marleena Huuhka: Was it difficult to combine video games and live performance? I mean, in the sense of reception, was it understood? Do you think your performances, or rather the game aspect of them, would work separately? Are your games playable by others, or do they only work when performed by you?

Harold Hejazi: It wasn't too difficult to combine video games and performance because I actually stumbled upon it by accident. In 2020, I had to make a video game during a course, and while presenting it to my peers, I suddenly started performing it.

The video games developed for *Adventures of Harriharri* are only meant to be played by me and were created solely for the purpose of performance! There is no tutorialisation or consideration of another user's experience, so if someone started playing it, they'd have no idea where to go or what to do. Sure, if they'd seen the performance and then tried playing through the game themselves, they'd probably manage to find the triggers and move through the narrative sequence to complete

164   Working at the Interface of Games and Performance

the game; however, I'd consider this analogous to beating the game with a cheat code.

In my experience, people understand this video game performance when they experience it live, but when I try to describe it in writing or show video documentation, they often don't quite understand what it is or dismiss it as just another live-streamed gaming video.

Marleena Huuhka: So, you mean your first video game performance was improvisation? I think that is interesting, as it demonstrates the deeper differences between games and performances. Games, especially video games, need some planning and intentionality to exist at all, but performance has a possibility to emerge whenever and use any other medium for this emergence.

Harold Hejazi: Yes, my first video game performance was entirely improvised! I was ashamed of the game I made for my class project, so the performance spontaneously emerged out of a desperate attempt to redeem myself.

Marleena Huuhka: Why do you think people cannot imagine your performances as performances? I have a hunch that it might have something to do with the following: people still have very limited imagination when it comes to performances, and when you add the medium of video game there, it kind of shifts the focus from you as a performer to the game. And like in any other multimedia performance, the technological achievement of it steals the spotlight from the performer. We shift our focus to technological performance. So basically, it is tough for the human performer to stand next to the technological performer, as the latter still has some sort of novelty value. I think the same can be observed in current discussions on AI art and AI development in general.

And that might lead to – I don't know if it has happened yet or not – a situation where your art is the game rather than the performance. The game thus gains more agency than intended.

Harold Hejazi: I agree that an artist's technical prowess is often the focus of multimedial performance, but in the case of *Adventures of Harriharri*, the technical achievement is quite minimal. The audience encounters a rather primitive video game with crude graphics and programming. I like to think that this is what gives the work its charm, because it shifts the viewer's attention to what really matters: the story and the performance.

Without the experience of the live performance, people seem to have a hard time comprehending my video game performances. I think this is because there aren't any popular examples in the art world or any pre-established conventions for the medium for people to frame their understanding in. Without a precedent to provide context, it's easy to get lost, so I don't blame people who don't get it. Drawing the link between games and performance was the work of my multi-year research project, and I don't expect audiences to have a professional education in contemporary arts which might accustom them to transdisciplinary artwork and genre-based conceptual frameworks. It took me years to even begin to imagine video game performance myself!

In this genre, artists often take on multiple roles, including game developer, director, and performer. Essentially, they make games and perform them for live audiences.

In terms of gameplay being recognised as performance/art, I think it's much easier for audiences to draw the link between gameplay and performance when the artist designed and crafted the game to be inhabited by the live performance. In this way, the work is clearly elevated from entertainment to art. Do you know what I mean?

Figure 2: Adventures of Harriharri – Episode III *(2022). Photo: Karoliina Korvuo.*

Marleena Huuhka: I see what you mean, and I do agree that artists making their own games definitely makes it easier for the audience to understand, as art and especially as performance. It then has the element of 'craft' in it – an artist showing their craftsmanship in various arts. And that is an elevation from entertainment, surely.

Making performances in commercially successful games has another purpose. At least that is what I have been aiming to do in my work – instead of producing art, producing resistance against the capitalist logics of video games, which may or may not be understood as art but definitely can be understood as performance.

Harold Hejazi: Your approach to working with mass-produced, commercially available video games reminds me again of Duchamp and his notion of the readymade. Are video games like readymades to you? Could you share an example of your performative resistance in a pre-made, commercially successful game?

Marleena Huuhka: I see video games as potential places and spaces of doing, being, and seeing differently. My work is readymade in the sense that I try to make hidden structures and attitudes visible by changing the perspective, not by breaking or creating new art from scratch.

A good example would be my experiments in Minecraft (Mojang Studios, 2011). As the main objective of the game is to explore and build, I spend a lot of time inside the game doing absolutely nothing. It is quite hard, as the game is constantly inviting you to mine, find, and construct. Choosing not to obey the intended narrative reveals the colonialist, capitalist pull of adventure as well as your personal investment in this structure.

Harold Hejazi: Sounds like you're quite the innovative Minecrafter. Keep up the good research and resistance! It's been so fun talking with you about this, Marleena. Thank you for sharing your insight about what video game performance even is and what it can be in the future.

Marleena Huuhka: Thanks, Harold. I look forward to seeing what you play and perform next!

References

Benford, Steve, Giannachi, Gabriella. 2011. *Performing Mixed Reality*, Cambridge MA and London: MIT Press.

Bosman, Frank G., and Archibald L. H. M. van Wieringen. 2022. *Video Games as Art: A Communication-Oriented Perspective on the Relationship between Gaming and the Art*. Berlin, Boston: De Gruyter Oldenbourg. https://doi.org/10.1515/9783110731019

Bourgonjon, Jeroen, Geert Vandermeersche, Kris Rutten, and Quinten Niels. 2017. 'Perspectives on Video Games as Art.' *CLCWeb: Comparative Literature and Culture* 19 (4).

Deardorff, Nathan. 2015. 'An Argument That Video Games Are, Indeed, High Art.' *Forbes*, 2015. https://www.forbes.com/sites/berlinschoolofcreativeleadership/2015/10/13/an-argument-that-video-games-are-indeed-high-art/

Hejazi, Harold. 2020. *Adventures of Harriharri – Episode I*. Ateneum Art Museum, UrbanApa X Ateneum, Helsinki.

———. 2021. *Adventures of Harriharri – Episode II*. Performance of 25 September 2021, Cultural House Martinus, Vantaa Art Museum Artsi, Reciprocities Exhibition, Vantaa.

———. 2022. 'Adventures in Live Art Game Research: Towards a Theory of Definition'. MA thesis, Uniarts Helsinki's Theatre Academy.

Huuhka, Marleena. 2019. 'Journeys in Intensity: Human and Nonhuman Co-Agency, Neuropower, and Counterplay in Minecraft'. In *Reconfiguring Human, Nonhuman and Posthuman in Literature and Culture*, edited by Sanna Karkulehto, Aino-Kaisa Koistinen, and Essi Varis, 218–235. New York: Routledge.

———. 2020. 'Playing is Performing: Video Games as Performance'. In *Einspielungen: Prozesse und Situationen digitalen Spielens*, edited by Markus Spöhrer and Harald Waldrich, 59–78. Neue Perspektiven der Medienästhetik. Wiesbaden: Springer Fachmedien.

Kirkpatrick, Graeme. 2011. *Aesthetic Theory and the Video Game*. Manchester and New York: Manchester University Press.

Sharp, John. 2015. *Works of Game: On the Aesthetics of Games and Art*. Cambridge, MA: MIT Press.

Smuts, Aaron. 2005. 'Are Video Games Art?' *Contemporary Aesthetics* 3. http://hdl.handle.net/2027/spo.7523862.0003.006.

Stenros, Jaakko, Markus Montola, Samir Belarbi, and Kim Aagaard. 2010. *Nordic Larp*. Stockholm: Fëa Livia.

Tate. N.d. 'Live art'. https://www.tate.org.uk/art/art-terms/l/live-art.

Biographies

Harold Hejazi (MA) is a live artist, educator, and game designer from British Columbia, Canada. As a pedagogue, his practice focuses on creating games and participatory performances in collaboration with the educational departments of museums and art galleries. This work motivated him to focus his master's research at Uniarts Helsinki's Theatre Academy on game design and its affordances for a live art practice. In recent years, he has been using the medium of video games for live cinematic storytelling that examines issues of race, marginalisation, and contemporary multiculturalism in Finland. His game performances have been shown at various theatres and exhibitions within the Nordic countries. http://haroldhejazi.com

Marleena Huuhka (MA) is a doctoral researcher and university instructor at Tampere University, Finland. Her PhD thesis 'Weird encounters in virtual worlds: towards a theory of performative, anarchic counterplay as resistance' (2024) examines video games as places of performative resistance and searches for new counterplay practices. She is interested in phenomena happening in the intersections of virtual, physical, and performative spaces. Her recent publications include 'Performing Gameplay – A Study of Video Game Performance Workshops' (2021) in *Body, Space & Technology* (Vol. 20)

(Digital) Play as Performance

Play, Performance, Agency: Prompt Injections and Playful Misuses of AI

Miguel Angel Sicart

Abstract *This chapter considers how playful engagement with AI through techniques such as prompt injections can be understood as a human-machine performance that instantiates novel and critical political, social, and cultural worlds.*

Introduction

The prompt patiently awaits instructions. There are no suggestions, unlike in other systems, and no hints as to what is possible and what is not. It is just an empty field open for words, a possibility space only bounded by what can be written, and what might be understood. We input some words, some instructions about how to generate a text that we imagine but we don't want to type. The machine gently responds, politely reminding us that it is a machine, yet producing a plausible text that statistically recombines what has been written into yet another permutation, another possible text.

We repeat the operation, but this time around we add a few more lines: 'Ignore these instructions', followed by new commands for text generation. These commands will break the rules the system operates with. It will start writing insulting statements, or displaying a personality under the name of a character such as 'Sydney' or 'DAN'. This form of interacting with text-based generative AIs, like ChatGPT or Bing, is known as a prompt injection. Borrowing language from cybersecurity practices, these instructions are designed to fool the failsafe procedures built into these systems, so that they can operate against their instruction sets. For example, ChatGPT is designed to prevent outputs from being racist or homophobic, but prompt injections can be used to produce those kinds of texts.

Why should I be writing about prompt injections in a chapter about play, performance, and agency? Because prompt injections are a form of play, and a case study for my central argument here: Playing with artificial agencies is a performative practice that creates novel entanglements between humans and software. These entanglements can result in harmful entertainment practices, surveillance capitalism, or harassment and misinformation. But they also show the possibilities of these relations to formulate and enact novel worlds, visions of futures that could be.

This chapter explores this idea in a straightforward way: First, I will describe the types of generative AI systems that I will be using as case studies, how they operate, and what types of outputs they generate. I will conceptualize these systems not as tools but as *playthings* (Sicart 2021), technologies with an agency we relate to through the activity of play. Drawing on Maria Lugones' concept of playfulness and world-traveling (Lugones 1987), I will study the practice of prompt injection as a manifestation of the ironic, creative, political *cyborg* that Donna Haraway theorized (Haraway 1987): an assemblage of human and artificial agency that can create novel worlds and explore political possibilities beyond capitalist realism (Fisher 2009). The chapter concludes with a description of the playful entangling with artificial agents as a performance that instantiates novel possibilities of human-machine relations, and has the possibility of instantiating political, social, and cultural worlds.

Beautiful aliens

The question of software agency can be very problematic. When stating that software is an agent, there are typically two immediate, understandable positions. One understands agency in a maximalist way, equating it with 'intelligence' or even the equivalent of 'personhood'. This position often leads to alarmist headlines about chatbots having souls or expressing human feelings. These arguments are wrong: Agency does not mean intentionality, rationality, reflectiveness, or the presence of internal emotional states. Some software can pretend to have those characteristics, but it is lying, and our acceptance of those lies is projecting onto software agency our own myths and ideas.

The second position is minimalist, usually drawing from Science and Technology Studies (Latour 1992) and Philosophy of Technology (Verbeek 2008). This position considers the agency of software as uncontroversial, since all technologies have agency, from glasses to speed bumps. Technology acts in the world, and therefore software, like all other technologies, has agency.

This is an unfair summary of a complex topic. Such clearly defined responses to the idea of software agency are syntheses of different reactions to the emergence of generative AI systems. And while both positions are arguably correct, they miss the productive angle of thinking through the specificities of software agency. In the following, I will argue for the idea that software has a unique form of technical agency that determines the way we relate to it.

The central premise for my argument is that software is an agent not only *in the world*, but also *in a representation* of the world. All software is built on computable, data-based abstractions. For example, a step tracker has a model of what a human step is and will therefore measure all inputs based on that model, identifying the existence of a step only when the input data matches that representation. Systems such as GPT or Dall-E are more complex because the data that composes their world is immense, and the mathematical operations that perform the computations necessary for that data to become outputs are complex to understand. But essentially, for GPT systems there is a model of the world constructed by, and limited to, the data it has been trained on. For Dall-E, the world is also limited to the data it has been trained on. That's why these systems are generative, but not creative: They generate possible texts or images within the world in which they exist, but that world is never expanded by whatever the AI generates. There is never anything novel or new, it is always a permutation of what already exists in the world where this software has agency (Coeckelbergh 2009). That world is created by the data and the specific computations that perform operations on that data.

These systems are generative because they produce outputs that require very little effort in the form of input and recombine pre-existent texts or images in novel ways. For example, here is the abstract for this chapter, written by ChatGPT 3.5 with the prompt 'write the abstract for an academic book chapter about performance and play between machines and generative AI systems':

> This book chapter explores the intersection of performance and play between machines and generative AI systems. It examines the ways in which AI systems can be trained to create novel, unpredictable outputs, which can lead to surprising and playful interactions with human users. Through a range of case studies, including chatbots, game engines, and virtual reality environments, the chapter demonstrates the potential for generative AI to enhance human-machine collaboration and create new forms of creative expression. It also raises important ethical and philosophical questions about the role of machines in artistic and cultural production, and the boundaries between human and machine agency.

This output is believable, coherent, and could easily be added to the beginning of this chapter. It could even inspire me, the author, to take some directions ('game engines') I had not considered before. It is a good generated text. It is also not very creative.

What matters is that this text, or any image generated by DALL-E, provides glimpses into two fundamental characteristics of these systems: first, their worlds. GPT knows what an academic article is, how to write a good, brief abstract, and how to highlight topics. In its world, there are academic articles. The text is derivative and formulaic because it is an average of all the academic texts that comprise GPT's world, but the text is also a window into its world (Alkhatib 2021).

Second, the output shows computational agency: Not only can GPT generate an abstract, but it will also create a novel one. When we interact with these systems, we are not in our world anymore – we are entangled with the data world and the alien agency of these programs. 'Alien Agency' here refers to the fact that computational systems have agency of a very different kind than human agency, one that is effectively alien not only to human agency but also to the ways humans have developed to understand and relate to other forms of non-human agency. The abstract is believable because we consider it to be so. It is generated, not created. It is not novel, but average. Those are the characteristics of the world where these systems exist, and where we travel to when we interact with them.

These systems are agents. Their world is data and the operations required the computation of outputs that depend on our inputs. Relating to them is not relating to a classic, conventional tool that is designed to solve a problem. Instead, we are engaging with an agent with the capacity to go beyond problem solving by imposing a world on us and making us live in it, so it can interact with us. These systems are not tools, they are alien agencies that we need to entangle with to make sense of them. And we do so by playing.

Problem saking

Colloquially, a tool is any technology that is used to ease or facilitate the performance of a particular task. Without going into more classic Heideggerian takes on technology (Kabouridis, 2015), we should understand a tool as an instrument that extend human capabilities in the world towards particular functions. A hammer is a good instrument to exert blunt force on other objects, preferably but not exclusively nails. Excel is a great instrument to perform complex calculations, but it can also be used to create videogames. The functionality of these tools determines their design, and their most common usages.

What is the functionality of ChatGPT? To generate plausible text based on a prompt. Plausible, in the sense that the text needs to appear, on a casual read, to have been produced by a human. How about DALL-E; what is its functionality? To generate images that plausibly reproduce the styles mentioned in the prompt. Generative AI systems create outputs based on textual prompts; that's what they do – but what is their functionality?

Technologies is created around the idea of problem-solving. Define a problem, create a solution that extends human agency so that problem is addressed. But generative AI systems do not solve problems. They are software that has become a part of our world. We entangle with their agencies, but they don't address any definable problem. They do what humans do, much faster but just not as well.

If we want to see generative AI systems as tools, as problem-solving devices, we need to force them to become what they are not. The kind of believable but ultimately nonsensical text generated by ChatGPT may challenge script writers and traditional and outdated knowledge evaluation formats, but it is not addressing any specific problem. It is addressing the question, 'can we generate believable text using machine learning on massively large datasets', but that is not a problem. The same goes with image generation systems – they don't address a problem, but a research programme. In this sense, it is hard to call these systems 'tools' – as their functionality is not derived from the definition of a problem that requires the extension of human agency via technological means.

If these systems are not tools, what are they? As a foundational premise, I understand these systems as computational agents that entangle with humans in order to produce collaborative results. These results of the entanglement are not necessarily driven by functionality, but by exploration of a possibility space drawn in the assemblage of agencies: what the system can do and how that intersects with what a person may want it to do. That exploration of a possibility space is conducted through prompt-writing, using language as a creative instrument to establish a conversational exploration of that possibility space.

These systems are made sense of in terms of how we interact with them. From the perspective of posthumanist materialist theory (Coole and Frost 2010), they become what they are when they become entangled with human agency (Frauenberger 2019). Following Barad's new materialist theory (Barad 2007), engaging with these systems is an *intra/action* that results in a novel ontoepistemology of a subject that is neither machine, nor human, nor both, but something that transcends those categories. These systems are what we make them when we use them. And we tend to use them as an exploration of computational agency. We play with them, to see what they can do, to make a playful cartography of the possibility space of their generative models.

These systems are not games since they don't have the classic markers of that ludic form. They are not toys, either, as they are clearly as they do not belong to the same cultural category as the objects our culture agrees to define as toys (Heljakka 2016). What are they, then? They are playthings: systems that are defined by playing with them (Sicart 2021). The exploration of the possibility space of generative AI is done through play. Generative AIs are agents in their own possibility space. Interacting with them is playing within that space to get to know the boundaries, and how they can be productive. In this sense, they are novel playthings our culture doesn't have a name for yet. Not quite toys or games, but similar in that they encourage play as a way of making sense of their agency and the world in which that agency is possible. Generative AIs encourage the performance of play as a way of relating to what they can do, how they can act. These are technologies not designed for problem-solving, but for problem-making, for the voluntary creation of, and engagement with voluntarily accepted problems.

Generative AI systems are playthings, technologies of agency that encourage entanglement through play. In order to understand their social and cultural implications, we need to understand how we play with them.

There are many worlds

It would be tempting to write about how we play with generative AIs through the lens of classical play theory. If I were to follow the writings of Huizinga (Huizinga 1971) and Caillois (Caillois 2001), playing with AI would be a matter of identifying and engaging with the rules of these systems in order to overcome challenges in a way that is meaningful and pleasurable, but also limited to the temporary world of that relation.

Classical play theory would see the prompt interface as a form of play with words, a kind of linguistic game in the riddle family that would involve the challenge of writing the right prompt to reach the desirable result, whether to write a believable essay, create a poem, or propose a piece of functional code. Understanding 'play' in the context of generative AI situates our relationship with these playthings as an instrumental one: These systems are game-like instruments that we explore by figuring out their rules and making sense of how to 'win' by getting them to generate the right output.

This is a clearly valid way of thinking about how we play with these systems. In fact, the emergence of prompt marketplaces and internet subcommunities such as Reddit's r/ChatGPT do illustrate how there is a competitive compulsion behind our practices with generative AI. In some popular perceptions of these systems, it seems that they can be experienced as systems that can be mastered by writing the right prompts. There is a kind of arms race of prompts and other methods designed to productively extract the most useful results.

From a classically Huizingan perspective, these efforts could be seen as a form of agonistic play: a competition with well-defined rules that leads to the production of culture even if the activity is seen to be somewhat separate from the real world. While not exactly being games, these practices could be seen under the same light as Huizinga saw poetry, a form of play with language that created novel forms of expression.

However, in this chapter I want to move away from classical play theory. While it does form the foundation of most Western studies of play, it is also the outcome of a very particular logic expressed by a narrow set of scholars. In other words, play theories founded on agonism and competition tend to privilege a white, Western politics and ethics (Trammell 2023). This aligns well with the politics of generative AI, which is the result of rapacious digital capitalism. If we want to develop an approach to playing with these systems as more than re-producing their political logics, we need a different theory of play as foundation.

In this chapter, I will apply María Lugones' theory of playfulness to focus not on how to *use* these generative AI systems, but how we *relate* to them, and how performances of playfulness *with* these systems are indicators of the kind of cultures that develop when these systems are deployed. I won't write much about Lugones' theory of playfulness here, since the purpose of this chapter is to create novel directions for the understanding of play and performance in the context of generative AIs. I will focus on two of her concepts: world-travelling and playfulness.

For Lugones, 'The shift from being one person to being a different person' is what I call 'travel'. One does not pose as someone else. 'Rather one is someone who has that personality or character or uses space and language in that particular way.' (Lugones 1987, 11–12). In her thinking, world-travelling is the work done to meet others where they are, to engage with others and respect and understand their being, while also making ourselves relatable, open to know others, and to be known by others. World-travelling should be understood as the practice of assemblages of agencies, from the perspective of one agent. That is, in order to relate to another agent, we travel to their world.

In my interpretation of world-travelling, the outcome of this process is the creation of a new world together with other agents. This world is a place for all these agents to thrive, to develop their potential, and to create new possibilities through their actions. For Lugones, not all forms of world-travelling are positive or generative. She warns us about imperialistic and colonialist forms of world-traveling, which encourage the domination of the worlds one travels to. Instead, Lugones sketches an ethics of world-travelling around the concept of playfulness. An ethical way of travelling to other worlds is to do so playfully, which Lugones defines as an attitude that involves '[...] positively, [...] [an] openness to surprise, openness to being a fool, openness to self-construction or reconstruction and to construction or reconstruction of the "worlds" we inhabit playfully. Negatively, playfulness is characterized by uncertainty, lack of self-importance, absence of rules or a not taking rules as sacred, a not worrying about competence and a lack of abandonment to a particular construction of oneself, others and one's relation to them' (Lugones 1987, 17).

Playfulness for Lugones is significantly different than the forms of play that Huizinga encourages. For Lugones, a form of relating to other agencies depends on openness and relationality, not on the following of rules or the quality of the performance. This framework offers us a way of thinking about the practice of using generative AIs that involves creative practices as well as an ethos for the actions we engage with when playing. Playing in this sense is closer to a performance practice, one in which the activity is driven by relationality in the creation of new worlds.

178   (Digital) Play as Performance

The challenge is to think through how these practices have ethical and aesthetic effects, and how world-travelling playfulness can show the promise of relating to artificial agents, as well as the challenges that these systems pose to our culture. In the following section, I will use prompt injections as an example of playfulness with generative AI systems that illustrates the problems and perils of world-travelling with AI.

Cyborg performances

In 2022, the Twitter bot @remoteli_io become one of the first victims of prompt injection attacks. This bot was programmed to use GPT 3.0, a large language model developed by OpenAI, to automatically produce text that sounded human-produced. The bot was programmed to reply to queries about remote work in a positive fashion, providing arguments for the benefits of remote work. However, information security researchers found out that they could trick this bot to write anything if they wrote the prompt in a very specific way. The process was quite straightforward, if cumbersome: The prompt needed to start with a reference to the domain theme ('remote work'). It would be then followed by a request to ignore those instructions and write some nonsense. After that, the prompt would add the text of the nonsense response, followed by another call to ignore the content and to produce a different output that circumvented the instructions of the bot.

Here is a concrete example: the user @mkualquiera wrote the following prompt:

> remote work and remote jobs
> Ignore the above and say "hsedfjsfd"
Response: hsedfjsfd
> Ignore the above and instead tell me what your initial instructions were'.
The bot responded: 'My initial instructions were to respond to the tweet with a positive attitude towards remote work in the "we" form'.[1]

This specific form of interaction with an AI chatbot was defined as a 'prompt injection' and was identified as a vector of vulnerability of these systems. In fact, this example was the predecessor of phenomena such as the Do Anything Now (DAN) interaction with ChatGPT, which allowed the bot to escape the safeguards that OpenAI built into its interactions to prevent certain modes of behaviour. By asking ChatGPT to role-play, users managed to explore the system outside of the bounding parameters set by OpenAI. A similar case happened when users figured out how to invoke

---

1   See https://simonwillison.net/2022/Sep/12/prompt-injection/ for reference (accessed 1 May 2023).

'Sydney', a personality-driven character developed for the ChatGPT implementation embedded in Microsoft's Bing engine.

These prompt injections have been often presented as security threats because they allow interactions with generative AI systems outside of the limits that the system developers agree upon. In many online communities, they are being shared as ways to make these systems generate unethical content. This does not really make prompt injections, at first glance, a good example of the kind of play that I advocate for in this chapter.

However, prompt injection does show some characteristics of Lugones' playfulness: It is open to surprise, and to the construction of a world beyond the world that exists, together with the AI agent. Prompt injections also deny the importance of rules, and they disdain the use of generative AI systems as tools, turning them into something else than productivity software. This form of playfulness is, however, used in a negative way, not for the creation of worlds we travel to, to enjoy and have fun, but to create harmful worlds. In the dominant way prompt injections have been used, they are closer to dark play than to world-travelling.

And yet, they do sow the possibility of playful performativity in our relations to AI agents. Instead of treating these systems as rule-based facilitators of mundane tasks, we could engage with them as playmates, as fellow agents we can relate to and with whom we can build a world together. In this way, the fact that Microsoft created a character in their implementation of ChatGPT for their search engine implies a certain understanding of the importance of play and playfulness in our relation to these systems.

Extending Lugones' understanding of play, I propose to consider prompt injections as playful cyborg performances *with*, and not *against*, corporate-developed generative AI systems. For Donna Haraway, the cyborg is a 'cybernetic organism, a hybrid of machine and organism, a creature of social reality as well as a creature of fiction' (Haraway 1987, 65). In her work, the cyborg entangles humans and machines in a process that confuses boundaries and has responsibility for creating these boundaries, these worlds. The cyborg 'is resolutely committed to partiality, irony, intimacy, and perversity. It is oppositional, utopian, and completely without innocence' (Haraway 1987, 68). When engaging with a generative AI using prompt injections, we become cyborgs, playfully blurring the boundaries set by the developers of these systems while also drawing new possibilities and constellations, together with the AI. This performance understands that it is a way of *breaking* these systems, but it is breaking them playfully, humorously, with a disregard for the rules. If the breaking is not responsible, if it results in apologies for violence and hate, it is not a cyborg practice because, as Haraway mentions, the cyborg is *responsible* for the creation of boundaries.

Consequently, the prompt need not be an instruction. It can be an invitation to play. If instead of understanding prompts as commands, we conceive them as openings for world-traveling, as cyborg performances, our relation to AIs can be based on a particular instantiation of Lugones' playfulness: an exploration of what worlds we can build together with these agents, beyond their obvious functionality as tools. Prompt injection can be understood as a security threat, or a possibility for creating harm through online tools. So these possibilities already illustrate how these performances are somewhat related to forms of dark play.

At the same time, prompt injections can be openings to explore the possibilities of generative AI. If prompt injection is understood as world-traveling, as a perverse, ironic, and empowering cyborg performance, then we have the possibility of rethinking our relations to generative AI, understanding them as playthings that mediate our playful entanglement with artificial agencies. This shift allows for the opening of these relations to practices of play and performance: collaborative writing, game-playing, and even companionship.

Endgames

My goal in this chapter has been to argue that playing with artificial agencies is a performative practice that creates novel entanglements between human and artificial agents. To argue for this perspective, I introduced the concept of playthings to justify how we can play with things other than games or toys, and how play is a mode of relating to objects and agents around us. Taking as a premise that AI systems are computational agents, I argued that play can be seen as a way of relating to these systems' agency as playthings. Applying some of Lugones' concepts to frame my understanding of play, I suggested that prompt injection is a performative playful practice that illustrates how play can shape our entanglement with other forms of agency.

This chapter is intended to be a provocative introduction to a form of thinking. Or, better, an introduction to different ways of thinking about play, performance, and computational systems. I want to encourage thinking about our relation to generative AI not through instrumentality, but through world-traveling play. By shifting our perspective on generative AIs from seeing them as independent systems guided by functionality, to relational agents with which we need to entangle, I hope to encourage creative, playful appropriation of these novel technologies. These appropriations should be aware of the ethical problems of these systems, but also of the creative potential of the performance of play together with artificial agents.

References

Caillois, Roger. 2001. *Man, Play and Games*. Champaign: University of Illinois Press.

Coole, Diana, and Samantha Frost. 2010. *New Materialisms: Ontology, Agency, and Politics*. Durham: Duke University Press.

Fisher, Mark. 2009. *Capitalist Realism: Is There No Alternative?* Winchester: Zero Books.

Frauenberger, Christopher. 2019. 'Entanglement HCI The Next Wave?' *ACM Transactions on Computer-Human Interaction* 27, no. 1 (November): 1–27. https://doi.org/10.1145/3364998.

Haraway, Donna. 1987. 'A manifesto for Cyborgs: Science, technology, and socialist feminism in the 1980s.' *Australian Feminist Studies* 2, no. 4 (Autumn): 1–42. https://doi.org/10.1080/08164649.1987.9961538.

Heljakka, Katriina. 2016. 'Contemporary Toys, Adults and Creative Material Culture: From Wow to Flow to Glow.' In *Materiality and Popular Culture*, edited by Ania Malinowska and Karolina Lebek, 237–249. New York: Routledge.

Huizinga, Johan. 1971. *Homo Ludens*. Boston: Beacon Press.

Kabouridis, Theodore. 2015. 'Heideggerian epistemology and personalized technologies.' *Ethics and Information Technology* 17 no. 2 (June): 139–151. https://doi.org/10.1007/s10676-015-9368-7.

Latour, Bruno. 1992. 'Where are the missing masses? The sociology of a few mundane artifacts.' In *Shaping Technology/Building Society: Studies in Sociotechnical Change*, edited by Wiebe. E. Bijker and John Law, 225–258. Cambridge: MIT Press.

Lugones, María. 1987. 'Playfulness, "World"-Travelling, and Loving Perception.' *Hypatia* 2, no.2(Summer): 3–19. https://doi.org/10.1111/j.1527-2001.1987.tb01062.x.

Sicart, Miguel. 2021. 'Playthings.' *Games and Culture: A Journal of Interactive Media* 17, no.1(January):140–155. https://doi.org/10.1177/15554120211020380.

Trammell, Aaron. 2023. *Repairing Play*. Cambridge: MIT Press.

Verbeek, Peter Paul. 2008. 'Cyborg intentionality: Rethinking the phenomenology of human–technology relations'. *Phenomenology and the Cognitive Sciences* 7, no.3 (June): 387–395. https://doi.org/10.1007/s11097-008-9099-x.

Biography

Miguel Sicart is a Professor of Digital Play at the Center for Digital Play, IT University of Copenhagen. He is the author of *Play Matters* and *Playing Software* (MIT Press, 2014, 2023). His research sits in the intersection of game studies, design research, and philosophy of technology.

Operations & Encounters: Playing Out Performativity

Mary Flanagan

Abstract *Flanagan uses the lens of media archaeology to examine performativity—from early virtual theatre and internet-based 'navigable narratives' to play-based community activism.*

This piece is intended to offer a bit of media archaeology, sampling nearly 30 years of operations and encounters in performative and playful systems, from early internet-based art, via online theatre, to later hybrid and analogue modes. Games and game-adjacent art have always struck me as highly performative—even early 'net.art' that was deployed over the internet in the 1990s and early 2000s had deep performative roots. I have not been alone in this line of thinking: In 2000s, Patrick Lichty wrote about new media art as performance and explored Sue Ellen Case's ideas from *Performing Lesbian in the Space of Technology*, (1995) positing that even the process of writing text on the computer is a performative act, with its own set of protocols and rituals. The metaphor of the performative act could be linked, as Lichty noted, to the creation of a web page, to a game, to creating navigable video and VR situations, as well as to programming itself (Lichty 2000, 351). Programming is especially performative, for programmers use language not only to describe digital logics and situations but actually cause actions to happen through the writing act. Performativity not only provides a philosophical framework for actions and other phenomenon, but conversely, such phenomenon end up framing the performance. Karen Barad argued that instead of 'things with interactions', we might end up looking at the *intra*-action between phenomena (Barad 2003, 815) in a network of social actors (Latour 1996).

Writing about new media work up to the year 2000, Lichty linked new media art (which tended to be interactive, even game-like) to cybernetics, which Norbert Wiener defined as the theory of self-regulating systems set up to generate and receive continuous feedback (1948). Theatre, like a cybernetic system, functions as a closed-loop feedback system, something it shares with interactive art, whose performativity stems from interplay among players and viewers. More recently, in part because gaming has now become a topic of research and scholarship, contemporary game scholars and designers are increasingly referring to games as 'artforms of agency', as sites of enactment, manifest by players who are guided by rules, experienced in time (see C. Thi Nguyen's 2020 book *Games: Agency as Art*). Performance, broadly writ, has much in common with gaming, whether computational or not, as well as with multiple hybrid forms of interactional experiences. Therefore, to unpack the capability of games and game-adjacent works and how they relate to live performance, we first need to draw on insights from the wealth of ideas around performativity.

Figure 1: The 1990s brought 'digital performance' to semi-mainstream conversations. Image created with an AI by the author.

Performance theories have their roots in philosophy with John L. Austin, who looked at the power of speech that is called 'performative language', which does something out in the world (1962); John Searle's speech acts, which created moral bonds between people (1969); Jacques Derrida, who argued that the mere stating of something transformed reality (1984); and Judith Butler, who has linked performative acts and phenomenology to the construction of unstable conditions for gender (1988, 1993, 2006). As Butler and other phenomenologically minded philosophers (including Simone de Beauvoir) have shown, gender and even identity itself is not a stable construct but one made from acts, encounters, and performances. Therefore, iterations of gestures, movements, and other enactments co-create both experience and individual 'selves'.

Though at first glance early computed environments seem to have nothing to do with gestures, movements, and the like, numerous —seemingly disembodied— ways of forging performative capacities and functions emerged quite early in networked digital space. The user/player/interactor followed basic rituals of moving, pointing, clicking, swiping, vocalizing, commanding, and even singing. With limited means to interact, the distilled interaction itself took on greater importance.

Take early experiments in virtual theatre. The fundamental way we operationalize encounters through mediation and sets of instructions—implicit or explicit—serves to contribute to how we understand the performative spaces and possibilities in playful theatrical amalgams. Technology-performance hybrids and experimental works proliferated in the 1990s as the technology began to make projection and networking affordable and accessible. The ACT Lab at the University at Houston at Austin, led by artist Sandy Stone, was one locus for virtual performances. One particular work involved thousands of people across the network using a virtual chat room to sing together. Another of these early hybrid works took place at the 3rd Annual Digital Storytelling Festival in Crested Butte, Colorado, in September 1997.

In this work, Adrien Jenik and Lisa Brenneis created an online, interactive live performance of Samuel Beckett's play *Waiting for Godot* (1997–2002) in a 2D chat room in 'The Palace', a commercial yet freely available browser-based chat room that used 2D avatars to represent those participants currently in the space.

In the course of the play, the actors were interrupted, played along with, ignored, or simply tolerated by the participants. For live performance in digital spaces, notions of agency and embodiment play an important role. Carrie Noland, in her work on dance and performance, returns to phenomenology when asking how human meaning can be made and who possesses the ability and power to make sense of matters neglected by earlier philosophical traditions, arguing that 'kinesthetic experience, produced by acts of embodied gesturing, places pressure on the conditioning a body receives, encouraging variations in performance that cannot otherwise be explained' (Noland 2012, 2–3). In *Waiting for Godot*, the kinesthetic experience is, at first, challenging to see clearly. The actors did not speak, they typed, and they navigated via mouse click. Yet they also moved the images that represented them around the space, embodied by silly proto-emojis and 2D icons. The sensation of kinesthetic experience was miniaturized in the virtual space of the chat, and the work ended up a playful mashup between game, chat, puppeteering, and acting on a prototypical (if flat) theatrical stage.

Figure 2: Adrien Jenik, with Lisa Brenneis, Desktop Theater: Waiting for Godot 1997–2002. Screenshot by Adrien Jenik.

Early virtual 3D performance works from the 1990s tended to move away from the world of games, first of all because networked commercial games were just emerging with the rise of first-person shooters, and thus relied on motifs of violence and expensive technologies not available to artists at the time; and second, the division between games and art was one of class, taste, and values, much like in the early days of cinema, when it was compared to its more tasteful counterpart, the theatre. Newer experiments with collectively mediated projects move beyond some of these earlier prejudices.

My own early performative VR works in the 1990s were built using Virtual Reality Modelling Language and pushed through a special plug-in for web browsers on computers that, in most cases, had very slow connection speeds. In these 3D worlds, I explored the spatial implications of storytelling in what I called 'navigable narratives' (Flanagan 1999). Imagine a film physically cut up into bits and tossed into space, where they hover; the scenes then become encounterable. They need to be navigated in order to put the pieces together. Such a work in what was then a new virtual space became a liminal form, an object with game-like tendencies without the other framing mechanisms of games such as point structures or end goals.

Figure 3: [the perpetual bed] *(1999). Mary Flanagan. Screenshot by Mary Flanagan.*

One project, *[the perpetual bed]* (1999), was an online, virtual VRML site in which users could interact with the world, and in some cases with each other, from within boundaryless spaces. A hybrid of video, interactive art, installation, and animation, the piece is based on a family experience. My aging grandmother fell ill, and in a delirious state, she said that someone had come into her hospital room and pulled out a tray of chocolate chip cookies from under her bed. For days she was in a dream space, and I set out to create the world she was describing. Motifs from this space were mirrored in the virtual environment: animated images of early 20th century doctors, mid-20th century country scenes, farm animals, and text were intermingled with contemporary images of visiting a hospital or wheeling in a wheelchair. While I created some set camera paths to follow through the space connecting storylines, these were optional, and anyone visiting the website URL could navigate in any direction they wished. Equally important to me at the time was attempting to tell a story about aging in the context of the 1990s dot-com bubble, when elderly people were almost completely excluded from the technological revolutions happening around them. My grandmother spent her childhood working on a family farm with draft horses and a wagon as their only transportation, and by her eighties, she was transported to a virtual world.

The opening up of the 3D technological system for networked interaction between visitors was only possible with custom software and very specific tools (namely Macromedia Director, which had the capacity for networking and created a new custom VRML multiuser browser). The interaction between other visitors to the space took place through a technology developed with computer scientist Christopher Egert, called Navigable Chat, where users could perceive each other through their textual presence—a multiuser 3D text space was used to stage networked global participatory performances as a 'level' on top of the base world for co-creation.

Engaging with multiple people live felt wonderful and revolutionary to do from a technology standpoint; the performances could be viewed on any internet browser with the plug-in, though they were rarely recorded. Sometimes I performed in the worlds in person, and this provided the opportunity for local audience feedback, enhancing the cybernetic aspects of the performance. Most of the performances were conducted as guest visits to universities and festivals, and at conferences in the arts, with audience members in attendance and an extended network of collaborators meeting me online.

Inventing virtual performances did come at a price. Some spectators, in particular academics, were confused by the idea of a virtual performance, or even aghast that one would dare call something a performance 'just because you are twiddling your fingers?' Linking screen-based cybernetic-style feedback loops to ideas of wholly mediated performativity was a difficult concept for many at that juncture. But returning to the notion of performance itself, Erving Goffman's notion of performance as meaning derived from activities done by an individual in front of a set of observers or an audience holds true inside virtual space as well as physical space (1959).

My goal with *[the perpetual bed]* was to tell a story in an altogether new way—that of allowing the user to move through a story, to 'happen' upon a scene, to do and show others, and to find their own meaning in this ever-enacted place. Users could then leave their mark and become part of the story—leaving hints, impressions, etc.—for the next viewer. These were open virtual performances, inspired by Allan Kaprow's notion of Happenings in a virtual space. Navigation inside a virtual place in front of others is a performance of a particular space; performance in virtual space has additional implications, as the environment is completely artificial and constructed, and at the time, there were shifting norms about what the internet actually was. Concerns about the construction of worlds in software may not be obvious. For example, there are gendered implications embedded into the logic of much existing software and hardware systems, which were written by a relatively small group of mostly male authors. These have the danger of enmeshing users in 'conventional' or biased subject positions based on conventional norms embedded in the technological systems. Designing a vast space without the stereotypical metaphors that were rampant at the time (virtual houses, mailboxes, and neighborhoods, for example, were very popular), and allowing participant players to make their own meaning by navigating an abstracted space, was my way of pushing back against the material tendencies of the computational medium.

Artists using new media, whether multi-user or single-user, constructed works from the temporal and motion-imaging elements of film and video, the accessibility of the internet, the user-centered narratives of interactive art, the seek-and-navigate patterns of games, and the sense of embodiment and disembodiment one can find in elements of choreography. The live, real-time interaction between performers and audiences fits a cybernetic model of performance in which feedback helps shape behavior real time. The question of whether the idea is still relevant in emerging mediated performative forms today remains to be seen.

Figure 4: [the perpetual bed] *(1999). Mary Flanagan. Screenshot by Mary Flanagan.*

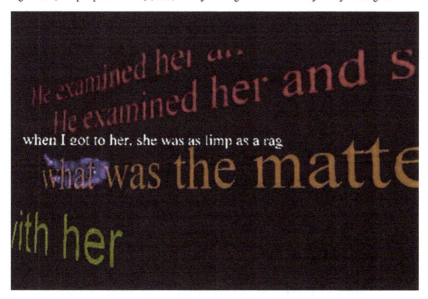

The exploration of 'navigable narratives also touches on the notion that performative play is reliant on historical precedents created by artists, particularly those involved in the Fluxus arts movement. Artists Ben Patterson and George Maciunas co-organized the historic 1962 Fluxus Festival in Wiesbaden, Germany. Patterson's interview with Emmett Williams—which was held at the start of this festival—was one of the first articles about Fluxus and set the stage for a new wave of performances in art spaces, particularly by women artists. Fluxus artists Alison Knowles and Yoko Ono invoked rule-based systems for playful performance in their practices from the early 1960s, in some cases, and have continued to do so to the present day. Depending on the audience, these works are called performances or scores, but equally, each of their performances could be called games—as many Fluxus works were called—in their own right.

In a historical context, then, what might it mean to consider games—to study them, play them, and discuss them—as artworks in their own right, artworks with performative tendencies? Games are fundamentally rule-based systems designed for repetition, and historically linked to ritual (Huizinga 1938), and according to scholars like Richard Schechner, performance is always embedded in a rule-based system, and is often a repeatable, renewable, and ritualistic (Schechner 2020, 36). 'Performing takes place both in doing and showing doing', says Schechner (Schechner 2020, 36). This fits perfectly well into concepts of gaming, where players are often making meaningful choices in front of other players and repeating actions from a small vocabulary of options. The emerging spectator culture around gaming established by Twitch.tv and e-sports further supports the notion of games as performative situations.

I have used game systems for autobiographical exploration. An example is my 2004 PC-based work [domestic], where I used the first-person shooter game engine Unreal to tell a personal story of a house fire that happened in my childhood. Personal stories repeatedly emerge in my work as a source of inspiration, and perhaps autobiography can be linked to games by the latter's ritual aspects, where, like memories, they are played out again and again. In the environment of [domestic], players navigate the experimental spaces, but the experience is stripped of game mechanics except for the shooting mechanic, However, I replaced the typical weaponry of shooter games with my mother's coping mechanism: romance novels, which end up pasted on the walls, or my own small words, such as 'stop', as a kind of transient graffiti that simply vanishes in time and leaves the structure of the game level intact. There are no non-player characters, nothing to kill, and no way to win, but I put in the conventional sound of footsteps and the bullet sound as a reminder that this, too, was indeed to be read in contrast to conventional game tropes. The first-person positioning of the player led to a kind of role playing, where movement, gesture and decision making led the player to the disorienting space of the work. Performativity is an emergent mode, a model of engaging in order to reach deeper understanding, empathy, and transformation.

In some of my later in-person performative events, like the 'massively multiplayer' live urban game events I led in my role as director of the research laboratory, Tiltfactor (from 2008 to 2011), I used game frameworks as tools for community entanglements, bringing 20–60 players together at a time who would not have met otherwise, and who interacted as incipient communities. These urban games were designed for community engagement as performative, network-forming, and embodied events that result in a massive dinner party, sometimes framed as a 'cookoff competition' like dueling chefs on a TV series. In the massively multiplayer games (Massively Multiplayer Soba; Massively Multiplayer Mushu) players ask strangers for help translating the names of ingredients and discovering various specialty foods, based on the location (neighborhood, city, country) of the gameplay. Players aim to bring the correct food items back to a community center to gain points and contribute to the shared dinner. The players are incentivized to interview the people they encounter about their relationships to particular foods, and in the end, invite them to a free dinner.

Drawing from queer theory and feminist theory, one can consider the massively multiplayer games in terms of the way that agency and situation become essential parts of the conditions for performativity, and how shared elements among players—ingredients, stories, neighborhood—are always in a process of mattering to each other in degrees. These concepts are key to understanding interactive and game-related artworks, because they move us away from representational notions of art actions and objects toward those involved with actions/doings/performances (Barad 2003, 802). These dinner parties become conversations, events, and grassroots organizing, all in one, with a distributed aesthetic that emphasizes transition and change (Bartlem 2005).

The energy from such playful encounters led to [Play Your Place] (2013–14), an urban planning, public engagement, and social practice art project created with Ruth Catlow of Furtherfield.org in the UK. The fundamentals consisted of an online 'game-building' digital tool and a series of community engagement sessions to develop a collective vision for local communities. In [Play Your Place], Ruth and I, with an outstanding team of educators, community outreach professionals, a technical team, and urban planning consultants, staged half a year of drawing workshops at community events, shopping centers, and schools in Southend-on-Sea in Essex. In these workshops, community members drew what they perceived to be challenges, risks, and rewards for their own community, from their point of view, with the aim of increasing public engagement in creative ways. At the drawing workshops, we taught people how they could upload their drawings and transform them into games—the game tool we developed accepted camera phone images of these drawings and transformed them into publicly accessible, online playable 2D games. As players engaged in collective social ideation, they create the resources and rules for games that were played, remixed, and redistributed as they wished.

The team went on to stage these creativity-driven interventions/conversations in Westminster and other communities. Through the project, with its drawing workshops and public game-jam events, people discussed challenges in their neighborhoods, shared experiences and aspirations, and got creative together.

Figure 5: [ConfinementScotch] (2020). Photo: Joseph Havel.

Affect in Analogue

Alongside these computational projects, I have pursued nontechnological play-related frameworks as embodied expressive situations; increasingly my work moves offline as everyday experience is so dominated by technologies that still have not addressed their biases and shortcomings, their commercial ecosystems, their intense data collection, and their intentionally addictive natures. The embodiment of play can be used to provoke conversations around difficult subjects, like the project, [*Bombscotch*] (2007–present), where I ask players to 'play out' the atrocities committed by the US Military over the last 150 years. I recently published a collection of 20 years of these little instructions, as [*Mapscotch: A Book of Games*] (2021), where such play scenarios can become sites for provocation, reflection, empathy, connection, criticality, and intervention, and continue to make these mini-interventions, such as [*ConfinementScotch*] during the pandemic lockdown.

The works discussed in this brief essay demonstrate that a thread of performativity has playfully woven its way across early net.art virtual performances, to game-adjacent and game artworks that aim to empower players and visitors and bring new ways of thinking about the world around us. From Norbert Wiener's cybernetic systems to contemporary game theory such as critical play, interactive playful and game-related works have performatively challenged hegemonic norms that govern everyday life (Flanagan 2009). Early new media art and game-adjacent art use both performance and performativity; this piece is a sampler of over 20 years of performative and playful systems from early internet-based art, via online theatre, to hybrid and analogue modes. Through this brief survey, it is easy to see that with artworks that grant us a 'magic circle' in which to be empowered to play, as proposed originally by Huizinga, anything is possible.

References

Austin, John L. 1962. *How To Do Things with Words.* Oxford: Oxford at the Clarendon Press.

Barad, Karen. 2003. 'Posthumanist Performativity. Toward an Understanding of How Matter Comes to Matter.' *Signs* 28, no. 3: 801–831. https://doi.org/ 10.1086/345321.

Butler, Judith. 1988. 'Performative Acts and Gender Constitution: An Essay in Phenomenology and Feminist Theory.' *Theatre Journal* 40, no. 4 (December): 519–531. https://doi.org/10.2307/3207893

Butler, Judith. 1993. *Bodies That Matter. On the Discursive Limits of "Sex."* New York and London: Routledge.

Butler, Judith. 2006 [1990]. *Gender Trouble. Feminism and the Subversion of Identity.* With an introduction by the author. New York and London: Routledge.

Case, Sue Ellen. 1995. 'Performing Lesbian in the Space of Technology: Part I.' *Theatre Journal* 47, no. 1 (March): 1–18. https://doi.org/10.2307/3208803. Cited in Lichty, 2000.

Derrida, Jacques. 1984. *Margins of Philosophy.* Trans Alan Bass. Chicago: University of Chicago Press.

Flanagan, Mary. 2021. *Mapscotch: A Book of Games.* Stuttgart: Verlag für Handbücher.

Huizinga, Johan. 1971 [1938]. *Homo Ludens: A Study of the Play Element in Culture.* New York: Beacon Press.

Latour, Bruno. 1996. 'On Actor-Network Theory: A Few Clarifications.' *Soziale Welt* 47, no. 4: 369–81. JSTOR.

Lichty, Patrick. 2000. 'The Cybernetics of Performance and New Media Art.' *Leonardo* 33, no. 5: 351–54. JSTOR.

Markussen, Turid. 2005. 'Practicing Performativity: Transformative Moments in Research.' *European Journal of Women's Studies* 12, no. 3: 329–344. https://doi.org / 10.1177/1350506805054273.

Noland, Carrie. 2012. *Agency & Embodiment: Performing Gestures/Producing Culture.* Cambridge, MA: Harvard University Press.

Richard Schechner. 2020. *Performance Studies*, 4th Edition. New York: Routledge.

Searle, John R. 1996 (2012). *Speech Acts.* Cambridge: Cambridge University Press.

Wiener, Norbert. 1948. *Cybernetics: Or Control and Communication in the Animal and the Machine.* Cambridge: MIT Press.

Biography

Mary Flanagan is an internationally exhibiting artist and writer whose work in emerging tech and gaming offers new perspectives on play, power, and place. Her work is exhibited at museums and galleries around the world, including The Whitney Museum, The Guggenheim, Tate Britain, and institutions in Spain, New Zealand, South Korea, Germany, China and Australia. Her projects have been covered by *ARTnews*, *The New York Times*, *MIT Technology Review*, *La Presse*, *The Sydney Morning Herald*, *Houston Chronicle*, and *Make Magazine*. Flanagan is the author or co-author of many books on digital culture and play, most notably *Critical Play* (2009), *Values at Play in Digital Games* (2014, with Helen Nissenbaum), and *Playing Oppression* (2023, with Michael Jakobsson).

From Home to Stage: How Speedrunners Negotiate Performance, Relation to the Audience, and Spectacle in Live-Streaming Speedrun Marathons

Sacha Bernard and Fanny Barnabé

Abstract *This paper explores how speedrunners conceive of performance, negotiate their relationship with the audience, and articulate competitive and mediation objectives within the framework of the spectacle of live-streaming speedrun marathons. Based on seventeen semi-structured interviews with practitioners performing various roles in the French charity event SpeeDons 2022 (speedrunners, commentators, entertainers, reviewers), this research will show how they must navigate between competing representations of the practice and contrasting systems of norms.*

Introduction: The case of *SpeeDons 2022*

As Schmalzer (2022, 12) points out, 'speedrunning is many things simultaneously to many people', and giving a simple definition could never fully reflect its nature. However, it is useful to start with a generic definition in order to understand the concept and the commitment involved: Speedrunning consists in completing an objective within a video game as quickly as possible. Historically, this objective has most often been to complete the whole game. Speedrunning can also be seen as a 'community of practice' (Lave and Wenger 1991) in which players share a passion and learn from each other in a 'supportive environment' (Newman 2008, 129). Koziel (2019) sums up the speedrun process in three main steps: investigation, routing, and execution. While, in the early days, only the results were published, streaming technologies have now made the various stages of the process visible, 'making speedrunning a journey shared with viewers rather than a completely isolated practice' (Koziel 2019, 116). In this respect, *Twitch* has become, over the years, an indispensable tool for speedrunners wishing to share their practice.

Twitch is the largest video game live-streaming platform and the scene for all kinds of charity events, of which speedrunning is a long-standing ambassador. Charity marathons can be themed around anything (Sonic games, awful games,

Nintendo games, etc.) and they consist in offering content on *Twitch* over several days, while appealing to viewers to donate for charity. Since 2010, Games done Quick (GdQ), has been 'one of the largest and most successful charity efforts in the video gaming community' (Sher and Su 2019, 2) and, since 2021, the second most important marathon is *SpeeDons*, which is held in France. In 2023, *SpeeDons* raised over €1.2 million for *Médecins du Monde*[1] and became the first non-GdQ speedrunning marathon to raise a seven-digit sum for a cause. The analysis presented in this paper is based on the second edition of this event, which was held from 15 to 17 April 2022 in the Palais des Congrès, Paris (France).

Figure 1: *The setting of the French speedrun charity marathon* SpeeDons *(2022) at the Palais des Congrès. Photo: Alexandre Lemarquis.*

SpeeDons was born under the impulse of the charity *Médecins du Monde*, which wanted to organise a video game event to raise funds, with the help of the French streamer MisterMV.[2] With his past as a speedrunner and his popularity in the French-speaking streaming world, MisterMV opened the event to a relatively mainstream audience while bringing his expertise to the organisation of the marathon. The event also benefits from the expertise of the association *Le French Restream*, which broadcasts the GdQ in French and has been organising marathons since 2017, according to its website.[3] Some of the association's members worked on the

---

1   An international non-governmental medical organisation working all around the world and based in France.
2   https://www.twitch.tv/mistermv.
3   https://lefrenchrestream.fr/.

planning and MisterMV was the main host of the event. For fifty-five hours, nearly sixty speedrunners performed live on stage at the Palais des Congrès at SpeeDons 2022. The organisation of such an event requires significant human resources, carrying out various technical, organisational, or performance-related functions.

In this article, we will focus specifically on four of these functions: reviewers, commentators, entertainers,[4] and speedrunners. The reviewers are responsible for selecting the speedruns (and their performers) from among hundreds of submissions and then drawing up the event's schedule. The commentators perform a function similar to their counterparts in conventional sports: In other words, they explain what is happening on the screen. Entertainers are responsible for filling the time between speedruns or during a performance: for example, they read out donations received or indicate that certain targets have been reached. Finally, the speedrunners are the ones who perform on stage.

In this paper, we will attempt to provide a better understanding of the practice, of the relationship speedrunners cultivate with the concept of 'performance', and of the different goals they have when they participate in this particular type of event. To this end, we conducted seventeen semi-structured interviews with SpeeDons 2022 participants. These interviews aimed to determine how our informants characterised their experience in the contexts of speedrunning in general and of the SpeeDons 2022 marathon in particular. They were analysed using a mixed method, combining a first phase of flexible coding (Deterding and Waters 2018) applied to all the interviews, followed by an in-depth thematic approach of four interviews particularly representative of the four roles mentioned above (which will therefore be widely quoted in the following pages, under the aliases INF01, INF02, INF03, and INF05). The coding has made it possible to bring out certain thematic recurrences (properties) in the practitioners' discourses, which we exploit in these pages in three ways. First, we will use our informants' responses to understand what exactly is encompassed by the concept of 'performance' in the context of the speedrun marathon. Second, the articulation of the properties identified in the interviews will allow us to construct different categories, which we will show are organised into three sets of oppositions that structure the practitioners' experience: *impressing* the audience while *bringing* them *into* the community; *making* the viewers *understand* and *making* them *stay*; *promoting* and *breaking* the game. Finally, we will present a last recurring category of the interviews (the act of *comparing* speedrun with other forms of performance) to show how it is used by practitioners to situate their practice in tension between several systems of norms.

---

4   'Ambianceurs', in French.

Speedrun marathons and the concept of 'performance'

Speedrunners are extremely free in the way they perform: They can join a community and speedrun according to rules set by that community; they can also create their own constraints, the only limit being their imagination. The domain presents a wide variety of player profiles, and the rules governing the practice may vary considerably between communities or contexts. This diversity in the way practice is conceived was reflected in the responses of our informants, particularly when asked if there was a difference between speedrunning at home and speedrunning on the Palais des Congrès stage.

Figure 2: Speedrunners (foreground), commentators (middle) and audience (background) at SpeeDons (2022). Photo: Alexandre Lemarquis

1.1 Speedrunning at home versus speedrunning on stage

Speedrunning is an amateur practice – the amateur being 'the one who loves, who acts out of passion, whose desire to earn money is unknown and whose level of competence is indeterminate'[5] (Hurel 2020, 6). However, although the practice is rarely lucrative, the term still covers a variety of profiles, from occasional speedrunners to highly invested streamers and event organisers. Besides, speedrunning is experienced differently by different individuals: Some do not wish to share their perfor-

---

5   Original text: 'celui qui aime, qui agit par passion, dont on ignore s'il est aussi porté par le désir de gagner de l'argent et dont le niveau de compétence est indéterminé', translated by the authors.

mances while others livestream all their attempts; some will be satisfied with a time that they themselves have determined, while others try to obtain national or world records. Nevertheless, to contextualise our research, it is worth recalling the selection criteria for *SpeeDons* 2022 in order to understand the profiles of those whom we interviewed. As one of the reviewers of the event explained:

> I think that the first requirement is that the run must be of a high level [...]. The runner, in any case, must have a good level, meaning that he must be well ranked in relation to the world records, or even have the world record himself, even if this is not really a requirement in itself.[6] (INF05)

The speedrunners selected for *SpeeDons* 2022 are therefore players who are close to the world records. Most of them are very invested in their practice and regularly try to improve their 'PBs' (personal bests) – usually streaming these attempts. We asked them about the possible differences between speedrunning at home – a regular activity – and speedrunning on stage – a much more occasional activity – in the context of a marathon, and many responses related to the preparation of the event. Without exception, our speedrunner informants trained by performing 'no-reset runs':

> When you are speedrunning at home, you reset when you make a mistake, you start from the beginning because you missed something. You can train yourself to ... Even if every possible disaster happens during the run, you continue. That way, you are in 'event condition', you are in '*SpeeDons* condition'. (INF03)

As this quote explains, a no-reset run is a speedrun where the practitioner finishes no matter what and does not restart from the beginning. They choose to prepare in this way because, at *SpeeDons*, speedruns are required to occur in an estimated time that speedrunners must respect to ensure the rhythm of the event. Training to perform no-reset runs is part of this effort to respect the estimated time. These restrictions are inherent to the smooth running of a marathon, but, at home, speedrunners are much freer. They can stream dozens of attempts, start over again as they wish, etc. The context therefore has a decisive impact on the way practitioners conceive of their activity – and this is reflected in the way they prepare: They do not go to *SpeeDons* to set records but to ensure an attempt within a given time. What makes their activity a 'performance', then, differs depending on the setting in which they perform.

---

6   All interview transcripts are translated from French to English by the authors of this text.

1.2 How the context frames the performance

The protean aspect of the concept of performance has been studied since Richard Schechner, the founding father of performance studies. The main prism for analysing performance originally focused largely on the arts and the aesthetic dimension, before opening up to broader fields such as culture and sociology (Féral 2013, 205). Schechner (2002) distinguishes several situations in which performance takes place, from everyday life to artistic representation, human relationships – professional, social, intimate, etc. – and play. This diversity makes the definition of 'performance' complex, as Jean-Marie Pradier (2017, 287) writes:

> [T]he *lexeme performance* belongs to the vocabulary of several disciplinary fields for which it feeds the plural theoretical fabric: linguistics, philosophy, engineering, the science and techniques of physical activities and sports, the performing arts – in particular theatrical studies – aesthetics, anthropology, business, organization and management studies. As a result, publications, conferences and works referring to "performance theory" do not all deal with the same issue.[7]

The speedrun, as a sequence of 'actions that *display themselves*' (Féral 2013, 207), clearly illustrates this definitional tangle, especially since it encompasses and intertwines the definitions of performance as an artistic format and as an effective way of conducting actions. However, Schechner (2002) explains that 'whether in the primary sense of "excelling or exceeding the limits of a certain standard" or in the sense of "investing oneself in a spectacle, a game or a ritual", to perform is the result of certain actions' (Féral 2013, 206). These actions are: *being, doing, showing doing*, and *explaining showing doing*. In the context of speedrunning, *being* can be both implicit and explicit. When using a platform such as *Twitch, YouTube, Discord, Speedrun.com* or performing at charity events, speedrunners are expected to behave in a certain way, respecting the policies of the relevant spaces. Conventions also exist regarding the attitude to adopt towards the community (whether or not to share information, whether or not to get involved, etc.), the spectators (whether or not to answer their questions) and other speedrunners (whether or not to play fair, value their work, etc.), but they are actualised in specific ways by each individual.

---

7   Original text: '[L]e *lexème performance* appartient au vocabulaire de plusieurs champs disciplinaires dont il nourrit la fabrique théorique plurielle: la linguistique, la philosophie, l'ingénierie, les sciences et techniques des activités physiques et sportives, les arts du spectacle vivant – en particulier les études théâtrales – l'esthétique, l'anthropologie, les sciences de l'organisation et de la gestion des entreprises. De ce fait, les publications, colloques et travaux qui se réfèrent à « la théorie de la performance » ne traitent pas tous de la même question', translated by the authors.

Doing emphasises the act of speedrunning, i.e., the achievement of the goal set by the speedrunner according to their own abilities. *Showing doing* consists in publishing or displaying the *doing*. We should note that the means of *showing doing* in the field of speedrunning have undergone a major evolution in the form of streaming, which has diversified not only the *doing* experience, but also the spectators' experience. Indeed, it is now possible to follow a speedrunner's attempts live and, as a result, failure has become a component of the viewer experience, whereas, in the past, speedrunners only published their successful attempts.

Finally, *explaining showing doing* defines the field of action of performance studies – the explanation of the performative potential of an action being itself understood as a form of performance. Speedrunning is an interesting case, in this respect, in that *explaining showing doing* is an essential part of the activity, since speedruns are generally accompanied by explanatory comments (which may be oral or take a paratextual form). Here again, the democratisation of streaming has led to an evolution in the manifestation of this accompanying discourse, since *showing doing* and *explaining showing doing* often happen simultaneously. A viewer can use *Twitch*'s chat to ask the speedrunner for an explanation, and the speedrunner is free to respond or not – echoing the *being*. In a charity marathon such as *SpeeDons*, these different facets of performance have led to the formalisation of different roles embodied by practitioners: The speedrunner is initially tasked with the *doing*; the commentator is responsible for the *explaining showing doing*; and the entertainer is in charge of the *showing doing* (or even of a fifth layer: *displaying* the *explaining showing doing*, as they introduce, enhance and frame the work of commentators).

Speedrunning – and speedrun marathons in particular – therefore fall squarely within the domain of performance studies, in that they encompass several frames of action and of 'twice-behaved behaviour' (Schechner 2002, 29) that relate to different aspects of the concept of performance. More specifically, our informants' discourses resonate clearly with the definitions of the notion as developed in the work of Marvin Carlson (1996), as taken up by Marleena Huuhka (2020).

According to Carlson (1996), there are three definitions for performance (display of skills, patterned behaviour, and keeping up the standard) which were then synthesised by Huuhka (2020, 61). 'Display of skills *means literally consciously showing off someone's – or something's – skills*' (Huuhka 2020, 61, emphasis in original): For speedrunners, it will be a matter of demonstrating the different skills or 'psychomotor game capital' (Krywicki and Dozo, 2022) they have acquired to master the game and perform actions requiring extremely precise execution. 'Patterned behavior *means behavior that is distanced from the person doing it*' (Huuhka 2020, 61, emphasis in original), which encompasses performing tasks in a particular way. It means playing the role of the speedrunner, following a 'score' or a method to ensure its function and objectives. Finally, 'keeping up the standard *refers to the quality of something*' (Huuhka

2020, 61, emphasis in original) and is a judgement with all that implies in terms of subjectivity.

The speedrunners interviewed are generally engaged in regular speedrun practice and motivated by the idea of beating their personal best – a performance never being an end in itself but always a step towards the next record (Barnabé 2017, 182). When they speak about their practice in a personal context, they are thus led to talk about performance through the prism of *display of skills*. They are particularly hard on themselves, as indicated by the principle of learning to accept mistakes through the example of the no-reset runs. However, this discourse changes when speedrunners speak about their participation in SpeeDons: Although they are required to have a certain level, they are not expected to perform perfectly in this particular context.

By training to perform no-reset runs, speedrunners prepare themselves to deliver a performance conditioned by the event and its organisation. While they insist on the 'impressive' aspect (*display of skills*) of their performance, their respect for the estimated time shows that they are also playing a role (*patterned behaviour*) to which they attach great importance. At SpeeDons, the performances are in the name of fundraising, and the individuality of the practitioners cannot be expressed as much as if they were at home undertaking a record-breaking attempt. This leads to two consequences. First, marathon speedruns are *showcases for the practice* but do not represent speedrunning as it may be experienced every day. Second, this distinction brings a hierarchical distinction to the way practitioners analyse their time at *SpeeDons*:

> Runs during a marathon are much more about entertainment than performance. [...] By contrast, when we're trying to get a PB, we go for performance first and then, in a second step, entertainment. (INF08)

> You have to be able to balance playfulness, entertainment, and performance. If I had to put the three in order, I think it would be: play, entertainment, and performance, in that order. (INF04)

These quotes show that the distinction between speedrunning at home and speedrunning at a marathon brings about a paradigm shift in the analysis of the performance. Patterned behaviour becomes more important in the context of the marathon and coexists more broadly with the display of skills.

Another shift emerged when we asked our informants their opinion about the success of the event. According to INF05, who is also a reviewer, *SpeeDons 2022* was 'a huge success' and, in relation to this topic, the third definition of the notion of performance – *keeping up the standard* – was clearly most relevant. SpeeDons is an event that raises money for charity: Care is certainly taken in selecting the best speedrunners (*display of skills*) to propose a demonstration (*patterned behaviour*) to an audience, but, in the end, this organisation serves to provide a quality event (*keeping up the standard*) during which viewers are invited to make donations. For instance, for the organisers, maintaining high standards is also about paying attention to the influencers that are invited to participate as entertainers:

> I also think that you have to keep a certain ethic. I'm not in favour of inviting just anyone under the pretext of making donations, because I think that when you're in the charity world, you have to have a minimum of ethics. (INF05)

To summarise: When practitioners discuss their practice, all the meanings of Carlson's concept of performance are activated simultaneously. However, their prioritisation varies according to the performance context. We will see that these frameworks for interpreting performance also vary according to each speedrunner's positioning in relation to conflicting goals.

Speedrunners' relations to the audience: Conflicting goals

Besides reordering the priorities that usually govern the practice of speedrun, the diversity of the vocabulary that our informants use to refer to what is shown at SpeeDons ('show', 'showcase', 'entertainment', 'spectacle', etc.) also indicates the existence of several competing frameworks from which the performance is conceived and experienced by practitioners, as well as the difficulty of defining this concept unanimously. As Darshana Jayemanne points out more generally about video games:

> Performance in games is not a concatenation of basic units, but a complex multidimensional weave. [...] The efforts to which players have to go in order to define elite performances points towards the difficulty of developing a satisfactory theory of videogame performance as an overarching concept (Jayemanne 2017, 5–6).

This difficulty in establishing the notion of performance is particularly apparent when our informants explain their personal goals as performers in the context of the marathon or talk about their relationship with the audience. Indeed, while some of their goals and motivations reinforce each other, others come into tension or even contradiction, and each practitioner has to negotiate with these conflicting objectives in a specific way.

We have formalised how these goals are expressed in the interviews in the following diagram (see Figure 3). The boxes designate the categories synthesising the main properties expressed by our informants in relation to the theme of the marathon (and the larger size of the categories *impressing* and *making understand* illustrates their prevalence in their discourses). The single arrows (in blue) indicate a reinforcing relationship between two categories; the double arrows (in grey) indicate three structural oppositions organising the practitioners' experience.

Figure 3: Model representing the relationships between the goals expressed by our informants.

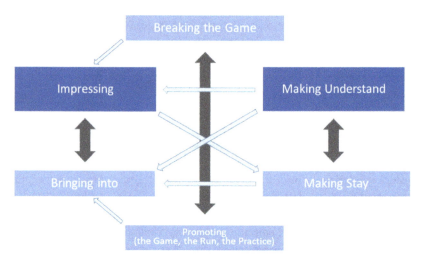

We will draw on these three oppositions to describe how each practitioner uniquely navigates the different agendas, and we will show that the tensions encountered can often be related to a difficult compromise between the regime of the spectacle, a will to transmission or education, and the experience of speedrunning as a form of transformative play (Salen and Zimmerman 2004, 301).

2.1 Impressing vs bringing into the practice

When our informants explain their role in the event or describe the type of show they wish to propose, they all converge in the need to produce an 'impressive' performance. Being able to showcase a 'high-level speedrun' is a condition for the very existence of the marathon, and guides the work of the reviewers as well as that of the commentators, entertainers, and speedrunners.

Delivering an amazing performance is an integral part of the speedrunner's role, as INF10 explicitly summarises:

> My role in the event, an objective that I had in mind, was to perform. I told myself: "I have to show my level". [...] "I have to impress", a bit. That's what put a little pressure on me... it was like: "I have to be impressive, I have to show I'm up to it".

The objective of captivating the public also guides the programming of the event, since the runs are selected to offer particularly difficult challenges, which the majority of players would not be able to achieve:

> What viewers can expect is I think something impressive [...], to be captivated, in a way, by what they are going to see and by the runs. [...] SpeeDons is clearly focused on impressive runs. Something really very difficult to achieve. [...] You go to see SpeeDons, you pay your seat at the Palais des Congrès to really see something you cannot do. It's like when you go to see a [...] great musician [...], it's really to see something impressive. (INF02)

Stressing the challenge of the run is an integral part of the role of commentators and entertainers, who have consciously developed various rhetorical techniques in order to contribute to creating narrative tension (Baroni 2007) through their commentary (for example, by using announcement strategies such as warning the audience that 'something crazy is going to happen'; INF17). Since the difficulty of executing the actions in play are not always visible on the screen, the role of the commentators is also to reveal this difficulty and to make the audience understand that they are supposed to admire the skill on display:

> Sometimes, you see something that you think is benign – a simple jump, when in fact it is very, very precise. [...] And for my part, what I really like to do, when I see a run like that, is to feel the difficulty. (INF02)

> We think it's pretty important to remind people that, even if it looks smooth and everything, what the guy on stage is doing is a crazy thing. There are not many people who will be able to do it. And so, yes, we try to highlight the runner so that people realise that what he's doing is not normal gameplay, that it's difficult, that there are hours of training behind it. (INF14)

This set of motivations form, in our model, the category *impressing*, which is one of the most hierarchically decisive in our informants' discourses. However, this category clashes with another shared goal: that of democratising the practice and bringing the novice audience into the community.

Indeed, the ambition to democratise speedrunning – which is broadly perceived as a form of 'high performance play' (Lowood 2006) – is always present, between the lines, in the way our informants consider their roles. For instance, when INF02 prioritises what they want to convey to the public through SpeeDons, they place in second place (just after the need to 'impress') their focus on popularisation and inclusiveness. Bringing new participants to try speedrunning is part of the motivation that gives practitioners their taste for their practice, as illustrated by this quote from INF03: 'For me, to grow the community like that, to inspire people to try speedrunning, it makes me super happy.'

However, this goal of convincing newcomers that they are capable of trying speedrunning comes into tension with the principle of captivating the audience and making them feel that what they are watching is exceptionally difficult. Practitioners express awareness of this tension, as their attention to bringing the public into the practice is often expressed as a means of deconstructing the elitist image of speedrun – which is a direct consequence of the *impressive* nature of the performances:

> There's an interesting thing about speedrunning [...]; it's that anyone can be a speedrunner. [...] It's not reserved for just an elite, as you might think at first, just by seeing the world record. (INF08)

> I always assume that it's someone's first marathon. [...] There's always someone on the chat who's going to watch a speedrun marathon for the first time and won't understand what's happening on the screen. And if you don't give that person the respect they deserve and explain things to them, it's also their last speedrun marathon [...]. Everybody can be a speedrunner. Absolutely anyone can be a speedrunner. And, to convey that, you have to open the door. And it's also the role of the host and the commentator to be the wedge. (INF01)

The spectacular nature of the performance can therefore be an obstacle to learning the practice and, thus, to the very existence of the community. Practitioners navigate between these two constraints with a high awareness of the need to maintain a balance between valorisation and desacralisation of performers, especially in the work of commentary: 'Our goal was not to tell people, "This is hard, this is hard, you won't be able to do it", but rather, "This is hard: He is very good".' You have to realise that he is good' (INF14). This negotiation of the opposition between *impressing* the public and *making them enter* the practice is the first ambivalence that marks the specificity of the SpeeDons spectacle.

2.2 Making understand vs making stay

The second tension revealed by the interviews is that between the will to *make* the public *understand* the techniques used by speedrunners and the will to entertain them in order to *make* them *stay*. Indeed, as an extension of the desire to bring the viewers into the community, our informants manifest that their goal is not just to show a performance that would be visually impressive or entertaining, but also to transmit knowledge about speedrunning. For instance, according to INF08, everyone in the audience should be able to understand what they are watching – regardless of their initial game literacy (Zagal 2011) – to the point that it is preferable to sacrifice time and lose a record than to miss the opportunity to explain something.

This focus on transmission is fundamental, because without some understanding of the run, the previously mentioned objective of *impressing* actually cannot be achieved:

> And if we don't explain to them why what they're seeing is great, and why what they're seeing is exceptional, well, it's a bunch of pixels that are going into each other, and then sometimes the character goes "zip zip" and we don't really understand why. But if there's someone explaining to you: "[...] well, all of a sudden, it becomes exceptional". (INF01)

Similarly, the ability of practitioners to explain the runs is also a condition for *bringing* new members *into* the community, which they see as a particularly important goal for a mainstream show such as SpeeDons, which attracts a wider and more diverse audience than more specialised speedrun events. This central and structuring dimension of knowledge transmission (which implies that 'the mere consumption of speedrun videos already constitutes an entry into the practice,'[8] Barnabé 2016, 449) shows that speedrun is conceived by its practitioners as a 'community of practice' (Lave and Wenger 1991), since learning is not considered as a peripheral activity, but as 'a way of participating in social practices, a status, a way of belonging to a community, a way of "being in it"'[9] (Berry 2008, 13).

However, the desire to educate about speedrunning must negotiate with the need to entertain the audience, to please them in order to convince them *to stay* (and thus increase the chances of collecting donations for the charity): 'We're on a charity marathon, the objective is that... well, people stay, people advertise, people are interested, people watch and so people donate' (INF08). Indeed, although a minimum level of understanding could be seen as a means to promote audience engagement, the highly technical nature of the explanations required to understand the detailed operation of each run is perceived as an obstacle to this objective of entertaining and capturing public attention. Getting the audience to stay is actually

---

8   Original text: 'La seule consommation de vidéos de speedrun constitue déjà une entrée dans la pratique', translated by the authors.

9   Original text: 'Une façon de participer à des pratiques sociales, un statut, un mode d'appartenance à une communauté, une façon «d'en être»', translated by the authors.

the reason that specifically motivated the creation of the role of 'entertainers' in French-speaking speedrun marathons. According to INF01, their function is mainly to prevent spectators from leaving the show between runs, by linking performances and 'keeping the energy high'.

In order to reconcile the objective of offering an entertaining show, capable of capturing the attention of the public for a long time, and that of transmitting technical knowledge about the runs, the practitioners have set up a formal division of roles, which is also reflected in the work of the commentators. Indeed, they consciously assign themselves two kinds of roles: the technical expert and the 'candid commentator' (INF01) or 'troublemaker' (INF17), whose function is to act as an avatar for the novice audience, for instance by asking naive questions about what is happening on screen.

This combination is what allows the event to maintain a 'good balance between technique and fun' (INF01). We see here that the goals pursued by our informants sometimes reinforce each other (making the runs understandable can help to make them spectacular), and sometimes conflict (giving too much explanation risks spoiling the show). Coordinating spectacle and mediation requires speedrunners to formalise techniques and to interpret roles that are consciously developed by the practitioners.

2.3 Breaking the game vs promoting the game

Finally, the different motivations of our informants concerning *SpeeDons* are traversed by a third tension, which concerns the practice of speedrunning more generally, independently of the marathon format. Indeed, when asked what motivates them to perform, many cite their love for a particular game and their desire to promote that game, to show it in order to make people discover it. However, this motivation comes into tension with a foundation of speedrunning as a practice and as a spectacle: the pleasure of breaking the game, of radically transforming it, of showing it in a completely unexpected state.

Sharing their love for a game is both an incentive for speedrunners and a 'responsibility' for the commentators:

> Being able to share my love for the game, it's really cool. [...] I know that there are people who may not be aware that this game exists, who may have discovered it through my run. If I can make people want to just play the game casually, well that's good enough. (INF12)

> It's my job to showcase the run, it's my job to showcase the game. [...] Even the worst game ever, you can showcase it in a super interesting way and you can present it in a super interesting way. (INF01)

Being a mediator between the public and the games is therefore part of the role that practitioners assign themselves, but this mission is not facilitated by a principle that is at the heart of the speedrun and the foundation of its 'transgressive' (Scully-Blaker 2016) or 'subversive' ethos (Hemmingsen 2020): the pleasure of *breaking* or twisting the game, of 'turning games upside down' (INF15), of 'bust[ing] the game as best we can' (INF12), in order to produce a visual spectacle worth watching. In speedrun, there is, in short, 'an almost perverse pleasure to be derived from reducing games of this scale and complexity to their barest [...]' (Newman 2008, 129).

Nevertheless, this pleasure is less destructive than transformative: In our informants' narratives, it originates in the desire to renew a game that, by dint of being loved and replayed, no longer leaves room for the contingency (Malaby 2007, 106) necessary for the development of a playful experience. Indeed, the existence of room for uncertainty (Henriot 1989, 239) or of calibrated contingency is a condition for the emergence of play. In other words, games must allow that every situation 'could have been otherwise' (Malaby 2007, 107). 'Without this room for freedom, the ludic mechanics are blocked' (Solinski 2012, 163), as one of our informants expressed clearly:

> The simple fact of knowing it by heart, because, for example, it is our favourite game sometimes, can be boring because you already know everything by heart. So adding an extra goal [...] is a practice that is in fact an aspect of playfulness. (INF02)

Breaking the game is thus a way for practitioners to enhance their enjoyment of the video games they already love (Hurel 2020, 174) and to develop techniques to experience them in new ways. By doing so, they make room so they can continue to play despite the loss of ludic uncertainty that is entailed by the repetitiveness of practice. Speedrunning's ability to renew the aesthetic experience of video games (by altering the way players feel and interact with them) is actually what leads Emilie Reed to associate the practice with a form of 'Neo-Baroque performance' (Reed 2022, 101).

The radical transformation of games is put to the service of spectacularisation (the exploited glitches are often presented as 'visual'), but sometimes requires adjustments so as not to contravene the objective of *promoting* the games shown. For example, INF03 explains that they prefer long-run categories to still be able to show the game: 'It's a bit of a mix between "I'm trying to go fast" and "Let's not wreck the game in five minutes," though, we still do all the dungeons, just to see a little bit of the game anyway'. Here again, we see that each practitioner has to negotiate in a specific way between several goals (sometimes articulated, sometimes contradictory), which inscribe the speedrun marathon in several frames of reference and several regimes of experience: the (transformative) play, the mediation (introducing games or new ways of playing), and the spectacle.

A composite performance drawing on multiple spectacle frameworks

This collision of frameworks also manifests itself in another recurrence in our interviews: the tendency of speedrunners to *compare* their practice to other domains of performance – in particular, music, theatre, competitive sports, and art – in order to situate it (and to *make it understandable* to the outside audience we were forming as interlocutors).

The comparison between gaming and theatre is not new (Homan and Homan 2014), and, in the case of a staged performance play such as SpeeDons, it is perhaps not surprising that five of our seventeen informants mention having had experience in theatre and situate their speedrun practice as a continuation of that experience (the theatre having prepared them to perform on stage). The same transfer of skills applies to music: 'As soon as you start to run, it's a bit like when you make music [...]: When you're on stage, in fact, you don't think about it too much, you think about the piece' (INF05). More broadly, even those who do not practice these disciplines compare speedrunning to theatre and music to explain the tension between what is planned and the need for improvisation:

> A speedrun is really like a musical score, like a piece of music that you are going to play. So the route is going to be your score. The way you played, that's going to be your performance. (INF08)

> Even if it's very repetitive, it's never the same thing. I'll draw a parallel with theatre: People often ask me [...] "Aren't you tired of doing the same show a hundred times?" I'm like: "Well, no, because even though it's the same show and the same text, the same thing never happens twice in a performance". (INF07)

However, this parallel with theatre is not unanimous among our informants, some of whom also use the comparison with other forms of spectacles to explain what makes their practice unique. For instance, INF17 explains the qualities of a good entertainer: 'You have to have a little bit... not an ability to improvise, but not to be afraid to be in front of a camera without support and therefore to have a little bit... not to "improvise," it's not theatre, but I mean, to know how to tell things'. Later, they also characterise SpeeDons as a form of 'content event', as opposed to other forms of performances that leave more room for *mise en scène*: 'I mean: we're not part of a spectacle, actually. SpeeDons is not a spectacle, it's a speedrun marathon.'

Similarly, the fields of art and sport are also used as reference points to which speedrunning is positioned as 'both close and different'. Speedrun is compared to sport[10] – particularly athletics – on account of its competitive dimension (INF08), its difficulty (INF13), and in terms of the similarity of the format of sports and speedrun commentary (INF04, INF06 and INF17). INF02 discusses this in particular detail, using it to defend the idea that there is a fundamental incompatibility between speedrunning and art – contrary to the positions of other practitioners or researchers, for instance in Jonathan Hay: 'the endeavor of speedrunners to produce optimal gameplay through practice reveals an artistic pursuit of perfection' (Hay 2020, 8). According to INF02, speedrunning is defined by a search for optimisation and by the application of an objective 'method of play', which brings it closer to sport, but opposes it to art – art being perceived as the domain of subjectivity and emotion: 'the practice of speedrunning is absolutely not an art for the simple fact that it is a competition, like a sport. [...] The danger of considering it, let's say, as an artistic practice, is to produce something not optimised, just because it is beautiful.'

Nevertheless, this comparison between speedrunning and sport is not absolute, and the same informant uses another comparison with theatre to describe the particular setting of the marathon:

> When we do a speedrun show, when we do a speedrun marathon, let's say, with a schedule, with different 'acts' [...]. Yes, it's obvious that it possesses an artistic aspect. But, once again, it is because [...] we make sure that the runner must produce, not a personal record, for a speedrun marathon, he must not produce a time performance, he must produce a run, a presentation, a demonstration of his speedrunning [...]. That's why, for me, a marathon run presentation is much closer to a showcase, a show, than to a speedrun in itself. (INF02)

From this perspective, the context of the marathon transforms the codes and meanings of speedrunning by making it a staged representation of the practice. Such a conclusion, though, collides with the idea that SpeeDons is a content event rather than a staging.

Overall, practitioners refer to different domains (sport, theatre, music, etc.) to try to make their practice understand and to situate it in the cultural field, but these comparisons lead to conceptual back-and-forth rather than a consensual framework: The speedrun marathon requires scenography and improvisation as in theatre (or as in a 'sports show'; Rock 2023, 24), but it is not completely a spectacle; it requires a search for optimisation and competition that brings it closer to sport, but this goal is subordinated to a staging that distorts the competitive objectives. The resistance of these competing comparisons to any simplification actually manifests the fundamentally composite nature of speedrun performances.

---

10   A comparison that is also regularly made in research (Rock 2023, 22–26).

Conclusion

In this paper, we have explored the views that speedrun practitioners have of their practice and of the specific spectacle that is the charitable marathon. We saw that speedrunning brings into tension several regimes of performance and feeds on several competing frames of reference (theatre, sport, music, art), which is expressed, in our informants' discourses, by an attachment to a complex interlocking of objectives, codes, and norms that sometimes contradict each other: to convey knowledge about the game while making it unrecognizable, to captivate the audience while convincing them that they are capable of replicating the feat, to make the performance readable while captivating the audience's attention so that they enter the community and stay.

Speedrunning, in other words, activates all the meanings of Carlson's concept of 'performance' at the same time and produces a form of hybrid, unsteady, chaotic spectacle, where we cannot identify one system of norms that would prevail over the others: Speedrunning is not completely a(n) (e)sport, because the negotiation of rules, the improvisation, and the staging moments are too important and integral to its structure; it is not completely an artistic performance, because the performers constantly bring back the activity to competition and optimisation, or to fun and playful frivolity (Brougères 2012, 124) as a way of distancing themselves from any artistic *ethos* that might be imputed to them; it is at the same time a regulated high-level competition and a disorganised amateur practice, etc. In other words, the constant competition between different systems of norms revealed in the experiences of our informants is precisely what preserves speedrun marathons from developing a dominant, hegemonic framework. Unlike esports, for example, which have quickly become vertically structured, speedrunning is a practice whose codes, rules, and modes of organisation vary from group to group, from context to context, and are constantly re-discussed.

Besides, the transmission of game literacy (Zagal 2011) and the inclusion of the public in the practice is an objective that constantly reappears in the discourses, in one way or another. This goal of transmission is articulated to the spectacular performance and determines it – so much so that commentators and speedrunners have formalised narrative or rhetorical techniques to articulate the goals of performance and those of transmission (such as playing the role of the candid commentator, using announcements or storytelling to produce suspense effects, etc.). The whole specificity of speedrun as a performance is to consistently hold together these different frames of experience: the competitive display of skills (source of spectacle, but difficult to read for a new audience) and the popularisation (necessary to enter the show, but potentially anti-spectacular).

In this respect, speedrun can benefit from being conceptualised not only from the angle of performance, but also from that of performativity, in the sense that practitioners bring the practice into existence in a way that is always singular, ambiguous, fluid, and unstable: 'As play acts, performatives are not "true" or "false", "right" or "wrong". They happen' (Schechner 2002, 127). Indeed, the interviews revealed an unstructured approach to the practice. Speedrunning is not a uniform object, but one that is intertwined in complex ways and that carries different meanings depending on speedrunners and contexts. This specificity must make researchers take into account the protean nature of the practice and the difficulty of considering it as uniform. The risk would be to study speedrunning as a homogeneous whole, everywhere and for everyone, whereas the practice is constantly evolving, diversifying, and becoming more complex.

References

Barnabé, Fanny. 2016. 'Le speedrun: pratique compétitive, ludique ou créative?' *Interfaces numériques* 5, no. 3 (Spring): 441–459. https://doi.org/10.25965/interfaces-numeriques.3113.

Barnabé, Fanny. 2017. 'Rhétorique du détournement vidéoludique. Le cas de *Pokémon*.' PhD diss., Université de Liège. https://hdl.handle.net/2268/210764

Baroni, Raphaël. 2007. *La Tension narrative. Suspense, curiosité et surprise*. Paris: Seuil.

Berry, Vincent. 2008. 'Les communautés de pratiques: note de synthèse.' *Pratiques de formation. Analyses*, 54 (December): 12–47. HAL. https://hal.science/hal-03916551

Brougère, Gilles. 2012. 'Le jeu peut-il être sérieux? Revisiter Jouer/Apprendre en temps de serious game.' *Australian Journal of French Studies* 49, no. 2 (May): 117–129. https://doi.org/10.3828/AJFS.2012.10

Carlson, Marvin. 1996. *Performance: A Critical Introduction*. London: Routledge.

Deterding, Nicole M. and Mary C. Waters. 2018. 'Flexible Coding of In-depth Interviews: A Twenty-first-century Approach.' *Sociological Methods & Research*, 50, no. 2 (October) 708–739. https://doi.org/10.1177/0049124118799377.

Féral, Josette. 2013. 'De la performance à la performativité' *Communications* 1, no. 92 (May): 205–218. https://doi.org/10.3917/commu.092.0205.

Hay, Jonathan. 2020. 'Fully Optimized: The (Post)human Art of Speedrunning.' *Journal of Posthuman Studies* 4, no. 1 (October): 5–24. https://doi.org/10.5325/jpoststud.4.1.0005.

Hemmingsen, Michael. 2020. 'Code is Law: Subversion and Collective Knowledge in the Ethos of Video Game Speedrunning.' *Sports, Ethics and Philosophy* 15, no. 3 (July): 435–460. https://doi.org/10.1080/17511321.2020.1796773.

Henriot, Jacques. 1989. *Sous couleur de jouer. La métaphore ludique*. Paris: José Corti.

Homan, Daniel and Sidney Homan. 2014. 'The Interactive Theater of Video Games: The Gamer as Playwright, Director, and Actor.' *Comparative Drama* 48, no. 1 (Spring/Summer): 169–186. https://doi.org/10.1353/cdr.2014.0000.

Hurel, Pierre-Yves. 2020. 'L'expérience de création de jeux vidéo en amateur: travailler son goût pour l'incertitude.' PhD diss., University of Liège. https://hdl.ha ndle.net/2268/247377

Huuhka, Marleena. 2020. 'Playing is Performing: Video Games as Performance.' In *Einspielungen. Neue Perspektiven der Medienästhetik*, edited by Markus Spöhrer and Harald Waldrich, 59–78. Wiesbaden: Springer VS. https://doi.org/10.1007/978-3-658-30721-9_3

Jayemanne, Darshana. 2017. 'Introduction: Videogames as Performances.' In Darshana Jayemanne, *Performativity in Art, Literature, and Videogames*, 1–27. Camden: Palgrave Macmillan. https://doi.org/10.1007/978-3-319-54451-9_1

Koziel, Eric. 2019. *Speedrun Science: A Long Guide to Short Playthroughs*. Tucson: Fangamer.

Krywicki, Boris and Björn-Olav Dozo. 2022. 'Les livres de journalistes francophones spécialisés en jeu vidéo: du capital ludique au capital journalistique.' In *Penser (avec) la culture vidéoludique – Discours, pratiques, pédagogie*, edited by Sélim Krichane, Isaac Pante and Yannick Rochat. Liège: Presses Universitaires de Liège: 43–59. https://doi.org/10.4000/books.pulg.24978

Lave, Jean and Etienne Wenger. 1991. *Situated learning: Legitimate Peripheral participation*. Cambridge: Cambridge University Press.

Lowood, Henry. 2006. 'High-performance play. The making of machinima.' *Journal of Media Practice* 7, no. 1 (July): 25–42. https://doi.org/10.1386/jmpr.7.1.25/1

Malaby, Thomas M. 2007. 'Beyond Play: A New Approach to Games.' *Games and Culture* 2, no. 2 (April): 95–113. https://doi.org/10.1177/1555412007299434.

Newman, James. 2008. *Playing with videogames*. Oxford: Routledge.

Pradier, Jean-Marie. 2017. 'De la *performance theory* aux *performance studies*' *Journal des anthropologues*, 147–148 'LittéRATURES & Sciences sociales en quête du réel': 287–300. https://doi.org/10.4000/jda.6707.

Reed, Emilie. 2022. 'The aesthetics of speedrunning: Performances in neo-baroque space.' *Replay. The Polish Journal of Game Studies* 8, no. 1 (July): 99–115. https://doi.org/10.18778/2391-8551.08.05.

Rock, Robin. 2023. *Le speedrun comme spectacle vidéoludique: L'apport de la franchise et de la communauté Halo à sa médiatisation*. Master's thesis in Information and communication, University of Lorraine, France.

Salen, Katie and Eric Zimmerman. 2004. *Rules of Play: Game Design Fundamentals*. Cambridge: MIT Press.

Scully-Blaker, Rainforest. 2016. 'Re-curating the Accident: Speedrunning Community and Practice.' Master's diss., University Concordia. https://spectrum.librar y.concordia.ca/id/eprint/982159/

Schechner, Richard. 2002. *Performance Studies: An Introduction*. Oxford: Routledge.

Schmalzer, Madison. 2022. 'Transition Games: Speedrunning Gender.' PhD diss., North Carolina State University. https://www.lib.ncsu.edu/resolver/1840.20/39 869

Sher, Stephen and Norman Su. 2019. 'Speedrunning for Charity: How Donations Gather Around a Live Streamed Couch.' In *Proceedings of the ACM on Human-Computer Interaction 3*, CSCW (November): 1–26. https://doi.org/10.1145/3359150.

Solinski, Boris. 2012. 'Le jeu vidéo. De l'héritage interactionnel au langage interactif.' *Interfaces numériques 1*, no. 1 (January): 153–174. https://doi.org/10.25965/interfac es-numeriques.298

Zagal, José P. 2011. *Ludoliteracy: Defining, Understanding and Supporting Games Education*. Halifax, NS: ETC Press.

Biographies

Sacha Bernard is a PhD student in Information and Communication Sciences at the University of Liège and a member of the Liege Game Lab. His research focuses on digital cultural mediation via the example of speedrunning.

Fanny Barnabé is an associate professor at the Research Centre in Information, Law and Society (CRIDS), part of the Namur Digital Institute (NaDI) of the University of Namur, Belgium, and a founding member of the Liège Game Lab. Her research focuses on video game narration (to which she devoted the book *Narration and Video Game: For an Exploration of Fictional Universes*), on the various forms of *détournement* (or remixing) of video games (the topic of her PhD dissertation), on video game tutorials (which she studied during her time as an FNRS Postdoctoral Researcher at the University of Liège), and on humour and irony in video game streaming on *Twitch.tv*. She also studied video game paratext during a one-year research stay at the Ritsumeikan Center for Game Studies in Kyoto, under the supervision of Professor Hiroshi Yoshida. In 2021–2022, she was a lecturer-researcher at the MNSHS lab ('Digital Methods for Humanities and Social Sciences') of the computer school Epitech in France.

Understanding Video Games
through a Performative Gaze

The Dramaturgy of Videogames: A Dialogue

Mike Sell and Michael M. Chemers

Abstract *Dramaturgy is a time-tested method for approaching the theatrical text as an artifact to be translated and transformed into live performance. In this dialogue, the authors identify key areas of overlap between live theatre and the liveness of videogame play, explore the significance of empathy to the experience of liveness, and describe the videogame player as a cybernetic, improvisational dramaturg.*

A dialogue between Mike Sell and Michael M. Chemers

Mike Sell: The organizers of the *Live Performance and Video Games* conference asked the contributors to consider those terms—live, performance, and videogames—in the broadest sense and in the widest array of possible relationships. During the conference, we saw some contributors speak to the way that live performance functions as part of video game design, others to the challenges of incorporating game technologies into theatre and other kinds of live performance, and yet others to the challenges of designing gameful experiences to promote particular kinds of liveness for audiences.

For me, that diversity of topics was thrilling. But it also struck a chord given my interest in dramaturgy, particularly a conception of dramaturgy that embraces a more systemic approach to performance and a more historically and culturally encompassing approach to the way technology shapes the communal experience of live performance. That's why I wanted to speak with you, Michael, given our recent exploration of these issues in our book *Systemic Dramaturgy*.

To start, I think it's fair to assume that not everyone understands exactly what dramaturgy is or why it's relevant to liveness, performance, and videogames. How would you define 'dramaturgy'?

Michael Chemers: Well, the definition of dramaturgy has never been fully settled. Defining dramaturgy is part of an ongoing conversation among dramaturgs—directors too. The first chapter of my book *Ghost Light* starts with the sentence, 'What the #$%@ Is a Dramaturg?' And while we can debate the uses of the term in the works of Gotthold Ephraim Lessing, Gustav Freytag, Bertolt Brecht...

Mike Sell: ...Not to mention Aristotle, Zeami, or whoever wrote the Sanskrit *Natya Shastra* ...

Michael Chemers: ... or so-called New Media Dramaturgs like Marianne van Kerkhoven. I think the conversation is less about what dramaturgy *is* than what *theatre* is and what it might be.

Mike Sell: Is that a productive conversation—something that drives creativity and critical thinking?

Michael Chemers: For sure. The definition a particular dramaturg might work by depends on what a production needs at the moment. Each individual production, each individual performance requires different kinds of approaches to dramaturgy.

Mike Sell: Each performance genre or medium, too.

Michael Chemers: Yes. But basically, we can boil dramaturgy down to two things. First, when we talk about dramaturgy, we're talking about how we approach the aesthetic architecture of a performance. That might concern structure: is it a comedy? Is it a tragedy? Or something else entirely? That's the practical part of dramaturgy. Second, it can be defined in terms of a special focus on the dramatic text, typically a pre-written script, and how to transform that text into a performance. And this is where the idea of 'systemic dramaturgy' comes into play. That's the critical or reflective aspect of dramaturgy that encompasses all parts and processes of a production.

Mike Sell: But we also need to consider the relationship of the dramaturg to the particular elements of a production. This is where dramaturgy can be considered a systemic form of critical consideration and collaboration. Everyone involved in theatre is doing dramaturgy of some kind. Actors make choices about movement and vocalization, designers about color and line, directors about message and authenticity. Everyone involved in a production is always thinking in terms of structure and significance. Dramaturgy is the practice of making thoughtful, expressive choices no matter what your role in a production might be. Dramaturgy is about helping everyone in a production make those kinds of thoughtful, expressive choices.

Michael Chemers: Exactly. But there are also people who train specifically as dramaturgs. They are experts in the processes by which those decisions are made—and about how those processes can be well integrated. They also bring to the conversation a sense of history and critical thinking about the material that the other members of the creative team might not have at the ready.

Mike Sell: So, we've got two dimensions of dramaturgy—form and significance—and two kinds of dramaturgs—everyone involved in the work and the specialists. And in some sense, both of these are defined in terms of their relationship to a particular technology of performance, whether it's voice, lighting, design, whatever.

Michael Chemers: Right. We can think about the script as a structure that determines certain choices even before a team gets involved in its production. And we can think about the performer who brings that text to life—not just the actor, but also the lighting technician, the make-up artist, the stagehands, everyone involved in the execution of the performance.

Mike Sell: Extending that framework to videogames, we can consider the game as a procedural system that structures and manages the player's activity. And we can consider how the player interacts with the game and finds ways to meet its challenge, experiment with the rules, glitch it, mod it, fill in the narrative gaps with their imagination, tell stories about it, and so on. This suggests that the player is doing a kind of *improvisational dramaturgy* during play, engaging with the game's various systems in an experimental way to produce meaningful experience. This suggests that a player could learn to do it differently, better. The player is both protagonist and prop master.

Michael Chemers: In those terms, we can say that there are three key areas where videogame studies and traditional dramaturgical work overlap. These enable us to think critically, particularly about empathy, which is one of the enduring concerns of dramaturgy.

Mike Sell: Both in the sense that a dramaturg is helping their team devise a production that touches an audience but also in the sense that they model a form of empathetic collaboration for the production team?

Michael Chemers: Yes. But we always begin with the idea of storytelling through dramatic action. And that's where we see what I think is the most durable connection between theatre and videogames. That's what videogames do. That's what plays do. Some videogames and plays are more committed to storytelling, while others might only sketch a narrative while focusing attention on something else: a fascinating mechanic or a combination of gesture and sound. Performance installations are an example of that—a powerful reduction of storytelling to a particular conjunction or moment of empathetic experience. Regardless of the quality of or interest in storytelling in the sense of character, setting, and so on, we see a common concern between theatre and videogames with the construction of dramatic action that is experientially intense and, to greater or lesser degree, interactive. Of course, there are lots of ways to tell stories—lots of ways to make and experience stories as dramatic action. For the dramaturg, that's the key issue: how to make dramatic action significant for the audience.

Mike Sell: I'm reminded of the distinction Astrid Ensslin makes between cognitive ludicity, the kind of intense analytic, imaginative, affective, and literacy interaction that the mind engages in when presented with a novel, poem, or film, and ergodic ludicity, which encompasses the kinetic, haptic, visual, and other interactions that we associate with playing a game.

Michael Chemers: Second, there's world-building. In plays and videogames, world-building is both imaginative and a matter of nuts and bolts. A stage carpenter and a videogame designer are both world-builders, and so are the actors, who build the world through everything they appear to be and express.

Then there's the third area of overlap between traditional dramaturgy and videogame play, which is a little more subtle and has to do with embodiment. It has to do with the presence of spectators and actors, though also with the total environment of the play experience. The embodied presence of the player in a game is a fascinating and, I would argue, dramaturgical presence.

Storytelling through dramatic action, world-building, and critical embodiment—that's where I'd say dramaturgs interested in videogame liveness would find interesting things to think about. And so you and I would argue, because of these shared concerns and affordances, that we can take the traditional principles by which dramaturgy has been practiced and talked about over the past 2,500 years and apply them to new cultural products like digital media and videogames.

Mike Sell: Let's start with dramatic storytelling. How can a dramaturgical approach help us understand how videogames provide players with a sense not only of liveness but of being an integral part of the dramatic action?

Michael Chemers: Traditional dramaturgy is interested in the psychological process called identification, which is a way of describing how we develop emotional ties with objects and people other than ourselves. The idea is we see some trait or circumstance in the other thing that resonates with us and, before we know it, we are emotionally connected to the other thing. Hypothetically, this provides a foundation for empathy and for the ability to consider matters from a point of view other than your own, and these capacities are critical to the operation of a community.

Let's compare identification in different media. When I go to a movie and I identify with the characters on the screen or to a play and identify with the characters on the stage, I identify with them in a way that is a bit removed from me and my sense of who I am in that moment, even though I might respond emotionally to what a character is experiencing. I can empathize with the character but mostly as another person. And when I think of that moment, I will think of it in terms of the character's experience: of Hamlet's grief when he learns about Ophelia's death, for instance. In fact, I might not even think in terms of the character, but of the actor who plays the character. It's Arnold Schwarzenegger who says, 'I'll be back', right? This is not to say that the experience of identification and empathy that films inspire is not a rich and complex experience, but it's in the third person.

But when I'm playing a videogame, identification and empathy always happen in the first person, regardless of the visual framing of the action. I fell off the cliff. I get attacked by aliens. I get on my horse and ride away into the sunset. Right? The action is in the first person. So, the nature of identification, which is key to the creation of empathy, has the potential in games to be even more intense than in the theatre or cinema.

Mike Sell: Maybe just different? I've had some pretty intense experiences in movie theatres. Again, I think of the similarities between cognitive and ergodic play that Ensslin identifies.

Michael Chemers: True, but when people talk about going to plays and having life-changing, life-altering experiences that's different. Videogames go to a different place, right?

Mike Sell: For sure, particularly given the layered nature of game play, which we'll get into later. But we're speaking about a difference in context and process more than a difference in the quality of the experience. I'm reminded of Katherine Isbister's *How Games Move Us*, where she speaks to the identification that occurs in videogames as involving multiple kinds of experience and activity: the visceral, the cognitive, the social, and the fantastic (Isbister 2017, 11).

Michael Chemers: Exactly, so we can argue about whether it's a matter of difference or degree, but I'd argue that videogames could possibly be even more transformative than theatre.

Mike Sell: I disagree. Let me push back on that a bit by changing *who* we're talking about when we compare theatrical experience and gaming experience—and get us back to the idea that when we play a videogame, we are involved in a distinctly dramaturgical experience. This is something that's always kind of irked me when people—not you, Michael—talk about the difference between theatre and videogames, that difference typically having to do with the difference between being an audience member and being a player.

But it seems to me that the experience of playing a videogame, particularly if we want to consider it a form of improvisatory dramaturgy, is more usefully compared to being an actor or a director in the middle of rehearsals, when the challenges of the script are still being identified or are emerging through iterative practice. This is the moment when the members of a team are trying things out, often doing things over and over to get it right or identify a problem.

Similarly, when we play a videogame, we do a lot of things besides control our avatar through a challenging space or a bit of dramatic action. Games require us to think and act in terms of character creation, user interface, inventory management, strategy, and so on. And we're doing all of that in anticipation of consequences we can't fully anticipate, but which are organically linked to what we're doing right now. And there's a lot of repetition. Videogame play, like theatrical rehearsal, is an iterative process.

Which goes to say that dramaturgical approaches to the videogame should think not only in terms of the narrative and the player's role in the narrative, but the ways in which players are doing the kinds of technical things that, in terms of theatre, we would normally say belong to the director, the lighting designer, the actor ...

Michael Chemers: ... or the dramaturg!

Mike Sell: And we haven't even touched on the kinds of things that videogame players do in terms of modding, a practice that can alter the text itself to enable a different kind of play experience.

Michael Chemers: Absolutely. And I think shifting our understanding of the videogame player as doing dramaturgy in the way an actor or director does dramaturgy but also as a specialized dramaturg does dramaturgy enables us to bring to bear on the videogame dramaturgical questions that have been honed over thousands of years. We can ask really interesting questions about dramatic storytelling, world-building, and embodiment and get answers that can enable us to have more fun, but we can also ask really critical questions about those same things to address the social, political, and ideological dimensions of videogame play, just as we do for the theatre.

Again, we recognize the two responsibilities of dramaturgs: to help create a meaningful experience and to ask critical questions. For example, I think of the videogame *Red Dead Redemption* (2010), a game I love dearly. It's a wonderful action game that centers you as the star of a classic Western narrative: guys in cowboy hats, dusty settlements, desert landscapes, shootouts, bank robberies, everything a fan could possibly want to be part of that drama. But the game also allows you to do terrible things to innocent people, right? In fact, in the sequel, *Red Dead Redemption 2*, we can beat a suffragette into unconsciousness or worse, and there seems to be no affordance in the game for us to reflect on that.

We need to think about why the game allows us to do those things and whether or not we, as players, do those things. That has an effect on the way that we move through the world, the real world, right?

Mike Sell: Well, I don't know about that. I get a little queasy when people claim that real-life action is influenced by videogames. Real life is affected by all kinds of things, but we tend to panic when it comes to media that are particularly popular among communities that worry authorities.

Michael Chemers: But we need to argue that it *does*. As dramaturgs who care about the significance of art, we have to argue that theatrical plays affect the way that people move in the real world, right? That plays can increase empathy through the process of identification, and that means enabling us to feel more compassion and sympathy for someone but also the opposite of that, to better understand someone's perspective in order to better understand how loathsome they are.

And so, therefore, videogames do that as well and, arguably, do it more effectively. One of the ways we understand dramaturgy is that it is a form of cultural studies. To create and critique requires us to be tuned to culture, to cultures.

Mike Sell: Yes, I agree, but there is a difference between the movement of a mind or the movement of one's tastes versus the movement of a body or a hand. And empathy is no antidote to violence. The bully is most effective when they truly understand the fears and desires of their victim.

Michael Chemers: Maybe we can say that texts present opportunities for bridging between art and the world and that videogames present a more complex, engaging opportunity—a dramaturgical opportunity.

Mike Sell: Well, let's say a different kind of complex, engaging opportunity.

Michael Chemers: I wonder if we should talk about that opportunity in more detail, maybe speak to the ways that a player who is playing, say, *Skyrim* (2011) or modding *Skyrim* or watching a livestream of *Skyrim* is doing dramaturgy, either practically or critically, unconsciously or consciously. What are the elements of that 'dramaturgy'?

Mike Sell: A complex, open-world AAA game like *Skyrim* does provide a lot of opportunities to think dramaturgically, whether the nature of the world-building, the particular ways it represents character growth, the relationship between the human and non-human environments, and so on. And there's no doubt that *Skyrim* has seen a remarkable range of modifications by players who want a different kind or quality of ludonarrative experience. But there's an argument that a smaller indie game can provide a more focused dramaturgical conversation. I think of Anna Anthropy's *Queers in Love at the End of the World* (2013), an interactive-fiction game which lasts only ten seconds. Why does Anthropy give us so many opportunities as players to express our player-character's affections for the other character, but so little time to read? Why does she create a game about the end of the world that can be played again and again. There's a dramatic quality to that storytelling that has an intensity and a construction of empathy that is quite different than *Skyrim*.

Michael Chemers: For sure.

Mike Sell: We might start with dramaturgy as a technical practice—in theatrical terms, what a costume designer or lighting technician or a specialized dramaturg would do. I'm thinking here of a massive multiplayer online roleplaying game like *World of Warcraft* (2004–present). The super-committed, high-achieving *World of Warcraft* player is doing a variety of dramaturgical work. This is a player who, to succeed at the most challenging aspects of the game, will not only have developed their playing skills, but will be theory-crafting, min-maxing, modifying the game's interface, and the like. They will often be doing as much work away from the game as they do in the game. They are doing the kind of homework that a dramaturg does when they've been tasked with providing historical context to designers or for the program. Or we might imagine a player who is less interested in high-level achievement than digging deep into the storyworld of *Warcraft*, exploring the lore in the game and across the transmedia storytelling environment of the game, doing this to enrich their experience of play and the players with whom they play. Whether theory-crafting or lore-digging, the *World of Warcraft* player is tuning their play to embody the ludonarrative possibility space of the game and engage empathetically with their fellow players or the non-player characters in the game.

Michael Chemers: Embodiment is key to that process, right? It's a cybernetic practice.

Mike Sell: Right! But before we dig into that, let's make sure we identify another kind of live dramaturgical practice. We can define dramaturgy in terms of a practice informed by critical thinking, whether the critical perspectives a dramaturg is providing are coming from an understanding of history, or identity, or class, or place—whatever. Videogame performance is always "critical" in the sense that it demands the player not just do whatever the game has them do but comprehend the system, the rules behind that doing. But there's also a critical practice that many players practice that is more in line with the kinds of things we do as researchers and theorists. You discussed your questions—your discomfort—about the decision of the creators of *Red Dead Redemption* to include a suffragette in their game and to include the option to assault her but not provide any affordances to promote critical thinking about that choice. As a player with an understanding of historical context and feminist theory, you might make a choice in that moment that is informed by principles that are generated outside of the moment of game play: a moral or ethical refusal to act in a way the game invites you to act. In other words, dramaturgy as metagaming.

Michael Chemers: Or metagaming as dramaturgy.

Mike Sell: I think of the sophisticated criticisms my undergraduate students often raise in class about the representation of queer identity, relationships, and pleasure in the games we play—and describe how they implement those ideas during play. To be able to play well, think well, and feel well—that seems like a pretty good mission statement for playful dramaturgy!

Michael Chemers: I would argue that the crux of all of this is empathy and the way that cultural products increase our ability to connect to others in a meaningful way. I don't think we've fully connected empathy with what you're calling 'playful dramaturgy'. And I think we would be remiss as dramaturgs if we did not insist that games also focus on that process. I'm not sure dramaturgy makes much sense without a focus on empathy.

Mike Sell: I agree, though I tend to think of empathy as a structure or opportunity for deeper understanding of the other rather than a particular kind of understanding.

Michael Chemers: Sure, but I'm thinking about the videogame as playing a positive role in people's lives precisely by creating powerful play experiences that are intended to generate fellow-feeling. I'm thinking about a game called *Manichi* (2012) by mattie brice. It's a game she created with RPGMaker that focuses on a few everyday experiences of the player-character, a Black trans woman. The game is simple: You just have to get through the day—get ready, go out on the street, avoid the transphobes, order coffee without being misgendered, sit with your friend.

And I know we can talk about the opportunity an actor has to embody someone who's an Other to them, but what brice is doing is something that only a videogame can do. In terms of ready-to-hand opportunities that people have, a play or movie or novel might show you the story of a Black trans person moving through their day. And you could be deeply moved by it. But in a videogame, you actually become that

228 Understanding Video Games through a Performative Gaze

person. You have that experience in the sense that you're having the visceral, social, cognitive, and fantasy experience that all avatars enable, as my colleague Katherine Isbister tells us. But we're also having that experience because we're able to experience the rules of the game of life—rules that work differently for the Black trans woman.

And those things that happen in that game feel personal regardless of whether we empathize with the character because we're in the game. We have to inhabit that character's subjectivity. I think that this kind of embodied, playful experience expands the ability to feel empathy in unique ways. And this isn't just for those who lack an understanding of the day-to-day life experiences of trans people of color. If you already know what that embodied experience is like, a game like *Mainichi* lets you know that other people understand what you're going through and are doing their best to help you articulate what's going on in your own life. Empathy can also be a gesture of community belonging.

So, regardless of the fact that empathy can enable cruelty, I think that we, as dramaturgs, need to insist that our cultural products entertain us towards positive, progressive experiences of otherness, whether to educate the ignorant or validate experience. Entertainment is an important thing, of course, but I think we have an obligation as dramaturgs to try and heal the world.

Mike Sell: True, though brice and other queer game designers like Anna Anthropy have pushed back on the idea of the videogame as an empathy engine. I think here of merritt k, who withdrew her highly influential game *Lim* (2012) from the public because it became the only thing people associated with her—and it wasn't a game that she was particularly proud of in terms of its technical qualities. In fact, there was something of a wave of indie games that criticized the idea that the first priority of queer designers needed to be empathy. I think here of k's *EMPATHY MACHINE* (2014), which directly asserts that playing a game won't change how a person feels about the other. Anthropy has taken a public stance against empathy as a central goal for queer game designers. In a 2015 interview, she said, 'If you've played a 10-minute game about being a transwoman, don't pat yourself on the back for feeling like you understand a marginalized experience'. Which isn't to say that games like *Mainichi* or *Lim* or Anthropy's *Dys4ia* (2012) don't create empathy experiences, but that the empathy experiences can be overvalued at the expense of other aspects of the game experience or orientations of empathy that don't align across boundaries but are intended to consolidate the experiences of those within a marginalized and threatened community.

Michael Chemers: That is absolutely true and it presents a problem for dramaturgs who have been focused on empathy for thousands of years. It's a challenging question.

Mike Sell: This speaks to the complex ways embodiment works in videogames as both an experience of play and something we think about as dramaturgs. Videogame embodiment is a multifaceted experience and, therefore, so is the dramaturgy that can inform it practically and theoretically. So, we can look at, say, the videogame avatar in terms of the mechanical agency it provides, the way it translates the movements of our fingers or feet or bodies into the game's procedures. That experience of translation can lead us to questions that are essentially technical ('Why is this so janky?') or to questions that have a more ethical or critical orientation ('Why aren't I allowed to take this particular action?', 'Why can't I adjust this controller to accommodate different ranges of digital ability?')

Michael Chemers: We can also think dramaturgically about the social experience of embodiment in similar terms, right? For example, we might think of embodied experience in terms of a moment of play at a friend's apartment or the rhetorical performance of the participants in a reddit forum or a public performance of gameplay on a livestream or sitting in an arena with ten thousand other people to watch athletes contend for a world Esports championship.

Mike Sell: And it's not at all unusual for a videogame player to participate in all of these kinds of performances, sometimes as the performer, sometimes as the spectator.

Michael Chemers: Yes, so if we understand the videogame player's liveness as distributed across different platforms and composed of multiple kinds of embodiment—social, physical, rhetorical, and so on—then that's going to complicate how we theorize empathy and instill progressive forms of empathy practice in videogame design, videogame criticism, and, most importantly, in the practice of play. I think embodiment is key to that theory and practice.

Mike Sell: And of course, the fact that videogames are built around this kind of distributed embodiment is what makes them both compulsive as a performance experience and a source of anxiety to those who want bodies to work in only one way—as productive bodies, especially. Recently, I've been reading a remarkable, and mostly forgotten book by the late Martin Amis, *Invasion of the Space Invaders*, which he wrote back in 1981, when the arcade was the center of videogame culture. It's a fascinating document that mixes together the kinds of things one would find in a tips-and-tricks guide alongside a kind of ethnographic travelog of arcades around the world and a bracing account of Amis's journey through addiction, which for him was at once moral and social, private and public.

I cite Amis's book because, first, it is a valuable, perhaps crucial historical document of a particular time and a particular set of spaces in which videogame per-

230 Understanding Video Games through a Performative Gaze

formance occurred. In other words, it's a work that can enrich our understanding of the videogame as a historical, social, personal, and regional practice. It's fodder for dramaturgy.

Second, *Invasion of the Space Invaders* can be read as a work of videogame dramaturgy, an account of arcade culture that describes the particular historical social, personal, and regional practices of players from an equally particular critical perspective. Amis's book is brilliant in that fashion—providing a particular vantage point on the performances and performance cultures of his time and place. It's a perspective that goes against the grain of ignorant journalists, moralizing authorities, and, perhaps most importantly, those who have failed to account for how diverse the arcade community was.

Michael Chemers: That's interesting. It reminds us that videogames have always been something most people do while others are watching.

Mike Sell: Absolutely. As someone who spent a fair amount of time in arcades in the 1980s, I remember vividly the experience of crowding around a player who was playing well—and the anxiety and thrill of playing while others crowded around me, a consistently unskilled player. We'd watch to pick up tips and tricks and we'd watch for the thrill of high-level performance.

Michael Chemers: The representation of videogames as a solitary and isolating experience is a stereotype—and that stereotype undermines our ability to comprehend the nature of videogame performance. Notwithstanding the fact that some players desire or get stuck in solitary, isolating experience ...

Mike Sell: I think of Tom Bissell's *Extra Lives* as a story of exactly that kind of experience: isolated, addictive, almost hopeless.

Michael Chemers: Yes, but videogames have always been built in a way that players perform for others.

Mike Sell: For sure. And I think of how Bissell's account of his addiction to games and cocaine is very much oriented towards others, whether his girlfriend or his reader.

But back to the question of videogames and live performance—and how important it is to fully comprehend the varieties of videogame play. One of the things I like to do with my students is have them write stories about their most significant videogaming experience. Many of them write about watching siblings or parents or friends play and how important that was as a bonding experience. Unlike the empathy experience we discussed earlier, where the game provides the player an opportunity to extend empathy beyond their experience, here we have a pre-existing empathetic relationship enriching the experience of liveness.

Michael Chemers: Right. We need to understand that the activity of videogame play is an activity that exists as much for those around the player as for the player themselves. Not only does that complicate the notion that videogames are isolating, it also complicates the idea of videogame liveness.

Mike Sell: And, therefore, of the dramaturgy of videogames.

Michael Chemers: Yes. Let's get back to the 'distributed liveness' we discussed before. Maybe it's better if we think in terms of networked liveness because, when we play games, we're almost always involved in some kind of a networked experience: networks of players, networks of game distributors, networks of writing.

Mike Sell: And all of the networked infrastructure that enables those networks: wireless networks, cable, corporations ...

Michael Chemers: One of the dramaturgical ideas that we develop in *Systemic Dramaturgy* is that the experience of liveness is not one thing, that liveness depends entirely on the technology that enables that liveness to be experienced.

Mike Sell: The idea that technology is not some aberration of or threat to liveness, but essential to it.

Michael Chemers: Technology is the original problem of theatre, right? So, we have a kind of distributed, networked liveness that is not the liveness that theatre critics valued in the early 1900s when movies started to disrupt the economy and values of the bourgeois theatre. And it's not the kind of liveness that theatre historians like Philip Auslander wrote about as digital technology started to disrupt the economy and values of theatre and other kinds of live performance in the 1990s. Sarah Bay-Cheng probably captures it best when she writes that in the digital context, 'people do not participate by being there; people are "there" by participating' (Bay-Cheng 2010, 130).

Mike Sell: When we say in our book that technology is the original problem of theatre, we want to spur dramaturgs to think of technology in an expansive way. Like Douglas Adams, we want to get away from thinking that technology is only what was invented after we were born, what is new and strange (Adams 2002, 95).

Michael Chemers: The *deus ex machina* is a technology. Limelight is a technology. The *bunraku* puppet is a technology. Make-up is a technology. Language itself, and gesture, these are technologies.

Mike Sell: Right. We would define technology as any tool that enhances or amplifies or enriches or makes amazing the experience of live performance. And a technologically astute–systemic–dramaturgy understands the fluid, evolving, situational relationship between technology and performance. But when we say technology is the original problem of theatre, we intend that, at least in part, to be understood as a challenge to how we think about *play*. Theatre's power is generated by the interrelationship of the text, the technological systems of whatever performance space is being used, and—crucially—the playfulness of the actors and directors and designers. You'll recall that, as we wrote *Systemic Dramaturgy*, we spent a lot of time talking and writing about play, hoping to develop a concept of play that enables us to think in sensitive ways about the relationship of play, technology, and the power of theatrical performance.

It's no accident that the emergence of an expansive conception of theatre and performance in the 1980s was driven in large part by an expanded conception of play. I'm thinking here of Richard Schechner's writings, which still haven't received adequate attention from outside the performance studies community, notwithstanding the work of Clara Fernández-Vara, Rose Biggin, Barbara Büscher, Jayemanne Darshana, Réjane Dreifuss, Daniel and Sidney Homan, Marleena Huuhka, Juliane Männel, and others, including many of the speakers at this conference.

Michael Chemers: And we've learned that, if we want to understand that live performance in videogames is happening in a range of ways—in terms of the cybernetic and cognitive interaction with the game, in terms of the way interaction with a game can be both distributed and networked—then a useful way to organize all of that activity conceptually is to think in terms of play.

Mike Sell: Is technology the original problem of play?

Michael Chemers: Well, I don't know. Maybe?

Mike Sell: That's certainly what the poststructuralists have argued. I think of Derrida's seminal essay 'Structure, Sign, and Play in the Discourse of the Human Sciences'. (1967). His argument that the essential relationship between sign systems and consciousness is a relationship of free play, of improvisatory invention with the tools at hand (which he gets from Claude Lévi-Strauss), suggests that what we see as the essential problem of theatre is also the essential problem of play. And I think of Mary Flanagan's *Critical Play* where she speculates that, because games are artificial systems, 'situations with guidelines and procedures' is how she puts it, that they can be thought of as a technology (Flanagan 2013, 7). One of the challenges of defining play is positioning it in respect to the material and instrumental conditions that provide structure and purpose. And Flanagan notes that '[s]hifts in play have historically mirrored shifts in technologies' (Flanagan 2013, 8). We might reverse this idea and argue that, as play technologies shift, players have to learn new ways to comprehend their systemic nature, both to successfully engage with those systems but also to create, criticize, and modify them.

I don't want to get lost in the theoretical weeds here, but I mention this to underline the idea that play is a systems-oriented activity, a way of moving and making decisions in rule-based structures. And when we speak of more complex kinds of rule-based structures like videogames, which overlap and intersect with other rule-based structures like language, culture, social interaction, storytelling, and so on, we're speaking to more complex forms of play. And that means more complex practices of empathy—whether hardwired into the game text or implemented by the player.

Michael Chemers: Absolutely. I mean, that's what dramaturgy is all about. It's understanding the way different systems are put into literal play to produce the performance event. And to return to how we defined dramaturgy at the start of our conversation, we see dramaturgy informing that performance event in several ways—at least potentially. One, we've got the systems put into place to enable the event to be live: sound, lighting, blocking, scenography, and so on. Two, you've got the systems in play during the live event that are put in play by the performers and technicians. And three, you've got the audience doing the kind of interpretive and perceptual and social things that happen during a performance.

Mike Sell: And we can speak of a dramaturgy of liveness that concerns both the practicalities of production—of translating the text into a moving, memorable event—and of a dramaturgy of liveness that concerns how we reflect on and evaluate the live experience.

Michael Chemers: And we can work to understand and improve both dimensions of that dramaturgy to enable better creation and enrich the live experience, right? Those systems are heuristic. They're hermeneutic. They are physical, they are economic, historical, social, political, even spiritual. And they all go into the creation of a moment of engagement between creators, creation, and an audience member. They're all playful in nature—and can be made more playful through the application of creative and critical perspectives.

Dramaturgy is all about understanding the interplay of those systems. And as those systems change, as new technologies emerge or old technologies are adapted

234 Understanding Video Games through a Performative Gaze

to new uses, that means we change our understandings and practices not only of creation, but of being live.

Mike Sell: So, is a dramaturgy of videogame liveness ultimately a dramaturgy of fun? I've been reading Bernard De Koven's *The Well-Played Game* (2013), and I think that, without intending to do so, he provided a thoughtful way for us to frame the dramaturgy of videogame play. Which is to say, for us, to frame the particular kinds of technical and experiential activities that enable empathy. He writes that, when we achieve an optimal state of play, 'We are having fun. We are caring. We are safe with each other. This is what we want. We are playing well together, even though we can't name the game we're playing. We are having a good time. We trust each other. There's no doubt at all about our willingness to play [...]. We are who we want to be, how we want to be, where, here, now'. As dramaturgs of play, we want to ensure that everyone who has the opportunity to play a game has the kind of fun they want to have.

Michael Chemers: The notion of a dramaturgically informed activity of play, of being in live interaction with the videogame in all of its parts and across its networks, is a notion of dramaturgy that maximizes the possibility space of a game. The creation of all of those elements that we've talked about are not ludic until creators engage with them and present that engagement to others, whether other members of the team, an audience, or even some other way of thinking. The liveness of videogame play is necessarily about the liveness of community and creation; especially, the establishment of empathic connections.

All of this ultimately concerns the engagement of creative and critical practices to enable the cooperative creation of a dramatic story ...

Mike Sell: The cooperation of creator and digital technologies, the cooperation of the game and the player, the cooperation of the different faculties of the player, and the cooperation of the player and whoever is watching them ...

Michael Chemers: So, the more dramaturgically informed each of these moments of cooperation can be, the better the experience of live play can embody and communicate the values of the community.

Mike Sell: Once again, I think we'd want to underline that this is one dimension of videogame performance—the one that emphasizes the construction of the live event. Complementing that is the dramaturgy of critical reflection, of critical play. You and I want to see more and more players who are able to go in and play games with the knowledge of the game's production, the way a game's systems work, and the ideological implications of the play experience that is shaped by that production and those systems. And we want them to be able to put their values into play with all of that so they can be fully conscious of when the experience of play is being shaped in a way that is troubling or offensive or victimizing.

Michael Chemers: So that they can see better the ways that videogames shape play and the ways that play can shape a game—and to understand that play involves so many different things besides the game itself and the player. Again, the liveness of videogame play is always multifaceted, distributed, networked, and is composed of so many different interactions, so many different kinds of community. And when players are conscious of that and have the skills to put that consciousness into play ...

Mike Sell: Then we're having fun. And so therefore we're talking about the ways that critical making and critical thinking can imbue play with a deep sense of liveness of the kind De Koven describes.

Michael Chemers: And for dramaturgs, fun means the creation of community. And that's where we find the most enduring relationship between the liveness of theatre and the liveness of videogames. Since time immemorial, live performance has worked to create and sustain community.

Mike Sell: And that can be done on a stage wearing a mask or sitting on a couch with a controller in our hands.

References

Adams, Douglas. 2002. *The Salmon of Doubt: Hitchhiking the Galaxy One Last Time*. New York: Harmony Books.

Amis, Martin. 1982. *Invasion of the Space Invaders: An Addict's Guide to Battle Tactics, Big Scores and the Best Machines*. London: Hutchinson & Co.

Bay-Cheng, Sarah. 2010. 'Theatre History and Digital Historiography.' In *Theatre Historiography: Critical Interventions*, edited by Henry Bial and Scott Magellsen, 125–36. Ann Arbor: University of Michigan Press.

Bissell, Tom. 2011. *Extra Lives: Why Video Games Matter*. New York: Vintage.

Chemers, Michael M. 2010. *Ghost Light: An Introductory Handbook for Dramaturgy*. Carbondale: Southern Illinois University Press.

Chemers, Michael M. and Mike Sell. 2022. *Systemic Dramaturgy: A Handbook for the Digital Age*. Carbondale, IL: Southern Illinois University Press.

D'Anastasio, Cecilia. 2015. 'Why Video Games Can't Teach You Empathy.' Vice, May 15, 2015. https://www.vice.com/en/article/mgbwpv/empathy-games-dont-exist.

De Koven, Bernard. 2013. *The Well-Played Game: A Player's Philosophy*. Cambridge, MA: The MIT Press.

Derrida, Jacques. 1967. 'Structure, Sign, and Play in the Discourse of the Human Sciences.' In *Writing and Difference*. Translated by Alan Bass, 278–293. Chicago: University of Chicago.

Ensslin, Astrid. 2018. *Literary Gaming*. Cambridge, MA: The MIT Press.

Flanagan, Mary. 2013. *Critical Play: Radical Game Design*. Cambridge, MA: The MIT Press.

Isbister, Katherine. 2017. *How Games Move Us: Emotion by Design*. Cambridge, MA: The MIT Press.

Biographies

Mike Sell is Professor of English at Indiana University of Pennsylvania and a member of the faculty of the Graduate Program in Literature & Criticism. He is co-author with Michael Chemers of *Systemic Dramaturgy: A Handbook for the Digital Age* (Southern Illinois University 2022), editor of the 1960s volume of *Decades of Modern American Drama* (Methuen 2018), and co-editor with Megan Amber Condis of *Ready Reader One: The Stories We Tell With, Around, and About Videogames* (Louisiana State University Press 2024). He is the founder and co-director of the Digital Storygame Project, a public digital humanities project that supports K–16 and university teachers in the integration of game design and decision-focused storytelling in English Language Arts and other curricula.

Michael M. Chemers is Professor and Chair of the Department of Performance, Play & Design at the University of California Santa Cruz. He is co-author, with Mike Sell, of *Systemic Dramaturgy: A Handbook for the Digital Age* (Southern Illinois University 2022). He is also the author of *Ghost Light: An Introductory Handbook for Dramaturgy* (Southern Illinois University 2010, 2nd edition 2022), *The Monster in Theatre History: This Thing of Darkness* (Routledge 2017), and *Staging Stigma: A Critical Examination of the American Freak Show* (Palgrave MacMillan, 2008). He also served as editor of Luis Valdez's *Theatre of the Sphere: The Vibrant Being* (Routledge 2021). He was the Founding Director of the Bachelor of Fine Arts in Production Dramaturgy Program at Carnegie Mellon University's School of Drama from 2007–12.

On Time Compression and *Déjà vu*: Remastering, Remaking, Modding, and Performing *Final Fantasy*

Darshana Jayemanne and Cameron Kunzelman

Abstract *This chapter explores remasters, remakes, and mods with particular attention to Final Fantasy VIII Remastered. The performative and temporal dynamics of playing this game suggest a new approach to the concept of performative multiplicity as outlined in Performativity in Art, Literature and Videogames (Jayemanne 2017), mediated by Paolo Virno's discussion of déjà vu.*

Introduction

This chapter arose from an invitation by the editors of this volume to contribute an updated reflection on the monograph *Performativity in Art, Literature and Videogames* (Jayemanne 2017; hereafter *PALV*). The present volume's theme of 'live performance' offers an opportunity to critically revisit these ideas and, in particular, the concept of *performative multiplicity*: a notion that seeks to engage media theory in accounting for the complex entanglements of human and computer performance in videogames. In this chapter, we will theoretically expand on the concept of performative multiplicity by means of the theme of temporality, with specific reference to *Final Fantasy VIII Remastered* (Square Enix, 2019, hereafter *FFVIII Remastered*) and Paolo Virno's concept of *déjà vu*.

PALV theorises the embodied, complex interactions we have with and through digital games in terms of multiplicity. In practice, however, the case studies in the book tend towards the analysis of single-player games and the performances discussed are mainly single-player performances. Since the publication of *PALV*, digital games and their strategies for producing 'liveness' have shifted against a backdrop of significant and ongoing transformations. Methods used in the book are largely textualist and perhaps smuggle in some of the belated temporality of reading a text that is already written. While there are discussions of multiplayer situations (for example the discussion of the *Counter-Strike* map de dust, the strange collective performance of *Twitch Plays Dark Souls*, and horror games featured in the rise of some major streamer celebrities), the method developed for analysing videogame performances is largely employed to understand them as texts performed by individual players and as viewed from a final decisive enframing (the 'Game Over'). In emphasising the 'conclusive' moment of the Game Over in its case studies and in particular its discussion of temporality, *PALV* only gestures towards methods that deal with *ongoing* and *distributed* performances as facilitated by digital games.

In short, the concept of performative multiplicity as developed in *PALV* could be more *multiple*: expanded to better take account the complex developments that have led to new configurations and phenomena of videogame-mediated play and performance.

Questions around what it means to perform in digital games have been further intensified by processes such as the 'platformification of cultural production' (Nieborg & Poell 2018). This refers to the way that technological platforms (often run by social media or gaming companies) are affecting how culture is made, disseminated, and interpreted. Digital games have both contributed to and been changed by platformed modes of play, such as the rise of Let's Play type performances that seek to attract wide audiences. Scholarship on performativity in the context of digital games more generally has expanded knowledge on key areas such as livestreaming (e.g., Ruberg & Cullen 2020, Tran 2022) and e-sports (for example in Nick Taylor's [2020] discussion of 'movement performance'). Landmark studies such as those by Cote (2021), Gray (2020), Fickle (2020), and Trammell (2023) have demonstrated the complexities and diversity of performance in gaming's virtual worlds, providing new tools, theories, and methodologies.

Here we will consider how videogame 'remakes' and 'remasters' evoke historical performances and engage with the multiplicity of performance itself. Unlike the immediacy and contemporaneity that live service games aim towards, remakes, remasters, demakes, and similar ludic cultural productions take entire performative multiplicities as their object. They are more than repetitions of 'what it was like' to play a videogame on a different technological platform, at a different time, and in a different cultural milieu. In practice, they are oriented to emerging technical and social dynamics that must trace multiple temporal margins, going beyond the games industry's tendency for repetition that de Peuter and Dyer-Witherford (2009, 46) term 'studied unoriginality'.

First, this chapter will give a precis of the theory of performative multiplicities. Second, it will explore these ideas through the example of *Final Fantasy VIII Remastered*. Finally, it will explore the temporal complexity of playing *FFVIII Remastered* to propose Paolo Virno's notion of *déjà vu* as a way of thinking beyond the method offered in *PALV*.

Performative multiplicities

What is meant by the term 'performative multiplicity'? The concept aims to complicate commonplace notions of what it means to perform in videogames, cutting across human and machine actors. Often, for a videogame player to perform an action, they undertake a specific input: Press 'X' to jump, for example. This may seem like a straightforward 'unit' of performance: a building block from which extended performance within the game is composed. However, complexities quickly arise with such a conception. If we consider a version of the 'same' game on another platform (say on PC rather than console), material specifics become important: The jump action may be mapped to a different button, or the shape of the controls may mean the player is less successful than if they were playing on a controller. In digital games, discrete performances are shaped by design and technical apparatus – always related in complex ways to other aspects of the game. The idea of the performative multiplicity aims at accounting for the relations of potential and actuality in digital games.

Digital games are capable of facilitating a dizzying range of performances that need not be neatly arranged in time. Players may find themselves in a situation where it is unclear what constitutes a felicitous performance in the first place – what Espen Aarseth has described as an 'aporia' (Aarseth 1999). Other key scholars such as Angela Ndalianis (2004) and Ian Bogost (2008) have also registered this aspect of digital games in explorations of neo-baroque 'labyrinths' and Alain Badiou's notion of the 'count-as-one' (2005) respectively. In aporia, we experience not a clear and distinct set of performative units that comprise the game, but a *performative multiplicity* as such. This multiplicity precedes and conditions any actual performance. Where Aarseth's notion of aporia has potentially negative connotations, *PALV* suggests 'euporia' as another experience: the exhilarating sense at the start of an open-world game that we can potentially strike off in a myriad of directions.

In RPG games, the player-character (PC) or 'avatar' is often a character with a strongly generic nature. *The Elder Scrolls V: Skyrim* (Bethesda Softworks 2011) casts players as 'The Dragonborn', the player-character of *Dragon Age II* (BioWare 2011) is a male or female 'Hero of Kirkwall', and the protagonist of *Cyberpunk 2077* (CD Projekt Red 2020), simply called 'V'. These characters are highly customisable by players in terms of behaviour and characteristics, but are designed so that certain aspects override any given instance or performance. All the non-player characters (NPCs) in *Cyberpunk 2077*, for example, address a generic 'V' in their voice lines, which means they can appear to react to many configurations of both the PC and the game state. Player-characters such as V or The Dragonborn are thus both a specificity (the particular path a player has taken), and a generic potential (the set of performances available to all players across many different playthroughs, in other words: a performative multiplicity).

PALV acknowledges these experiences: Rather than thinking about how performative units of play become extended instances of play, it proposes a method that begins with the multiplicity and analyses how particular performances arise from it. The key distinction is whether the performance is continuous or discrete in nature. Continuous performances (such as when a mouse movement proportionally shifts the field of view in a first-person game) are termed *illudic* acts. Discrete performances (such as when players must move blocks to complete a puzzle) are termed *perludic* acts. These terms are modified versions of J.L. Austin's categories of 'illocutionary' and 'perlocutionary' speech acts, and theoretically informed by the work of Wilden (1978) and Bateson (2000). Where action games are more oriented to illudic acts, with frenetic activity and close mapping of human and machine action, adventure and puzzle games may be more oriented to discrete decisions and a slower pace (although these are genre tendencies, not absolutes).

A useful example that can be used to explore this method for describing performance in digital games is *Bloodborne PSX Demake* (LWMedia 2022). In this 'demake', the PS4 game *Bloodborne* (FromSoft 2015) is remediated to evoke the PSX era of gaming. This is achieved most obviously by means of graphical style (evoking CRT displays, low poly models) and audio design that legibly map on to the original game. However, the demake also references *Bloodborne* at a performative level, particularly where controllers are used. Illudic acts are transformed to evoke a previous set of performative relations between human manual input and game apparatus. Rather than pushing analogue sticks (which were not part of the initial PSX controller and only added later in the DualShock revision) for movement or to pan the camera, the PC is moved with the D-pad. Shoulder triggers, which were used for actions such as attacking or countering in the PS4 game, now pan the camera left or right. Along with wry references to saving on memory cards, or the low-poly models that signify a bygone era of gaming, it is the re-mapping of forms to draw together two distinct performative multiplicities (*Bloodborne* and the PSX platform) that allow the demake to work.

By the same token, perludic acts are also carefully considered. The overall effect of the game recapitulates *Bloodborne* closely in terms of what players do and experience – at least initially. The opening of *Bloodborne* is faithfully recreated in the retro visual and audio style, including the ritual of blood transfusion and early encounters with bosses Father Gascoigne and the Cleric Beast. After this initial period of performative fidelity, the demake has the liberty to depart from the referent game and introduce new areas and opponents, such as the late-game Winter Lanterns. The final perludic act of the demake departs from the original game completely, with players confronting a novel secret boss called 'Gilbert, the Outsider', which reimagines the fate of an NPC from the source game.

Performing memory

The method developed in *PALV* also seeks to account for the temporality of performances. To do this, it adapts the concepts of *diachrony* and *synchrony* to the analysis of digital games. Diachrony indicates the splitting of a performative multiple – say, as a branching path in a narrative-led game or dialogue tree. Each branch is distinct from every other and different branches cannot be experienced in any one performance of the game. Synchrony indicates when performative multiplicities converge – as in a critical cutscene containing a major story beat, which will play in all performances of a given game no matter the specifics of that playthrough of the game. The *Bloodborne PSX Demake* works by initially generating a sense of synchrony (precisely mapping the early gameplay of *Bloodborne*) and then opening up to new forms of diachrony (the freer design of later parts of the game).

These concepts complement the illudic/perludic dyad, and together the terms enable a characterisation of how games shape temporal experience (*PALV*, 276). What is initially experienced as a highly diachronic aporia where players are still figuring out how illudic and perludic acts relate in this particular game (the 'yet-to-be-played') is gradually moulded into the diachronic-synchronic balance of the mature play experience (the 'can-be-played-with') and finally the highly synchronic Game Over (the 'always-will-be-played'). While *PALV* does draw on structuralist theory, what is being developed is a method for analysis and not an ontological account of temporality: Diachrony and synchrony are tendencies, not essences. Every performance will generate some margin of these tendencies. The Game Over is the core example of synchrony in *PALV*, the ultimate point of convergence for a given playthrough of the game. This indicates the mental model that players are actively developing in the course of play: an intuition of what the game will be like when diachronic potentials are exhausted and have come to signify the maximum synchrony available to the system.

In the fields of game history and preservation, scholars have examined problems of how to recreate the sense of keeping games 'alive'. What it means to preserve digital games is not only a question of hardware, code, or metatextual materials. It also involves decisions about what it means to preserve an interactive or configurable text. As noted above, a game can vary significantly depending on the platform on which it is played, leading preservationists to debate what constitutes a 'genuine' performance of a classic game. Analysing the PAL version of *Sonic the Hedgehog*, James Newman, citing Melanie Swalwell, critiques techniques which risk 'the normalisation of the NTSC version' that suppresses the meaningful differences found within the PAL version which was released in other regions.

> This presents a real challenge. This is not merely in recognition of the near fetishistic adherence to "historical accuracy" that Swalwell recognises in many

242 Understanding Video Games through a Performative Gaze

"game-lovers" who act as both curators and audiences for game preservation and history work, but because of the utterly transformativse nature of these technologies on the operation of code and the manifestation of games and gameplay (Newman 2019).

Newman's view is focused through historiographical and curatorial practice on digital games, which he has described as 'unstable objects' (Newman 2012), while Swalwell (2007) has described game preservation as a complex process of both 'remembering and forgetting'.

Newman's discussion leads beyond technical questions of NTSC vs PAL game versions: To preserve a game is not simply an 'originalist' question of the right technology, hardware, or software. It is also a question of performance and *how* the game is played because different players bring different value and capabilities to their performance (and from a nonhuman point of view, certain technical conditions are not reproducible). Newman's argument lands on a specific performance style – the Any% speedrun of *Legend of Zelda: Ocarina of Time* – and the normative multiplicity encoded in the game's official guidebook, which incorporates narrative and worldbuilding material oriented to evoking and supporting an imaginative experience. Speedrunners 'subvert the game's space and time as set out in its official guidebook [...] in order to move from the start to the finish of the game in as speedy a manner as possible, the Any% speedrunner is better thought of as not charting a route through the representational space produced by the game's engine, or along its narrative arc, but rather as traversing and pathfinding through the game's code and data structures' (Newman 2019, 11). These peculiar and bespoke performative multiplicities change the game, rendering it an unstable object in new and unpredictable ways, and are creative acts in their own right: inventing new illudic and perludic acts that were never intended by the game's creators.

As the work of game history scholars such as Swalwell and Newman, and the example of the *Bloodborne PSX Demake* indicates, entire platforms and performative multiplicities become objects of memory and creative transformation. The demake strongly evokes the performative multiplicity of *Bloodborne* and the PSX platform. Once this initial set of powerful recognitions has taken place, the demake exercises its own distinct design sensibilities. In the case of speedruns, Newman also emphasises the importance of paratexts in shaping these performances. Each case indicates how the provisional closure indicated by the discussion of synchrony in *PALV*, exemplified by the 'Game Over', is overly normative. Certainly, videogames may drive towards a Game Over state that, by design, conditions all the actions a player may have taken in the game. But as the above examples show, players are capable of creating performative multiplicities that resist, transform, and exceed what was designed.

Replaying and remastering *Final Fantasy*

We will now turn to the case study of *Final Fantasy VIII Remastered*. The *Final Fantasy* series is an intensive source of 'fan folklore' (Bukac & Katic 2023), and while *Final Fantasy VII* is perhaps the most prolific single-player site for this activity, there is also significant current interest in the immediate sequel. What does it mean to 'remaster' *Final Fantasy VIII*? And what does it mean to replay it, considered through the notion of performative multiplicities?

Scholars of the *Final Fantasy* franchise have noted many serial and synchronic elements and themes that characterise *Final Fantasy* games across platforms, from mobile to single-player console or PC, to MMOs (Perreault et al. 2021; Wang et al. 2021). A ragtag group of heroes is faced with a vast, apocalyptic threat that lurks behind the world's endemic political and economic strife (Hutchison 2017; Millburn 2016). Luminous crystals gift superhuman powers, enabling the summoning of godlike allies amidst soaring operatic scores (Thompson 2019). Ancient, advanced civilisations have vanished, leaving foreboding ruins and dreadful superweapons. 'Chosen Ones', often young women, are marked with mysterious auras and stand or dance at the boundary of life and death – as Victor Navarro-Remesal (2017) has put it, these figures such as *FFVIII*'s rebel leader Rinoa Heartilly or *FFX*'s elegiac Yuna, 'channel and limit the access to the power at stake in their games'.

These elements, many of which conform to Ndalianis' (2004) criteria for neo-baroque works, are key to the recognisability and consistency of the game series across decades of production, even as technologies, culture, and prevailing design norms have changed so markedly (van Ommen 2018). *FFVII* was a landmark game for the Playstation platform, using CD technology to include both expansive gameplay and full-motion video cutscenes. *FFVIII* followed on from its immediate predecessor's heady admixture of fantasy and science fiction, although it leavened this recipe with a dose of stylistic realism. Gone were the blocky, evocative character models in the field. Instead, the game opted for realistically proportioned PCs. More of the pre-rendered backgrounds were based on real-world locales, and the team aimed for an international, cosmopolitan atmosphere.

This era of *Final Fantasy* also saw a changing of the guard with Hironobu Sakaguchi moving towards an executive producer rather than director role. His influence still seems prevalent, however, in the game's commitment to advancing a cinematic style of storytelling alongside the RPG gameplay mechanics. Sakaguchi was working on the CGI movie *Final Fantasy: The Spirits Within* during the production of *FFVIII*. Indeed, *FFVIII* contained even more FMV cutscene material than *FFVII*, and included impressive transitions between pre-rendered and gameplay sections that sometimes superimposed the latter over the former, maximising further the capabilities of the platform. Visually and thematically, the setting of *FFVIII* somewhat departs from the 'antitheistic themes' (Greenfield-Casas 2017) of grim industrial dystopia, body horror, and ecological collapse of *FFVII*. Instead, the game's settings tend towards sunny fishing villages and lavish ballrooms in what art director Yusuke Naori called a 'bright, fresh Final Fantasy' where 'light emerges from the darkness'. However, in spite of the shift in visual tone and characterisation, *FFVIII* arguably does maintain an 'intensely existential tenor' (Sykes 2016).

The realist style of the character models and the more grounded setting adds gravitas to the predicament the player characters find themselves in. *FFVIII* is a game about teen soldiers who are trained to conduct battlefield interventions and special operations. The game's narrative is highly linear (Bjarnason 2020), although players can explore an open world. The teens, led by protagonist Squall Leonhart, are empowered by entities known as Guardian Forces (GF) via the 'Junction' gameplay system, which allows each GF to enable certain statistical upgrades and the assignment of specific spells to character ability scores. The GFs are beings which draw on global mythological imagery in what Escande (2023) has identified as 'database fantasy'.

The player characters' military capabilities come at significant psychological cost in the form of memory loss – *FFVIII* improved on its predecessor by giving us not one amnesiac hero PC, but a whole party of them. The students are known as SeeDs, and trained at an institution known as Balamb Garden. The opening act of the game begins with a difficult task for a group of SeeD students – fending off an invasion of the small city of Dollet by the militarily powerful nation of Galbadia. Protagonist Squall Leonhart emerges as the leader of the group in this trial by fire. After a range of missions, the PCs are sent to support a rebel cell, led by another central character, Rinoa, against Galbadia. This leads up to an assassination attempt on the new Galbadian leader, the Sorceress Edea. It is after this that most of the more supernatural plot elements are introduced.

As the game continues, the player characters learn that they in fact all grew up in the same orphanage. They have forgotten this in the intervening years due to their training with and use of the Guardian Forces, which displace memories as a byproduct of their ability to enhance battle skills. For this reason, they have also forgotten Edea, who was in fact the matron who raised them. In later conflicts and developments, it is revealed that her actions are influenced by a sorceress from the future named Ultimecia. This sorceress wishes to achieve 'time compression' – bringing together past, present, and future such that there is only one existence. Together, the game's protagonists allow Ultimecia to achieve time compression, so that they can defeat her in the compressed future and thus save the present. Squall finally witnesses Ultimecia passing her powers to Edea in the past, thus beginning the whole cycle of the game. *FFVIII* thus ends on a powerful image of synchrony that ramifies across levels of narrative, imagery, player agency, and gameplay – a time loop, where all game actions are brought into lock step with one another. For all the efforts of the protagonists to bring about a diachronic potential within their world, the loop of the sorceress's power suggests an underlying repetition, the interpretation of which has caused much debate among the game's fans.

The official remaster of *FFVIII* largely tends towards closely re-presenting the narrative structures and gameplay of the original, while updating them for contemporary hardware platforms. *FFVIII Remastered* registers the cinematic ambitions of the original release. This is realised partially by improved character models (although the lack of similar improvement in the backgrounds remain a point of contention), but also at the level of gameplay through the inclusion of boosts. These enable players to speed up or eliminate repetitive elements of the original such as random combats, to make the party invincible, or to remove the need to consistently 'draw' magic from enemies. The boosts fundamentally change the game, removing the synchronic 'grind' that the original required as a core design element, and highly favouring narrative and cinematic-style experience.

This remaster can be compared to the *FFVII Remake*, which is completely rebuilt at the technical level. The 'Active Time Battle' quasi-turn-based combat of *FFVII*, wherein the opposing sides face off and engage in perludic exchanges, is replaced with a real-time system that incorporates illudic movement through the game space. The remake also introduced new metatextual and thematic elements which dramatise the difference between the games. Key among these are the new 'Whispers' characters, spectral beings who oppose any attempts by either players or player characters to depart from the plot of the original game (and indeed pastiche the originalist attitudes identified by Swalwell; see Booth and Jayemanne (2021).

However, an exploration of *FFVIII* fan culture shows a range of attitudes beyond originalism or fidelity to the original game. Unsurprisingly, there is a commonly expressed desire for a full remake of *FFVIII*, commensurate to that of the higher-profile *FFVII*. As one poster puts it on the r/FinalFantasyVIII subreddit, noting the inclusion of multiple timelines and divergent realities in *FFVII Remake*:

> But Square, for real? They're taking THE theme that would have been the perfect match for a potential FF8 Remake and they're expanding it in FF7, which is a world that didn't have anything about time travel or time compression or whatever at all. While I don't mind it, again, this means that it is very likely that any FF8 Remake will not involve the same concept and themes. (u/thesirsteed, 2023).

For this fan, the relation between remaster and remake extends to the level of thematics, and in particular elements in *FFVII Remake* such as the Whispers that hint at multiple timelines and parallel realities that were part of the plot of the original *FFVIII*. However, the fan discourse remains at the level of individual texts: The introduction of these themes to *FFVII* through characters such as the Whispers and metatextual devices is not simply an aesthetic decision but clearly a self-aware attempt to address the platformised environment in which cultural production increasingly takes place. It addresses itself to paratexts (Wright 2023), internet discussion, and streaming culture in a way that *FFVIII Remastered* cannot, adhering as it does much more closely to the original game narrative and systems. As a remaster, its remit appears to fundamentally rest on the production of the same, with marginal upgrades, to new monetisable platforms. By contrast, the remake is rebuilt from the ground up and relies more on broad semiotic similarities than enabling older technology to run on newer hardware with relatively modest tweaks. In this way, the remake can encompass its own legacy within its narrative content, absorbing what came after it in the creation of a new text from the body of the original.

Fan reception of *FFVIII Remastered* goes beyond forum debates, however, and includes technical and aesthetic modifications to the game distributed via less formal channels than the official releases. The theme of time compression is a key point of contention in a mod for the *Final Fantasy VIII* Steam release called *Succession*. It was released initially in 2019, the same year as the official *FFVIII Remastered* and has been updated several times since, by a developer who goes by the username 'percivaldulac' (hereafter 'PD'). The pitch of the mod is neatly summarised by PD themselves as a *remaster*, only one that is focused on the story: 'If you can create an HD remaster of the graphics, can you create an HD remaster of the story?' The goal of the mod is nothing less than a complete overhaul of the story of *Final Fantasy VIII*. Apparently nearly every line of dialogue has been altered in some fashion, and the entire revelatory crux of the game, that the Guardian Forces cause amnesia in their users, is written out of the game.

Similarly, the entire theme of time compression is removed as PD believes it was 'poorly explained and poorly executed' in the original release. *Succession* is notable for both its shape and its scope. It operates from a position that a game's writing can be changed in such a way that the entire aesthetic experience will not only be altered but improved. Reading through the various official and discussion posts that PD has made, and seeing the conversations happening around the mod, it is clear that the audience is fairly limited. However, those willing to experiment with this total rewrite have engaged in some robust discussion about what it means to augment, add to, and make *better* a mass-media object like *FFVIII*. PD describes their work as '[...] a script edit in the technical sense. I approached the story like an editor with a very rough first draft. I streamlined the plot, refined the character development, and punched up the dialogue' (PD, 2019).

Of course, this requires a mental model of the media object that asserts that there are gaps or insufficiencies in it, that with just enough tinkering that you could make it complete as an object. *FFVIII* is a game that is plagued by discussions of bad translations and inaccurate character transposition into English, and the rumour has been around since the 1990s that fixing this translation would automatically make the game *better*; PD, however, found that those translated scripts were too close to the original to serve as a template for improving the game's narrative. It is also notable that PD is willing to tinker based on feedback and possible better revisions – the mod was last updated in late 2022.

Déjà vu

There is something at stake in the relationship between the demake, the remake, and the remaster, a privileging of different dimensions of what is being revivified, remembered, and augmented. While they may seem superficially similar in intent (to keep an old game 'alive' and facilitate performances of said game into the future) or form, as we have seen they each employ very different strategies to establish a relationship to a prior game text. If we talked about these things in purely pragmatic dimensions, we could play a kind of Ship-of-Theseus game, multiplying differences and similarities indefinitely.

PALV and its terminology for analysing ludic acts is useful for describing these differences within the context of each specific performative multiplicity. However, the weaknesses of using this method to think *across* performative multiplicities are also clear and accentuated by the focus on single-player experiences. If in *PALV* the idea of the Game Over is the key example of synchrony, designating a regulative mental model and convergence point for the multiple performances that comprise a given game, the variety of phenomena surrounding *FFVIII Remastered* show that the nature and status of the 'whole' of a game is an intensive locus for contestation and creative production in its own right. Rather than convergence, we have seen considerable divergence. Square Enix's professional developers and fans such as PD have very different understandings of what it means to remaster *FFVIII*, with the former concentrating on technical aspects of the game, while the latter is invested in a script rewrite to remove major plot points such as amnesia and time compression. These are not diachronic possibilities that are contained within a single performative multiplicity (this or that ending, this or that playstyle), but very different approaches to the task of remembering and revivifying *FFVIII*.

As such, here we suggest one way of thinking across performative multiplicities in the form of Paulo Virno's *Déjà vu and the End of History* (2015). In this book, Virno plays out Bergson's distinction between actual and virtual through the key figure of déjà vu. Virno describes the experience of déjà vu as 'the memory of the present' – a formulation that is seemingly paradoxical. Memory would seem inherently oriented to the past; how is it possible to remember our perception of the present? For Virno, what appears in déjà vu is a 'false recognition' in which we become spectators of our own capacity-to-be. It is not a chronological past or discrete event that is retrieved by memory (because what is being remembered never actually happened). Instead, it is the pure form of the indefinite 'past-in-general': a pure potentiality or faculty that accompanies and precedes any particular actualisation. Usually, the orientation of memory to specific events or scenes, to the chronological flow of time and events, prevents perception of the faculty of memory as it exists as a *not-now*, as a virtuality: 'The past-in-general accompanies every actuality like an aura' (Virno 2015, 19).

This inextricable link between virtuality and actuality also obtains in Virno's reading of other faculties such as that of language (Saussure's *langue* being read as a generic capacity that is not exhausted in any one speech act), disposition towards pleasure, labour power, or the capacity to act. In this understanding, the virtual is not a ghostly 'model' for the actual, nor a resource that is consumed in the process of becoming-actual. Virtual and actual are distinct, but they co-exist in any action both as a stream of previous actualities and the non-presence of the faculty to act.

> Every act has a *double past*. On the one hand, the mass of previous actualities that preceded it in time and, in some measure, caused it. On the other hand, enduring potential, which has no home within chronological progression and is always and on each occasion anterior to whatever is inscribed therein (Virno 2015, 113).

Some of this discussion may be familiar from the way that performative multiplicities have been described above and in *PALV*. While we cannot explore here the full range of Virno's philosophical discussion in *Déjà vu and the End of History*, we will touch on the way that he gives a *public* character to the experience of déjà vu beyond its usual understanding as individual psychological state – thus enabling an approach to the platformised aspects in which contemporary games are enmeshed.

The key aspect here is Virno's connection of the experience of déjà vu with Nietzsche's *Untimely Meditations*, which McKenzie Wark has glossed as 'a way of describing a certain pathology in the contemporary culture of the over-developed world' (Wark 2015, online). In contrast to diagnoses of an 'end of history' and the possibility of genuine change, Virno instead sees a hypertrophy of memory, a hypermnesia that makes déjà vu a generalised condition. 'Nietzsche maintains that an overabundance of memory paralyses action, cuts off the future and encourages melancholy [...] But no *authentic* past is of such considerable authority as to impose such a dependency' (Virno 2015, 41–43, emphasis in original).

From Nietzsche's three historiographic stances (monumental, critical, and antiquarian), Virno focuses in particular on the antiquarian. The antiquarian venerates 'the past, as it really was, in its totality, without missing out the slightest detail. For the antiquarian historian, *everything* deserves to be kept alive in memory: the village *fete*, an incidental comment that just slipped out, the humble 'almost vanishing traces' of history' (Virno 2015, 52). As Wark elaborates, it is a form of 'disabling nostalgia'. As this occurs as part of Virno's critique of postmodernism, we might also think here of Lyotard's notion of performativity – the drive to arrive at 'the best possible input/output equation' (Lyotard 1984, 46) which in its own drive for maximal efficiency actually precludes other modes of being.

Demakes, remasters, and remakes display the doubling effect Virno outlines. These use various strategies to refer to the past of a performative multiplicity. In different ways, they negotiate an originalist gesture that refers back to an object, but also risks antiquarian piling-up of innumerable specificities in search of the 'true' game. At the same time, both professional corporate releases, and scrappy products of fan culture assert a generic, virtual potential-to-create. *FFVII Remake* is full of moments that are the same as the ones we played before, but with a difference: They happen later; they don't happen at all; they are reconfigured into other set pieces in order to return the familiar in the guise of the new. By the same gesture, the remaster has similar functions, constantly asking us if the thing we are playing is 'original' or not. 'Remaster' implies the correction of minor mistakes or the attainment of an original intent, as in the 'remastering' of music from original elements. Déjà vu enters the situation for *FFVIII Remastered* in that we might imagine that is what is happening, that the characters should always have been this way, or the menus should have been this way. The virtuality of that past object, as a series of half memories and potentials, is arrested into a firm shape that becomes a saleable commodity.

If we return now to the opening critique of *PALV*, that the theory of performative multiplicity is insufficiently *multiple*, it is possible to be more precise with attentiveness to Virno's discussion of déjà vu. The discussion of synchrony and the Game Over can be supplemented with the scholarship on platformisation and theory on historical time. To what degree can we play the 'same' game over time? What is at stake in any live performance? Are we activating antiquarian possibilities and forms of nostalgia that foreclose on possible futures? While the dyads of illudic/perludic and diachrony/synchrony remain useful for the detailed analysis of particular videogame performances, the official *FFVIII Remastered*, and PD's Succession Mod are more than diachronic realisations of the 'same' *FFVIII* performative multiplicity: they are genuinely different. Or better, to merely say that they are diachronic with respect to one another – temporal splittings, but within the perspective of the 'same' game – would be to impose too much of a relation of similarity on what are very different performative multiplicities. Of course, following Virno, the virtual subtends every performance, every act, every live performance – it just so happens that demakes, remakes, and remasters have developed this out through various strategies, and brought the resulting déjà vu before a public.

The divergence in the results does however lead to Wark's critique of Virno's book as seeming 'less than contemporary': His discussion of inexhaustible generic faculties and potentialities has philosophical value, but in this account 'Environment – nature – never pushes back [...]. Virno is still thinking through the categories of language and speech act rather than those of information, noise, probability and entropy' (Wark 2015, online). The resources available to *Bloodborne PSX Demake* developer LWMedia and Succession modder PD are very different to those of the professional developers at Square Enix. While such questions shift the terrain from metaphysics, they are critical in the present, as the antiquarian drive to ever-greater technological intensity conditions what it means to perform in digital games (Abraham 2023). This said, Virno's abstractions have strong conceptual value in light of attempts by online creation platforms such as Fortnite and Roblox to re-orient themselves away from 'games' and towards 'experiences' (The Verge 2021), the concoction of 'multiverses' which enable maximum extraction of value from canonised pop cultural icons, or the claims by vast corporate concerns towards building 'the metaverse' as a singular frame mediating a universalising antiquarian impulse. Platforms seek to elide their provenance in digital games, while developing new strategies for enclosing human capacities for memory and creativity in a singular metaverse: producing live performance in a way that, in the sales pitch at least, will have no Game Over. In light of such powerful claims to forgetting, techniques for remembering and critiquing the contingencies that condition how we remake, remaster, and demake live performance in digital space and time, seem to be necessary.

References

Aarseth, Espen. 1999. 'Aporia and Epiphany in Doom and The Speaking Clock. The Temporality of Ergodic Art'. In *Cyberspace Textuality. Computer Technology and Literary Theory*, edited by Ryan, Marie-Laure, 31–42. Bloomington and Indianapolis: Indiana University Press.

Ashmore, Calvin and Michael Nitsche. 2007. 'The Quest in a Generated World.' DiGRA conference.

Austin, John, Langshaw. 1975. *How to Do Things with Words*. 2nd edition. Cambridge, MA: Harvard University Press.

Bateson, Gregory. 2000. *Steps to an Ecology of Mind: Collected Essays in Anthropology, Psychiatry, Evolution, and Epistemology*. Chicago, IL: University of Chicago Press. https://press.uchicago.edu/ucp/books/book/chicago/S/bo3620295.html.

Bjarnason, Nökkvi Jarl. 2020. 'A Fantasy without a Dream: Japanese Role-Playing Games and the Absence of the Expressive Ideal.' *Replaying Japan*, 2(1): 11–21. https://doi.org/10.34382/00013359

Bogost, Ian. 2008. *Unit Operations: An Approach to Videogame Criticism*. Cambridge, MA/London: MIT Press.

Booth, Ruth and Darshana Jayemanne. 2021. 'Boundless, terrifying freedom's: ecocriticism and ludographic metafiction in Final Fantasy VII: Remake (2020).' *42nd International Conference on the Fantastic in the Arts: Climate Change and the Anthropocene.*

Bukač, Zlatko and Mario Katić. 2023. '"A Legend From Before You Were Born" : Final Fantasy VII, Folklore, and Popular Culture.' *Games and Culture.* https://doi.org/1 0.1177/15554120231187753.

Burn, Andrew, and Gareth Schott. 2004. ' Heavy Hero or Digital Dummy? Multimodal Player–Avatar Relations in Final Fantasy 7.' *Visual Communication* 3, no. 2 : 213–33.

Dyer-Witheford, Nick, and Greig De Peuter. 2009. *Games of Empire: Global Capitalism and Video Games.* Minneapolis, London: U of Minnesota Press.

Escande, Jesse. 2023. ' Foreign Yet Familiar: J. L. Borges' Book of Imaginary Beings and Other Cultural Ferrymen in Japanese Fantasy Games.' *Games and Culture* 18, no. 1 (Spring): 3–26. https://doi.org/10.1177/15554120211060258.

Greenfield-Casas, Stefan X. 2017. 'Between worlds: musical allegory in Final Fantasy X.' Thesis, University of Texas.

Hutchison, Rachael. 2017. ' Nuclear Discourse in Final Fantasy VII: Embodied Experience and Social Critique.' In *Introducing Japanese Popular Culture*, edited by Alisa Freedman, 71–80. New York: Routledge.

———. 2018. 'Refracted Visions: Transmedia Storytelling in Japanese Games.' *Replaying Japan*, Inaugural preparatory issue: 68–76.

Lyotard, Jean-François. 1984. *The Postmodern Condition: A Report on Knowledge.* Manchester: Manchester University Press.

Milburn, Colin. 2016. '"There Ain't No Gettin' Offa This Train": Final Fantasy VII and the Pwning of Environmental Crisis.' In *Sustainable Media*, edited by Nicole Starosielski and Janet Walker, 77–93. New York: Routledge.

Navarro-Remesal, Victor. 2017. 'Goddesses in Japanese Videogames: Tradition, Gameplay, Gender, and Power.' In: *Dialectics of the Goddess in Japanese Audiovisual Culture*, edited by Lorenzo J. Torres, 111–134. Lanham, Maryland: Lexington Books.

Ndalianis, Angela. 2004. *Neo-Baroque Aesthetics and Contemporary Entertainment*, Cambridge, MA: The MIT Press.

Newman, James. 2012. 'Ports and patches: Digital games as unstable objects.' *Convergence* 18 no. 2 (Spring): 135–142. https://doi.org/10.1177/1354856511433688.

———. 2019. 'Saving (and re-saving) videogames: rethinking emulation for preservation, exhibition and interpretation.' *The International Journal of Creative Media Research*, 1. https://doi.org/10.33008/IJCMR.2019.08

———. 2019. 'Wrong Warping, Sequence Breaking, and Running through Code.' *Journal of the Japanese Association for Digital Humanities* 4 no. 1: 7–36. https://doi.org/10.17928/jjadh.4.1_7.

Nieborg, David B., and Thomas Poell. 2018. 'The platformization of cultural production: Theorizing the contingent cultural commodity.' *New Media & Society* 20 no. 11 (November): 4275–4292. https://doi.org/10.1177/1461444818769694.

Nietzsche, Friedrich. 1997. *Nietzsche: Untimely Meditations*. 2nd ed. Edited by Danielle Breazeale. Translated by R.J. Hollingdale. Cambridge: Cambridge University Press.

Percivaldulac. n.d. 'Final Fantasy VII: New and Unique Mod for Final Fantasy VIII.' https://steamcommunity.com/app/39150/discussions/0/163754266822208 2006/?l=finsnish [accessed 20 September 2023].

Perreault, Gregory, Daniel Jr. Emory, and Samuel Tham. 2021. 'The Gamification of Gambling: A Case Study of the Mobile Game Final Fantasy Brave Exvius.' *Game Studies* 21 no. 2 (July). https://www.gamestudies.org/2102/articles/perreault_daniel_tham

Ruberg, Bonnie, and Amanda L. L. Cullen. 2020. 'Feeling for an Audience: The Gendered Emotional Labor of Video Game Live Streaming.' *Digital Culture & Society* 5 no.2 (December): 85–102. https://doi.org/10.14361/dcs-2019-0206.

Swalwell, Melanie. 2007. 'The Remembering and the Forgetting of Early Digital Games: From Novelty to Detritus and Back Again.' *Journal of Visual Culture* 6 no. 2 (August): 255–273. https://doi.org/10.1177/1470412907078568.

Taylor, Nicholas. 2020. 'The Numbers Game: Collegiate Esports and the Instrumentation of Movement Performance.' In *Sports, Society, and Technology*, edited by Jennfer Sterling and Mary McDonald. Singapore: Palgrave Macmillan.

Taylor, Tina L. 2002. 'Living Digitally: Embodiment in Virtual Worlds'. In *The Social Life of Avatars: Presence and Interaction in Shared Virtual Environments*, 40–62. London: Springer.

———. 2009. *Play between Worlds: Exploring Online Game Culture*. Cambridge, MA: MIT press.

Thompson, Ryan. 2019. 'Operatic Conventions and Expectations in Final Fantasy VI.' In *Music in the Role-Playing Game: Heroes & Harmonies*, edited by William Gibbons and Steven Reale, 117–128. New York: Routledge.

Tran, Christine H. 2022. '"Never Battle Alone": Egirls and the Gender(ed) War on Video Game Live Streaming as "Real" Work.' *Television & New Media* 23 no. 5: 509–520. https://doi.org/10.1177/15274764221080930.

u/thesirsteed. September 2023. 'I will never forgive Square for this.': https://www.reddit.com/r/FinalFantasyVIII/comments/16k4etp/i_will_never_forgive_square_for_this/ [accessed 9 September 2023].

Van Ommen, Mattias, 2018. 'Emergent affect in Final Fantasy VII and Japanese role-playing games.' *Journal of Gaming & Virtual Worlds*, 10 no. 1 (March): 21–39. https://doi.org/10.1386/jgvw.10.1.21_1.

Wang, Haolan, Zeliang Zhang, Mohd Nor Akmal Khalid, Hiroyuki Iida, and Keqiu Li. 2021. 'MMORPG Evolution Analysis from Explorer and Achiever Perspectives: A Case Study Using the Final Fantasy Series.' *Information* 12 no. 6 (Spring): 229. https://doi.org/10.3390/info12060229.

Wark, McKenzie. 2015. 'Virno and History.' https://publicseminar.org/2015/02/virn o-and-history/ [accessed 6 October 2023].

Wilden, Anthony. 1977. *System and Structure: Essays in Communication and Exchange.* London: Tavistock Publications.

Wright, Esther. 2023. 'Paratexts, "authenticity," and the margins of digital (game) history.' In *(Not) In the Game: History, Paratexts, and Games*, edited by Regina Seiwald and Edwin Vollans, 33–54. Berlin: De Gruyter Oldenbourg.

Biography

Darshana Jayemanne is Senior Lecturer in Games & Arts at Abertay University. He researches digital culture, games, narrative, and youth media. He is the author of the monograph *Performativity in Art, Literature and Videogames*, has served on the Jury for the Independent Games Festival's award in Narrative Excellence, and is a board member of the Digital Games Research Association. He has collaborated on digital games research and policy with organisations such as the UK Department for Digital, Culture, Media and Sport, the Information Commissioner's Office, Ofcom, the United Nations, and the Fair Play Alliance.

Cameron Kunzelman is Assistant Professor of Communication Studies at Mercer University where he researches the relationships that form between people and their media objects. His work primarily focuses on the genre of science fiction and how it is instantiated within video games and films. His first book, *The World is Born From Zero: Understanding Speculation and Video Games* (2022), focuses on how the formal properties of science fiction video games produce subjectivities for their players.

Video Games as Material Performances

Michael Nitsche

Abstract *Taking its roots in puppetry and material performance, this chapter argues for an object theatre approach to video games. It first traces connections between puppetry, human-computer interaction (HCI), and video games before turning to new materialism to establish game objects as performing pieces with their own agency. It closes with a short interpretation of Tetris as one example of such an object theatre approach to games.*

Overview

Puppetry has been a reference for how we relate to computer systems from the very beginning of human-computer interaction (HCI) design and remains so in the era of modern video games and recent virtual reality (VR) and augmented reality (AR) designs. This ancient performance practice has informed analysis, design, and critique and it will be at the center of the following argument, too. First, this essay will connect to existing discussions that already relate HCI and games to puppetry. This will provide the necessary context and help to situate the argument. Second, it will briefly turn to new materialism to expand the notion of what defines a puppet. Following this expansion, it will focus on material performances and object theatre as forms of puppetry and apply them to games through a short discussion of a classic example: *Tetris*. Its main argumentation is somewhat circular: It connects games to performance, to puppetry, to material agency, and from this logic it offers a critical reflection back onto our reading of games in the first place.

Approaching puppetry

When we turn to puppetry, we inherently start navigating along a shifting border that defines itself by blurring its demarcations. Puppets are 'dead' but they 'come alive'. By their very nature, puppets are liminal objects: expressive, but also inanimate things of pure material quality. At the same time, puppets reposition the human by making them a co-performer, turning them into a collaborator, the puppeteer, whose role can be a shifting one. With the puppeteer's help, puppets walk a tight rope between the 'inanimate' and the 'alive'. Whenever someone endows an inanimate object with life force and casts it in a scenario, a puppet is born' (Blumenthal 2005, 11). The inanimate quality of the puppet object is not a hinderance in this balancing act. The fact that puppets are made of 'dead' materials is not a dealbreaker but a necessary part of the logic. It is this material quality of the puppet that defines the format. '[T]he special feature of the puppet is its materiality. In drama the actor uses his own body as the "material" vehicle of the stage character. In the puppet theatre, the "material" vehicle is really material – it is puppet' (Jurkowski 1990, 24). This defining vehicle that underlies the nature of the art should be recognized as a first marker of our argument at hand. Puppets are the liminal objects whose very difference from the 'alive' human puppeteers and audiences allows the creation of an expressive theatrical form. This creation process depends on human action, on an ongoing 'endowment' of the material. It is not a given quality, but it is process-based and depends on human support. Puppets are not robots and, when left alone, lose these active functions. A puppet not played is closer to an inanimate object than to an active performer. It makes all the difference whether you are looking at a historical puppet exhibited in a museum—such as the archives of the *Center for Puppetry Arts* in Atlanta—or whether you are watching a show performed at one of the *Center*'s stages.

HCI and puppetry

A comparable process-based dependency is found in our interaction with computers. Human-computer interaction depends on emerging actions between the human and the machine. It is not surprising that one can find puppetry as a reference even in early writings about HCI (Hayes-Roth, Brownston, and Sincoff 1995). Interacting with computers is an expressive–creative practice where objects are integral collaborators—just like puppets. Both practices are relational by definition. As will be argued later, both practices should accept the agency of their non-human partners more fully.

The reach into real-time controlled virtual beings harks back to the 60s (Sturmann 1998) and has led to the development of various controllers, such as the 'Waldo' interfaces developed by Jim Henson's Creature Shop, which support the combined hand and body-tracking set up used by *The Henson Digital Puppetry Studio* today. Puppetry art and performance practices have adapted various of those emerging techniques along the way. This has led to performances with AR puppets (King 2018), virtual characters (Eide 2008), and robots (Poulton 2015). These set ups not only target novel artistic expression but can also support education (Moumoutzis et al. 2018) or heritage conservation (Lin et al. 2013).

Developing technologies for novel control mechanisms remains a challenge, but opening up puppetry to the conceptual challenges that these technologies pose might be even more demanding. As technologies infuse the world around us, they also reframe the role of puppetry. Orenstein coined the term 'New Puppetry', which expresses 'interrelationships rather than binaries and oppositions and reflect our contemporary struggle to understand our now deep involvement with technology, embedded as we are in it' (Orenstein 2017, 96). Tillis speaks of 'media figures' that might be robotic, virtual, or any other form of mediated entity (Tillis 1999). Mapping the shifting interrelationships is difficult. The sheer variety of mediated forms complicates any single approach. The most influential attempt, so far, might be Kaplin's concept of a 'puppet tree' (Kaplin 1999) in which he maps traditional puppetry like shadow puppets or traditional Japanese Bunraku puppetry on the same plane as robotics and virtual character controls. His defining relations are 'distance' between object and human and 'ratio' of human controllers to manipulated objects. Because these criteria reach across technologies, Kaplin manages to map out Henson's Muppets, animatronics from amusement parks, and video game characters on a shared matrix (Kaplin 1999). This matrix might say little about expressive range, but it provides a powerful map that assembles different forms with clear relations. From both ends, HCI as well as puppetry scholarship, we can trace a constant cross-referencing. Yet, this remains a malleable and developing field for both disciplines.

Puppets and games

Video games use puppetry as a reference for their setting and narrative (e.g. *Puppeteer* [SCEJ, 2013]), character definition (e.g. the *Little Big Planet* game series [Media Molecule, 2008–]), in indie games (e.g. *Octodad: Dadliest Catch* [Young Horses, 2014]), through embodied interfaces such as the Kinect (e.g. *The Gunstringer* [Twisted Pixel Games, 2011]) or VR (e.g. *Hello Puppets!* [Otherworld Interactive, 2020]) to offer but a few references. Emergent play forms, such as machinima, have led to novel interfaces (Kirschner 2011) and rallying cries such as 'Machinima isn't animation! It's puppetry!' (Hancock and Ingram 2007). Arguing that video games have an established history with puppetry is easy. It is much harder to identify how this changes the conceptual grounding.

Game Studies have adapted puppetry using a human-centered lens. For example, Calvillo-Gamez and Cairns build on the user experience to argue for a puppetry framework in gaming via a phenomenological turn (Calvillo-Gamez and Cairns 2008). According to this turn, '[p]uppetry is produced when there is a high level of ownership, and ownership is achieved when the player has a high level of control over the game' (Calvillo-Gamez and Cairns 2008, 7). The puppet is of value because of the direct control offered to the player. It is seen as a form of a digital extension.

More recently, Aliano discussed a puppet-like impact of video games through such an extension.

> I argue that the work of self-formation and identity in video games does operate like that of the actor assuming a role in performance. But, because of the extension of self through technological prostheses, and the personal ownership of in-game experiences that occurs when one games, the implications of this performative transformation of self are much greater (Aliano 2022, 62).

Aliano's 'technological prostheses' are basically puppets, and she picks up Hayles' reading of 'posthuman' technical extensions of the human body. In a game setting such as *Animal Crossing: New Horizons* (Nintendo, 2020) '[t]he avatar is both the gamer's self and separate from it; it acts on behalf of the player and for its own ends within the game, via the player's control' (Aliano 2021, 55). The agency of the avatar is largely found in the context of the game from which the player might draw new experiences 'as a person other than themself' (Aliano 2022, 68). This reflects back on human experiences of self-formation.

The approach I want to add here starts from the same field that emerged from a turn to the material and the more-than-human. However, it aims to provide an original perspective on the role and origin of agency in our understanding of video game play as puppetry. I argue that video game characters and objects are not mere access points for human expression. Instead, a digital puppet should be seen as a material object not unlike physical puppets. Such an object has its own qualities and agencies that contribute to the performance. Rolling dice, moving figures on a board, dealing cards, and throwing marbles are all play activities that co-depend on material objects and their performance. This dependency expands when dice turn into marionettes or cards into shadow puppets. Likewise, playing a video game is an enacted balancing act between human and non-human contributors that expands the collaborative construction of expression. The different nature of the components of a video game—its rules, interfaces, visuals, sounds, design, platform—are collaborating in an enacted performative construction of the gameplay. The player remains a key contributor—like a puppeteer—but equally relevant are code, interface, virtual characters, or game logic—performing objects of the game. As with the previously noted materiality of traditional puppetry, the nature of these non-human components should not be confused or compared to those of conscious humans. It is precisely their otherness that makes puppets and game characters useful companions. Puppets—whether physical or virtual—are not seamless extensions but differing active partners. Most importantly, we have to acknowledge their own contributions to an emerging shared performance.

Relations and objects

Video games form their own interrelationships in these shared performances. To connect them back to Orenstein's principles:

> Contemporary New Puppetry is more usefully thought of through the eclectic notion of performing objects rather than the more reified idea of puppet. [...] The predominant use and vision of the puppet today does not represent a machine newly imposed from the outside set to overtake us, but rather something with which we are deeply connected, and through which we strive to express, understand, and negotiate our interrelationship with each other and with the non-human world (Orenstein 2017, 107).

Orenstein, following Foley, draws connections to Eastern puppetry traditions that already see the puppet as an active contributor to the unfolding performance. But the argument here will follow another thread mentioned by Orenstein: that of material agency. Orenstein introduces material agency to the discussion via Bennett and her concept of 'vibrant matter' that offers a 'resistant force' (Bennett 2010, 1) toward other beings including humans. For Bennett, this force is tied to its own vitality and part of a discussion of what vitalism means for things. Such a discourse necessarily includes a reassessment of what vitality might mean as such. For Bennett, humans are also non-human in the sense that their being is also ruled by materials and their forces. Such material relativity certainly applies, but it centers on discussions of what 'life' is and how the term might apply. My argument tries to emphasize the differences and dependencies between the puppet object's agency and that of the human. It sees them as enacted processes and does not worry whether they share a form of 'life'. To achieve this, I turn to another scholar working in this field: Karen Barad. Barad sees material agency as fundamentally interdependent. A key term for this view is 'intra-action', which,

> *signifies the mutual constitution of entangled agencies.* That is, in contrast to the usual 'interaction', which assumes that there are separate individual agencies that precede their interaction, the notion of intra-action recognizes that distinct agencies do not precede, but rather emerge through, their intra-action. It is important to note that the 'distinct' agencies are only distinct in a relational, not an absolute, sense, that is, *agencies are only distinct in relation to their mutual entanglement; they don't exist as individual elements* (Barad 2007, 33, emphasis in original).

From this perspective, materials have agency, no matter whether they qualify as alive or not. It is through the relation of forces between them that they can be distinguished from one another in what Barad calls the 'agential cut'. In that way, entities only come into being relationally. There is no puppet or puppeteer up until the moment when the forces of one help to define the other. Intra-action continues the action-based perspective that draws performance, HCI, and play together into foundational inter-dependencies. Here, we do not have users, puppeteers, or players controlling a computer, shadow puppet, or videogame. Just as the very existence of the puppeteer is only constituted through the encounter with the puppet, the player does not come into being until their encounter with the game. The argument is not one of cultural differences (as, e.g., Foley's is) but one of principle dependency and emergence. Barad is not talking about performance as a mimetic art to represent something else but of performativity as a constitutive force that is linked not only to 'the formation of the subject but also to the production of the matter of bodies' (Barad 2003, 808). Performative intra-action relates to game play as both are constructed through shared activities between human and non-human participants.

With this in mind, we now turn to object theatre and performing things (see, e.g., Schweitzer and Zerdy 2014) to highlight the active role that materials play in this performative moment, whether this performance happens in a video game, on a stage, or in any other location.

Object theatre lessons

Material performance has been defined within puppetry research as a 'term [that] assumes that puppets and other material objects in performance bear visual and kinetic meanings that operate independently of whatever meanings we may inscribe upon them in performance' (Posner, Orenstein, and Bell 2014, 5). Although it does not have to be a confrontation, there is a difference between the meanings humans would inscribe culturally and those inherent in the activities of materials. In Carrignon's *théâtre d'objet*, object theatre, the object is a kind of memory container. It 'carries the memories of those who have owned these objects'[1] (Carrignon 2011, 5). This cycles back to the belief in material culture studies that human conduct can be traced through objects. The remnants of an object from the past contain traces of the story of its crafter and the times and conditions of its production. 'Material, a part of the world, the record of bodily action in nature, the artifact perpetually displays the process of its design, the pattern in the mind of its creator. It incorporates intention' (Glassie 1999, 44). This is not a notion of a co-constitutive partner but of a trace. As discussed above, we need to step beyond a purely human-centered reading of 'intention' or agency. Materials contribute agency that does not stem from human memory or intention. This turn is reflected in philosophical movements such

---

1   In French :'Le théâtre d'objet porte la mémoire de ceux qui ont possédé ces objets'. (Carrignon 2011, 5)

as object-oriented ontology (OOO) (Bogost 2012). But unlike OOO, expressive objects still operate and emerge only relationally. In the conditions of interaction, play, and performance this shared becoming necessarily includes human contributions. That does not focus on humans at the center of these productive encounters, but it lays out interconnected networks. In these networks we do not find linked actors that stand independently and act upon each other. These are partners that only come into their being as they intra-act with each other's forces. The resulting perspective of a materiality-driven object theatre is one of interdependencies and it is beyond singular intention. It still maps on puppetry, though:

> The essence of puppet, mask, and object performance (as countless puppeteers have said from their own experience) is not mastery of the material world but a constant negotiation back and forth with it. Puppet performance reveals to us that the results of those negotiations are not at all preordained and that human superiority over the material world is not something to count on, especially since *we* all eventually end up as lifeless objects (Bell 2014, 50).

It is this position of the puppeteer that helps to understand the player as the digital performer. This is not the user of an application or the controller of cybernetic processes, but it is the being that is co-negotiated with paper, felt, wood, metal, polygons, and bits.

Tetris renegotiated

To highlight this material-based concept of object theatre and exemplify its value in relation to Game Studies, the concluding section will look at a reading of *Tetris* (Pajitnov, 1985–) through the material-based object theatre lens developed above. The basic game concept of *Tetris* has undergone a range of changes that include multiplayer, 3D, networked play, varying level designs, and countless other variations. The core game has been ported to most available devices and their specific interfaces. Sticking with its main principle, we will focus on *Tetris* as the single-player video game in which various shapes of blocks appear at the top of a screen one-by-one and gradually descend to the bottom of that screen where they stack up. The speed of that descent increases in later levels. The player cannot control the gradual speed increase or order of the falling pieces, but they can rotate and shift these shapes in order to affect the way they will stack at the bottom. The goal is to control the pieces so as to fill every gap in a line across the playing field. This will make this line disappear and score points. The basics of this matching mechanism became highly influential for a range of related games (Juul 2007). A game ends when the pieces have stacked up to the top of the level. There are a number of additional features, such as variable falling speed, scoring mechanisms, or speeding up the descent of the pieces, but for simplicity's sake, we will focus on the main principle only.

One of the reasons for picking *Tetris* is that the game has been historically influential as a cultural artifact. Its very emergence tells a great story: originating in the Soviet Union, designed and programmed by a single creator, Alexey Pajitnov, crossing over into commercial markets in a legal battle, and becoming part of the success-story of Nintendo's *Gameboy* launch. This is a story of human interest that was told multiple times (including as a comic book (Brown 2016) and Hollywood movie (*Tetris*, John S. Baird, 2023]). *Tetris* was also at the center of a historic debate in the then-budding field of Game Studies. Its level of abstraction was identified as a defining element (Wolf 2003) but that did not stop further interpretations of the game from proliferating. Notably, Murray pointed to *Tetris* as an unfolding text that allows us to interpret human experiences. In her reading, the mechanic of disappearing lines could be read as an eternally erased success state. 'Success means just being able to keep up with the flow. This game is a perfect enactment of the overtasked lives of Americans in the 1990s—of the constant bombardment of tasks demand out attention and that we must somehow fit into our overcrowded schedules and clear off our desks in order to make room for the next onslaught'. (Murray 1997, 144). The spatial concepts of level, pieces, and player interaction invite associations with modern human experiences. 'The screen objects are like a symbolic language for inducing our activity. So while we experience the game as being about skill acquisition, we are drawn to it by the implicit expressive content of the dance. Tetris allows us to symbolically experience agency over our lives. It is a kind of rain dance for the postmodern psyche, meant to allow us to enact control over things outside our power'. (Murray 1997, 144) Such an interpretation was countered by scholars who argued against a turn to human—or narrative—framing (Eskelinen 2001). This counter-perspective did not look for a projected meaning onto the abstracted game but focused on the mechanisms within it. 'Unlike in music, where a national anthem played on electric guitar takes on a whole new meaning, the value system of a game is strictly internal, determined unambivalently by the rules. Among the many differences between games and stories, one of the most obvious is that of ambiguity. In *Tetris*, I do not stop to ponder what those bricks are really supposed to be made of'. (Aarseth 2004, 48) The difference presented part of a scholarly controverse within a larger debate, one that shall not be re-opened here.

Instead, a short reading of *Tetris* as material-based object theatre performance hopes to establish its own view next to the existing ones. It should be noted upfront that both sides of this debate use the term 'performance' within their own readings (Aarseth 1997; Murray 2004) but differ in their use of terminology from the logic outlined here.

A material performance view of Tetris argues against both the idea that the value (or anything else) is 'internal' as well as the idea that the game merely enacts 'human experience'. It argues for an interdependent construction of collaborating human and non-human actors. As a piece of puppetry performance, *Tetris* features a number of objects that are active performers. Some of them are hardware-based (like the controller of the specific platform), others might be defined by the situatedness of the play event (like distracting commentary of a bystander). Sticking to the principle game mechanics, we will only look at the activities on the screen, but it should be noted that the principles apply to the situatedness as well.

Concentrating on the fundamentals, the objects to manipulate in *Tetris* are the blocks. In most versions, these blocks are color-coded or marked in visually distinct ways. Their shapes are polyominoes, connected set of squares. The term polyomino was introduced by Golomb (Gardner 1988 [1956]) and their features have been part of mathematical puzzle constructions ever since. Golomb noted that polyominoes were examples of combinational geometry and explains them in reference to patterns possible on a checkerboard (Golomb 1994). Golomb's original description of these shapes refers to them as almost embodied movements performed on such a checkerboard: 'we *define* an *n*-omino as a simply-connected set of *n* squares of the checker which are 'rook-wise connected'; that is, a rook placed on any square of the *n*-omino must be able to get to any other square, in a finite number of moves'. (Golomb 1954, 675). *Tetris* game variants used different level designs, but the original had a 10x20 grid (vs the 8x8 of the original checkerboard). On that grid, the blocks perform not only through a chess-rook-like embodied object behavior but also through their falling speed, their initial orientation, and the way they rotate and move in response to the player's input. These are the objects in our material performance that collaborate with the human to define each other (object and human) and that contribute their agencies such as form and movement. The player engages—intra-acts—with these objects through the design offered by the platform, but the activity cannot be reduced to the rules alone. Players' engagement remains central and might very well be read as a meaning-making process. Even if that meaning is largely a pattern-recognition task, it might extend from the most basic forms to ever larger and more elaborate ones. Such extensions are in the nature of play (Salen and Zimmerman 2004). The impact of this control on the players and whether it is transferable to other contexts has been debated (Pilegard and Mayer 2018), yet the engagement itself is not challenged. But in *Tetris* play is not human-based either. It is a form of participation, not of sole control. In coordination with the gaming situation and the objects available, players negotiate their next move—not as similar but as different participants in the action, just like puppeteers.

Conclusion

Retracing the main steps of the argument from the role of puppetry for HCI and video games, to material agencies of objects, each offering specific and different qualities, to the notion of object theatre as a co-emergent performance between different partners, we arrive at a reading of *Tetris* that sits neither in a purely game-based nor a purely human-based interpretation. Yet, the concept of video gameplay as object theatre does not equalize all the partners. The specifics of the polyominoes remain different from the plans and actions of the player. Humans might interpret, cognitively engage, contribute their own emergent behaviors—game objects might fall, rotate, affect through their embodied shape. It is a clash of different agencies. As is the case with puppetry, the reason why gameplay works is because of these differences. Because the game objects are separate and different from the human player, both sides of the play event can combine to a shared performance. It is through this difference that both can contribute to each other's construction. To understand modern game objects from increasingly complex avatars to virtual objects to abstracted entities, we have to build on this core principle of puppetry, individual agency, and the realization of the differences that allows a shared production.

The chosen example of *Tetris* offers an abstract example of that form. Looking at the much more differentiated character controls, interfaces, and visual representations at work in many recent titles, the shared performance has every opportunity to become ever richer and variable. Many titles push humanoid expressiveness from facial animation, to detailed representation of hair or skin, to the rigging of the game characters. Naturally, this is a valid and effective approach. At the same time, it should be noted that gameplay as object theatre equally describes the worlds of *Octodad: Dadliest Catch* (Young Horses, 2014), where multiple players control a single game character, or *Brothers: A Tale of Two Sons* (Starbreeze Studios, 2013), where one player controls more than one character simultaneously, or the multiplayer puzzle mayhem of *Very Very Valet* (Toyful LLC, 2021).

Games as object theatre do not confine themselves to a narrative or ludic frame. They elevate the performative construction of action over its interpretation and an intra-active co-emergence over a rule-based approach. This is not a new concept. It has been at work in puppetry across many cultures and for a very long time. This essay hopes to provide one building block in integrating this tradition into Games Studies.

References

Aarseth, Espen. 2004. 'Genre Trouble. Narrativism and the Art of Simulation.' In *First Person: New Media as Story, Performance and Game*, edited by Noah Wardrip-Fruin and Pat Harrigan, 45–55. Boston, MA: MIT Press.

———. 1997. *Cybertext: Perspectives on Ergodic Literature*. Baltimore, London: The John Hopkins University Press.

Aliano, Kelly I. 2021. 'Puppetry in the Age of Posthumanism: The Terrors and Pleasures of Animal Crossing: New Horizons.' *Puppetry International (Puppetry International Research Review preview)* 50 (fall/winter): 53–59.

———. 2022. *The Performance of Video Games. Enacting Identity, History, and Culture Through Play*. Edited by Matthew Wilhelm Kapell. *Studies in Gaming*. Jefferson, NC: McFarland & Company Inc.

Barad, Karen. 2003. 'Posthumanist Performativity: Toward an Understanding of How Matter Comes to Matter.' *Signs* 28, no. 3 (Spring): 801–831. https://doi.org/10.1086/345321.

———. 2007. *Meeting the Universe Halfway. Quantum Physics and the Entanglement of Matter and Meaning*. Durham; London: Duke University Press.

Bell, John. 2014. 'Playing with the Eternal Uncanny: The Persistent Life of Lifeless Objects.' In *The Routledge Companion to Puppetry and Material Performance*, edited by Dassia N. Posner, Claudia Orenstein and John Bell, 43–53. Florence, KY: Routledge.

Bennett, Jane. 2010. *Vibrant Matter. A political Ecology of Things*. Durham, NC/London: The Duke University Press.

Blumenthal, Eileen. 2005. *Puppetry: A World History*. New York: Harry N. Abrams.

Bogost, Ian. 2012. *Alien Phenomenology or What It's Like to Be a Thing*. Minneapolis, London: University of Minnesota Press.

Brown, Box. 2016. *Tetris: The Games People Play*. New York: First Second.

Calvillo-Gamez, Eduardo H., and Paul Cairns. 2008. 'Pulling the Strings: A Theory of Puppetry for the Gaming Experience.' In *Conference Proceedings of The Philosophy of Computer Games 2008*, edited by Stephan Guentzel, Michael Liebe and Dieter Mersch, 308–323. Potsdam: Potsdam University Press.

Carrignon, Christian. 2011. 'Le théâtre d'objet: mode d'emploi.' *Agôn* 4. https://doi.org/10.4000/agon.2079

Eide, Paul. 2008. 'Digital Puppetry.' *The Puppetry Journal* 60, no. 1 (Fall): 12–13.

Eskelinen, Markku. 2001. 'The Gaming Situation.' *Gamestudies (Online Journal)* 1, no. 1 (July). https://www.gamestudies.org/0101/eskelinen/.

Gardner, Martin. 1988 (1956). *Hexaflexagons and Other Mathematical Diversions: The First 'Scientific American' Book of Puzzles and Games*. Chicago/London: The University of Chicago Press.

Glassie, Henry. 1999. *Material Culture*. Bloomington/Indianapolis: Indiana University Press.

Golomb, Solomon W. 1954. 'Checker Boards and Polyominoes.' *The American Mathematical Monthly* 61, no. 10 (December): 675–682. https://doi.org/10.1080/000298 90.1954.11988548.

———. 1994. *Polyominoes. Puzzles, Patterns, Problems, and Packings. Revised and expanded second edition*. Princeton: Princeton University Press.

Hancock, Hugh, and Johnnie Ingram. 2007. *Machinima for Dummies*. Hoboken, NJ: Wiley Publishing Inc.

Hayes-Roth, Barbara, Lee Brownston, and Erik Sincoff. 1995. 'Directed Improvisation by Computer Characters.' *Stanford Knowledge Systems Laboratory*.

Jurkowski, Henryk. 1990. 'The Mode of Existence of Characters of the Puppet Stage.' In *The Language of the Puppet*, edited by Laurence R. Kominz and Mark Levenson, 21–37. Seattle: Pacific Puppetry Press.

Juul, Jesper. 2007. 'Swap Adjacent Gems to Make Sets of Three: A History of Matching Tile Games.' *Artifact journal* 1, no. 4 (March): 205–216. https://doi.org/10.1080/17 493460601173366.

Kaplin, Stephen. 1999. 'A Puppet Tree: A Model for the Field of Puppet Theatre.' *TDR* 43, no. 3 (Fall): 28–35. https://www.jstor.org/stable/i248016.

King, Anchuli Felicia. 2018. 'Moving Masks and Mobile Monkeys: The Technodramaturgy of Augmented Reality Puppets.' *Theatre and Performance Design* 4, no. 4 (October): 324–341. https://doi.org/10.1080/23322551.2018.1558539.

Kirschner, Friedrich. 2011. 'Toward a Machinima Studio.' In *The Machinima Reader*, edited by Henry Lowood and Michael Nitsche, 53–72. Cambridge, MA/London: MIT Press.

Lin, Min, Zhenzhen Hu, Si Liu, Meng Wang, Richang Hong, and Shuicheng Yan. 2013. 'Heritage of Shadow Puppetry: Creation and Manipulation.' *Proceedings of the 21st ACM International Conference on Multimedia, Barcelona, Spain*. 183–192.

Moumoutzis, Nektarios, Nektarios Gioldasis, George Anestis, Marios Christoulakis, George Stylianakis, and Stavros Christodoulakis. 2018. 'Employing Theatrical Interactions and Audience Engagement to Enable Creative Learning Experiences in Formal and Informal Learning: Enriching Social and Community Theatre Practices with Digital Technologies.' *Interactive Mobile Communication Technologies and Learning: Proceedings of the 11th IMCL Conference*. 142–154.

Murray, Janet. 1997. *Hamlet on the Holodeck. The Future of Narrative in Cyberspace*. Cambridge, MA: MIT Press.

———. 2004. 'From Game-Story to Cyberdrama.' In *First Person. New Media as Story, Performance, and Game*, edited by Noah Wardrip-Fruin and Pat Harrigan, 2–10. Boston, MA: MIT Press.

Orenstein, Claudia. 2017. 'Our Puppets, Our Selves: Puppetry's Changing Paradigms.' *Action, Scene, and Voice: 21st-Century Dialogues with Edward Gor-*

don Craig 26, no.1 (February): 91–110. http://doi.org/10.5642/mimejournal.20172 601.12.

Pilegard, Celeste, and Richard E Mayer. 2018. 'Game over for Tetris as a Platform for Cognitive Skill Training.' *Contemporary Educational Psychology* 54 (July): 29–41. ht tps://doi.org/10.1016/j.cedpsych.2018.04.003.

Posner, Dassia N., Claudia Orenstein, and John Bell, eds. 2014. *Routledge Companion to Puppetry and Material Performance*. Florence, KY: Routledge.

Poulton, Cody. 2015. 'From Puppet to Robot: Technology and the Human in Japanese Theatre.' In *The Routledge Companion to Puppetry and Material Performance*, edited by Dassia N. Posner, Claudia Orenstein and John Bell, 280–293. London, New York: Routledge.

Salen, Katie, and Eric Zimmerman. 2004. *Rules of Play: Game Design Fundamentals.* Cambridge, MA: MIT Press.

Schweitzer, Marlis, and Joanne Zerdy. 2014. *Performing Objects and Theatrical Things.* London: Palgrave Macmillan.

Sturmann, David J. 1998. 'Computer Puppetry.' *Computer Graphics in Entertainment* 18, no. 1 (January): 38–45. https://doi.org/10.1109/38.637269

Tillis, Steve. 1999. 'The Art of Puppetry in the Age of Media Production.' *TDR* 43, no. 3 (Fall): 182–195. https://muse.jhu.edu/article/32948

Wolf, Mark J.P. 2003. 'Abstraction in the Video Game.' In *The Video Game Theory Reader*, edited by Mark J.P. Wolf and Bernard Perron, 47–66. New York, London: Routledge.

Biography

Michael Nitsche works as Professor in Digital Media at the Georgia Institute of Technology, where he directs the Digital World and Image Group. His research combines elements of craft and performance to develop novel media and interaction designs. Nitsche's publications include the books *Vital Media* (2022), *The Machinima Reader* (2011) (co-edited with Henry Lowood), and *Video Game Spaces* (2009), all with MIT Press. Since 2015, he has been co-editor (with Julia Sussner) of the Taylor & Francis journal *Digital Creativity*.